THE
IDEA OF PROGRESS

AN INQUIRY INTO ITS ORIGIN
AND GROWTH

J. B. BURY

*Regius Professor of Modern History and Fellow of King's College,
in the University of Cambridge*

Introduction by
CHARLES A. BEARD

DOVER PUBLICATIONS, INC., NEW YORK

Published in Canada by General Publishing Company,
Ltd., 30 Lesmill Road, Don Mills, Toronto, Ontario.
Published in the United Kingdom by Constable and
Company, Ltd., 10 Orange Street, London WC2H 7EG.

This Dover edition, first published in 1987, is a republication of the 1955 Dover edition, an unabridged and
unaltered republication of the 1932 edition as published by
The Macmillan Company. This Dover edition is published
by special arrangement with St. Martin's Press.

Manufactured in the United States of America
Dover Publications, Inc., 31 East 2nd Street, Mineola,
N.Y. 11501

Library of Congress Cataloging-in-Publication Data

Bury, J. B. (John Bagnell), 1861–1927.
    The idea of progress.

    Reprint. Originally published: New York : Macmillan,
1932.
    Includes bibliographical references and index.
    1. Progress.   2. History—Philosophy.   I. Title.
[HM101.B865   1987]   303.4'4   86-29369
ISBN 0-486-25421-6 (pbk.)

Dedicated

to the memories of

Charles François Castel de Saint-Pierre,

Marie Jean Antoine Nicolas Caritat de Condorcet,

Auguste Comte,

Herbert Spencer,

and other optimists mentioned in this volume.

Tantane uos generis tenuit fiducia uestri ?

PREFATORY NOTE TO THE AMERICAN EDITION

The extended discussion of the idea of progress in recent American writings and the decision of the trustees of the centennial celebration at Chicago to dramatize it in "A Century of Progress Exposition" make it fitting to bring out an American edition of Professor Bury's volume. Here is a scholarly survey of the history of the idea, which all Americans who write or speak about the subject should read. Those who imagine that the idea of progress was lately discovered by the promoters of business enterprise and those who suppose that it is a superficial concept adopted by a superficial age will do well to widen their knowledge and enlarge their understanding by a study of these sober and thoughtful pages. The original text has been reproduced exactly as Professor Bury left it, but an introduction dealing with some of the implications of the theme has been added.

CHARLES A. BEARD.

New Milford, Connecticut,
December, 1931.

INTRODUCTION

By CHARLES A. BEARD

The world is largely ruled by ideas, true and false. Although a British wit has declared that the power which a concept wields over human life is nicely proportioned to the degree of error in it, only a sharp eye can discern the dividing line between truth and falsehood. Moreover we often discover that an idea which is not in accord with historical facts may become true in practice, at least partially. For example, when Jefferson wrote that "all men are created equal," it was easy for his critics to point out obvious discrepancies in physical and mental endowment and in social position, but nevertheless Jefferson's idea wielded a wide empire over the human spirit, worked for the liberalization of institutions, and has become a reality in so far as all men (and women) are theoretically equal before the law.

At all events an idea contains potential energy in no mystical sense. As Fouillé says, it is "the conscious form taken by our feelings and impulses; every idea covers not only an intellectual act, but also a certain direction of the sensibility and of the will. As a consequence, in a society as in an individual every idea is a force tending more and more to realize its individual end." In other words it is not a mere intellectual conception; it contains within itself a dynamic power to move individuals and nations, to drive them in the direction of effecting the ends and institutions implicit in it. While ideas are sometimes formulated by powerful persons for ulterior designs, they also frequently arise from obscure sources, are cherished for a term by the weak and unimportant, and finally make headway against indifference and suppression to a place of dominance in a whole epoch of civilization.

Although apparently academic and remote, all this has a very practical bearing. Constitutional and democratic government is impossible unless the significance of ideas is recognized. It is founded on the assumption that all social conflicts will be fought out within the framework set by the fundamental law through the exchange of ideas. To government by opinion there is no other alternative except government by violence.

It is not only in politics that ideas are important. They are regnant in every department of civilized life—in art, letters, economy, and social custom. One might almost say that peoples are civilized in proportion as they mingle ideas with their labors and aspirations. Form alone does not give influence and immortality to poetry or prose. Every great writer, as Morley says, gives expression in thought to immense movements of mankind, foreshadowing as well as reflecting. And the ideas of every epoch in history are related, usually with one dominant concept setting the key-tone for the others. Indeed, historians, with good reason, break the story of mankind into ages according to their characteristics—to the outstanding ideas disclosed in events, actions and philosophy. Thus we have an age of despotism, an age of reason, and an age of democracy. Though there is danger of over-simplification in such arrangements, there can be no doubt that whole periods are marked by particular types of thought, particular conceptions of life and its values. Neither statesmen nor artists nor writers can escape their pressures.

Now among the ideas which have held sway in public and private affairs for the last two hundred years, none is more significant or likely to exert more influence in the future than the concept of progress. With a few exceptions ancient writers were imprisoned in a vicious circle: they thought that mankind revolved in a cycle through some series of stages. In the Middle Ages thought and practice were cramped by the belief that man was a sinful creature born to trouble as the sparks fly upward, that the world would come to a close sometime, and that life on earth was not an end in itself but a kind of prelude to heaven or hell. It was not until commerce, invention, and natural science emancipated humanity from thralldom to the cycle and to the Christian epic that it became possible to think of an immense future for mortal mankind, of the conquest of the material world in human interest, of providing the conditions for a good life on this planet without reference to any possible hereafter. In due course, when conditions were ripe, the idea of progress arose in the Western world, and in the volume before us is told in clear language the story of the germination and growth of this fruitful concept.

The author of this volume, the late Professor John B. Bury, of Cambridge University, was a profound scholar and a philosophic thinker. Emphasis must be laid on both aspects of his life and work.

He was rigorous in his insistence on exacting research, a critical handling of sources, and the use of scientific methods in ascertaining the truth about persons and events. For the rhetorical historian or philosopher Professor Bury had no patience whatever. In language that could not be mistaken, he condemned all the theorists who tried to conjure explanations of mankind's evolution out of their inner consciousness without reference to the hard patterns of facts which constitute the inescapable substance of history. The attempts of Hegel and Krause to disclose the "rational element in the general movement of humanity," Bury characterized as "splendid failures," because their systems were "marked by insufficient knowledge of facts and details," and both writers sought to impose on the story of social development a rigid framework or scheme which did not fit the realities. The clue to what Hegel called the ultimate design of the universe must be sought, Bury contended, must be found, if at all, in the substance of human experience called history, always with due reference to the facts in the case.

Yet while emphasizing in his own researches the necessity of adhering with rigid exactness to historical facts, Bury exhibited his high quality as a thinker by searching far and wide for clues to their inner relations and meaning. "I cannot imagine," he said in his address before the Congress of Arts and Sciences at the St. Louis Exposition in 1904, "the slightest theoretical importance in a collection of facts or sequences of facts, unless they mean something in terms of reason, unless we can hope to determine their vital connection in the whole system of reality."

This opinion was strengthened by his conviction that history assumes "a different meaning from that of a higher zoölogy, and is not merely a continuation of the process of evolution in nature. If thought is not the result, but the presupposition, of the process of nature, it follows that history, in which thought is the characteristic and guiding force, belongs to a different order of ideas from the kingdom of nature and demands a different interpretation. Here the philosophy of history comes in. The very phrase is a flag over debated ground. It means the investigation of the rational principles which, it is assumed, are disclosed in the historical process due to the coöperation and the interaction of human minds under terrestrial conditions. If the philosophy of history is not illusory, history means the disclosure of spiritual reality in the fullest way in which it is cognisable to us in these particular conditions. And, on the other hand, the possibility of an interpretation of history as a movement of reason, disclosing its nature in terrestrial circumstances, seems the only hypothesis on which the postulate of 'history for its own sake' can be justified as valid." Yet it is to be noted that in making this assertion Bury does not deal in transcendent mysteries but keeps close to the earth of known and recorded human experience. Hence even the "toughest" scientific mind can scarcely quarrel with his position.

In searching for a scheme of ideas upon which to thread the bewildering facts of human development, Bury early became aware that history as a science could not be confined to a story of wars and politics, but must be extended to cover the whole range of civilization in its movement through time.

"One of the features of the renovation of the study of history," he remarked in his inaugural lecture at Cambridge, "has been the growth of a larger view of its dominion. . . . The exclusive idea of political history, *Staatengeschichte,* to which Ranke held so firmly, has been gradually yielding to a more comprehensive definition which embraces as its material all records, whatever their nature may be, of the material and spiritual development, of the culture and the works, of man in society, from the Stone Age onwards. . . . The growth of the larger conception was favored by the national movements which vindicated the idea of the people as distinct from the idea of the state; but its final victory is assured by the application of the principle of development and the 'historical method' to all the manifestations of human activity—social institutions, law, trade, the industrial and the fine arts, religion, philosophy, folklore, literature.

"Thus history has acquired a much ampler and more comprehensive meaning, along with a deeper insight into the constant interaction and reciprocity among all the various manifestations of human brain-power and human emotion. Of course in actual practice labor is divided; political history and the histories of the various parts of civilization can and must be separately treated; but it makes a vital difference that we should be alive to the interconnection, that no department should be isolated, that we should maintain an intimate association among the historical sciences, that we should frame an ideal—an ideal not the less useful because it is impracticable—of a true history of a nation or a true history of the world in which every form of social life and every manifestation of intellectual development should be set forth in its relation to the rest, in its significance for growth or decline."

Could the riddle of the universe be solved by this method? Could any indubitable conclusion as to the scheme of the whole be drawn out of the tangled and multitudinous facts? Wise in his day and generation, Bury first familiarized himself with the writings of the great thinkers in his field —Hegel, Ranke, Marx, and Lamprecht, for example. Cautious in announcing his views, Bury avoided a pontifical tone. Yet he courageously ventured a guess.

After spending many years in the study of the voluminous records of mankind, he came to the conclusion that there were two great discoveries in the history of thought which were significant for the task he had assumed. The first was made by a Greek poet. "There is no passage, perhaps, in the works of the Greek tragedians so instructive for the historical student as that song in the Antigone of Sophocles, in which we seem to surprise the first amazed meditation of man when it is borne in upon him by a sudden startling illumination, how strange it is that he should be what he is and should have wrought all that he has wrought—should have wrought out, among other things, the city state. He had suddenly, as it were, waked up to realize that he himself was the wonder of the world."* Thus in the fifth century B.C. man had become conscious of himself as a wonder-working force in the world—a conqueror of the beasts of the field, the fowl of the air, the wind of the sea, and the patient earth.

* Marvin, *The Living Past*, p. 74.

A second great stage in human evolution was reached when mankind became conscious of what could yet be done, when the idea of progress broke in upon the belief in the vicious circle or contentment with status. Sometime in the course of his wide searches in ancient and modern civilization, Bury came upon this concept and began to apply it in the prosecution of his studies. From the meager records of his intimate life now available to us, it is impossible to learn just when he discovered this instrument of thought, but it seems that the ground lines of the idea of progress were laid in his mind by the time he had reached middle life. At all events the concept had been a fundamental part of his intellectual equipment long before he issued in 1920 the volume which is now reprinted.

Support for this interpretation of his work is to be found in the inaugural address which Bury delivered on assuming the Regius Professorship of History at Cambridge in 1903, long before his treatise on the idea of progress was formulated. On that occasion he said in language that could not be mistaken: "A right notion of the bearing of history on affairs, both for the statesman and for the citizen, could not be formed or formulated until men had grasped the idea of human development. This is the great transforming conception, which enables history to define her scope. . . . The world is not yet alive to the full importance of the transformation of history (as a part of a wider transformation) which is being brought about by the doctrine of development. It is always difficult for those who are in immediate proximity to realise the decisive steps in intellectual or spiritual progress when those steps are slow and gradual; but we need not

hesitate to say that the last century [the nine-
teenth] is not only as important an era as the fifth
century B.C. in the annals of historical study, but
marks, like it, a stage in the growth of man's self-
consciousness." In other words, a clue to the mystery of history is to be found in the concept of development, or progress. If so, then that is evidently
a discovery as important as the human mind has
ever made, with implications for mankind that
almost transcend imagination.

Having brought the idea of development to the
center of his thinking about history, Bury was naturally quick to grasp the importance of organic
evolution, of Darwinism, for the elaboration of his
hypothesis, and in an essay published in 1909, entitled "Darwinism and History," he explored its
significance. Thoroughly acquainted with the
course of historical writing and thinking from
Herodotus to Lamprecht, Bury realized at once that
the procedure of natural science which had led to
the doctrine of organic evolution was in keeping
with a similar procedure in historiography. "The
growth of historical study in the nineteenth century," he said, "has been determined and charac-
terised by the same general principle which has
underlain the simultaneous development of the
study of nature, namely, the *genetic* idea. The 'historical' conception of nature, which has produced
the history of the solar system, the story of the
earth, the geneologies of telluric organisms, and
has revolutionised natural science, belongs to the
same order of thought as the conception of human
history as continuous, genetic, causal process—a
conception which has revolutionised historical research and made it scientific. . . . The genetic

principle, progressive development, general laws, the significance of time, the conception of society as an organic aggregate, the metaphysical theory of history as the self-evolution of spirit—all these ideas show that historical inquiry had been advancing independently on somewhat parallel lines to the sciences of nature."

The theories of human development already being worked out by the historians were reinforced by Darwinism. "The prevailing doctrine that man was created *ex abrupto* had placed history in an isolated position, disconnected with the sciences of nature. Anthropology, which deals with the animal *anthropos,* now comes into line with zoölogy, and brings it into relation with history. Man's condition at the present day is the result of a series of transformations, going back to the most primitive phase of society, which is the ideal (unattainable) beginning of history. But that beginning had emerged without any breach of continuity from a development which carries us back to a quadrimane ancestor, still further back (according to Darwin's conjecture) to a marine animal of the ascidian type, and then through remoter periods to the lowest form of organism. . . . This conception of a continuous progress in the evolution of life, resulting in the appearance of uncivilised Anthropos, helped to reinforce, and increase a belief in, the conception of the history of civilised Anthropos as itself also a continuous progressive development."

Looking upon Darwinism with wide-open eyes, Bury did not attempt to apply, naïvely and uncritically, the proffered explanations of organic evolution to the history of civilization. He recognized that historians could make use of Darwinian theo-

ries—adaptation to environment, struggle for existence, natural selection, survival of the fittest, etc.—
in explaining certain phases of human development,
but he did not think that these ideas could carry us
very far on the way to understanding the evolution
of mankind. Indeed he added a specific caution:
"It may be said that, so far as concerns the actions
and movements of men which are the subject of
recorded history, physical environment has ceased
to act mechanically, and in order to affect their
actions must affect their wills first; and that this
psychical character of the causal relations sub-
stantially alters the problem. The development of
human societies, it may be argued, derives a completely new character from the dominance of the
conscious psychical element, creating as it does new
conditions (inventions, social institutions, etc.)
which limit and counteract the operation of natural selection, and control and modify the influence
of physical environment. Most thinkers agree now
that the chief clues to the growth of civilisation
must be sought in the psychological sphere."

From natural science Bury also developed
another idea which was of deep significance for
his thinking about the evolution of mankind—
the idea of an immense range of time in front of
us. "Science," he says, "tells us that—apart from
the incalculable chances of catastrophes—man has
still myriads and myriads of years to live on this
planet under physical conditions which need not
hinder his development or impair his energies. That
is a period of which his whole recorded history of
six or seven thousand years is a small fraction."

Unlike most historians, whose faces are turned
resolutely to the past, Bury was ever mindful of
time to come. "The dark imminence of this un-

known future in front of us, like a vague wall of
mist, every instant receding, with all its indiscern-
ible contents of world-wide change, soundless revolutions, silent reformations, undreamed ideas, new
religions, must not be neglected, if we would grasp
the unity of history in its highest sense. For though
we are unable to divine what things indefinite time
may evolve, though we cannot look forward with
the eyes of

'the prophetic soul
Of the wide-world brooding on things to come,'

yet the unapparent future has a claim to make itself felt as an idea controlling our perspective. It
commands us not to regard the series of what we
call ancient and mediæval history as leading up
to the modern age and the twentieth century; it
bids us to consider the whole sequence up to the
present moment as probably no more than the beginning of a social and psychical development, whereof
the end is withdrawn from our view by countless
millenniums to come. All the epochs of the past are
only a few of the front carriages, and probably
the least wonderful, in the van of an interminable
procession."

Although Bury made efficient use of the bearing
of one aspect of natural science, that represented by
Darwinism, upon the idea of progress as the clue
to history, he did not dwell upon the significance
of another branch, applied science, for his philosophy of interpretation. Yet technology is the
fundamental basis of modern civilization, supplies
a dynamic force of inexorable drive, and indicates
the methods by which the progressive conquest of
nature can be effected. Important as it is, even

viewed superficially, technology has received little attention from historical thinkers and from those social observers who scan the horizon of the future. Preoccupied with practical tasks, technologists have neglected the philosophical aspects of their work. They report their findings usually in terms of physics and mechanics—machines, kilowatt hours, mileage traversed, and commodities produced. Seldom do they touch upon the effect of their labors upon mankind, the social adjustments made necessary by their operations, and the potentialities ahead.* But of all the ideas pertinent to the concept of progress, to the interpretation of what has gone on during the past two hundred years and is going on in the world, none is more relevant than technology.

The immediate effects of what is called "the industrial revolution" have been traced, of course, in many works by economic historians—the introduction of rapid transportation and communication, the rise of the factory system with its huge urban agglomerations, the division of labor, and the erection of capitalism upon the ruins of feudalism. But such treatises generally suffer from two limitations. They do not trace to their utmost ramifications the influences of technology upon the very woof and warp of civilization, including poetry and art. And they usually deal with the industrial revolution as an accomplished fact. Indeed the very term "revolution" is misleading in this connection for it implies that one order has been overturned and another substituted for it. Such analogies do not apply to the case before us. A peasant class may

---

* For a technological view of the modern world, see the collection of essays, *Toward Civilization* (ed. C. A. Beard), by eminent engineers.

revolt, overthrow landlords, burn castles, and establish an agrarian democracy, but the revolution wrought by technology in pre-machine economy was no such qualified affair. It did facilitate the conquest of landed aristocracies by the bourgeois, but that was an incident in its march, not the goal or end of its achievement. Rather was that the beginning of an evolution of indefinite scope, bound by no reach of time. A hundred years after the so-called "industrial revolution," technology was evidently only at the opening of its career. By that time it had undone many of the effects brought about by the crude steam engine and started another "revolution" with the internal combustion engine and the dynamo. Hence in dealing with the effects of technology upon social evolution we are not confronted by accomplished work alone, but also by a swiftly advancing method for subduing material things.

What then is this technology which constitutes the supreme instrument of modern progress? Although the term is freely employed in current writings, its meaning as actuality and potentiality has never been explored and defined. Indeed, so wide-reaching are its ramifications that the task is difficult and hazardous. Narrowly viewed, technology consists of the totality of existing laboratories, machines, and processes already developed, mastered, and in operation. But it is far more than mere objective realities.

Intimately linked in its origin and operation with pure science, even its most remote mathematical speculations, technology has a philosophy of nature and a method—an attitude toward materials and work—and hence is a subjective force of high tension. It embraces within its scope great constellations of ideas, some explored to apparent limits and others in the form of posed problems and emergent issues dimly understood. Though historically associated with the type of economy generally known as Western capitalism, technology by its intrinsic nature transcends all social forms, the whole heritage of acquired institutions and habits. It serves with impartiality Japanese samurai, American industrialists, and the Russian soviet state. Universal in its reach, it cannot be monopolized by any nation, class, period, government, or people. In catholicity it surpasses all religions. As an instrument of work engaging human energies in a manner far surpassing the lure of war, as a social dissolvent and readjuster, and as a philosophy of action, technology must be brought into the main stream of history, if the course of history is to be surveyed correctly and "the dark imminence of the unknown future" is to be in any way penetrated.

It is this dynamic character of technology that makes it so significant for the idea of progress. The latter assumes that mankind has been slowly advancing from a crude stage of primitive civilization; the former demonstrates what can be accomplished by exhibiting its achievements and disclosing its working methods. What was once Utopian becomes actuality. What appears to be impossible may be surmounted. The ancient theory that mankind revolves in a vicious circle is destroyed by patent facts. The mediæval notion of a static society bound to rule-of-thumb routine is swept into the discard by events.

But will the drive of technology fail? Bury suggests that the idea of progress may itself pass and be supplanted by another philosophy of history and life. Yet there is something intrinsic in technology which seems to promise it indefinite operation. First of all there is nothing final about it. The solution of one problem in technology nearly always opens up new problems for exploration. Activities in one specialty produce issues for its scientific neighbors. A discovery in chemistry shakes something loose in physics. Then the passionate quest of mankind for physical comfort, security, health, and well-being generally is behind the exploratory organs of technology. Until people prefer hunger rather than plenty, disease rather than health, technology will continue to be dynamic. At all events it has behind it man's insatiable curiosity which leads him to search the heavens with telescopes, dive to the bottom of the sea, and explore atomic worlds. Curiosity would have to die out in human nature before technology could become stagnant, stopping the progress of science and industry.

In another particular technology is geared into the interpretation of history formulated under the idea of progress. In discovering laws of nature it must deal with masses, with the interrelations of an immense number of particles, reducing the apparent idiosyncrasies of individual particles to averages and general rules. So with history.

In human societies founded upon war and politics, the leadership of a single masterful personality may be essential to victory or perdurance. So "chance" reigns here, and certain writers, observing the play of this phenomenon, shape their interpretations around the great-man theory: the masses of people count for nothing, are pawns in the game, and God, chance, or fortune sends heroes now and then to guide them, save them—or perhaps get them into wars where they perish by the million.

In societies founded on technology, the warrior, priest, and political leader sink into the background or at all events can operate only in accordance with the economic realities produced by the machine. Thus technology reinforces the social, as distinguished from the individual, aspects of historical evolution. Henceforward history must deal with masses of people, organized in associations, governed by laws of averages. Consequently statistical measurement, so fruitful in technology, becomes possible in tracing historical movements.

Owing to the meager character of records previous to the nineteenth century, historians can do little with the statistical method in exploring early ages, but the immense quantity of authentic data now being accumulated under public and private auspices will make it possible for the historian of the future to draw with a firmer hand the course of social development. For example, is there progress in public health? Indisputable materials warrant the conclusion that in specific areas the death rate is declining. In the year 2000 A.D. it will be possible to answer many fundamental questions concerning which we can merely guess at present. If there is progress it will be mass progress, measurable in averages and susceptible of graphic presentation.

It seems reasonable to assume also that technology is producing other social effects which will make a return to an exact past impossible. Through the press, the radio, the railway, the post office, and enormous educational plants, it extends literacy, distributes information, widens the social consciousness of masses of the people. Censorships and tyranny may delay the process here and there, now and then, but the disintegration of mass ignorance will proceed apace. So it becomes inconceivable that a basis of mass ignorance can ever be laid again, such as existed for the slave-owning aristocracies of Rome or the clerico-feudal régime of the Middle Ages. According to this apparently warrantable assumption, whatever may happen in the future, there will be no reduplication of the distant past. In this light the process of civilization becomes no Sisyphian enterprise. Viewed in the large, history reveals a great gulf between the primitive savagery with which mankind began and the best of modern social orders. This may be said without overlooking the tragedy and cruelty that mark the way from the beginnings; and technology by continually demonstrating potentialities, will surely strengthen the idea of progress until a new synthesis is provided which may enormously accelerate the blundering pace inherited from the past.

But after all this has been said, does the idea of progress take on the validity of a law of nature—the law of gravitation, for instance? Is it a conclusion drawn from the facts of history that imposes itself upon us as inescapable? The answer must be negative. Bury was no dogmatist here. As the editor of his *Selected Essays,* Mr. Harold Temperley, remarks, "the idea of progress was a useful one but it was not strictly scientific nor identical with the Darwinism conceptions. Bury speaks indeed of the 'countless stairs' man must ascend in the future, and believed perhaps that the movement would be upward. But his belief in the future was rather a hope than a conviction. And even if he had felt a conviction, he would not have maintained that it was scientifically defensible."

In the following pages (335-6) Bury makes this view clear: "Evolution itself, it must be remembered, does not necessarily mean, as applied to Society, the movement of man to a desirable good. It is a neutral scientific conception, compatible either with optimism or pessimism. According to different estimates it may appear to be a cruel sentence or a guarantee of steady amelioration, and it has actually been interpreted in both ways." His entire Epilogue (pp. 351-2) is a warning against "the illusion of finality." The last word has not been said. In the long train of the ages ideas succeed one another, hold the allegiance of multitudes for a time, pass into the heritage, and make way for novel conceptions of the great mystery—"the ultimate design of the universe."

If, however, the idea of progress cannot be set down as representing a purely scientific interpretation of history, that does not require a rejection of it as a guiding principle for statesmen and economic leaders. Many historical theories now exploded by critical scholars have exerted a powerful influence on the course of history. Every nation is inspired and given direction by what it thinks its past to be. Perhaps it may be said that every piece of large historical writing has been determined, in part at least, by the author's conception of the present and future. If the past as interpreted has been unsatisfactory, it may be reinterpreted in such a way as to help shape the ages to come. Strange as this may seem, it is true. For example the founders of the German romantic movement, so powerful at the opening of the nineteenth century, sought in the past of the nation's history the sign posts for a better future. Few other thinkers contributed more to the formation of modern Germany under Prussian leadership than Treitschke who employed history as his supreme implement of interpretation and prediction. Each step in the widening of democracy in England, from the sixteenth century onward, was justified by appeals to a more or less mythical tradition. This very intellectual operation, so distinct from the reasoning processes of the French Revolution, has served to give continuity to English development, to force a growth for which scientific history could offer no realistic authority. So it may be ventured that if the idea of progress is not a stubborn outcome of true history, it may, as a faith in possibilities, actually *make* history.

Yet it is not to be overlooked that the idea of progress differs from all fixed ideas of the past. It contains within itself the germs of indefinite expansion. It makes room for other conceptions within the wide reach of its sweep. Being a philosophy of change, it provides for change and, though it may be discarded from the vocabularies of mankind, it may continue to be a description of reality. If the Catholic Church which brought Galileo to book can widen its horizon to accept what it once rejected, surely a concept of history as catholic as the idea of progress will not be dropped in the march of events. Covering a wide range of known realities and potentialities, it cannot disappear entirely from human thought. Since a return to a belief in a completely static human society seems to be as impossible as anything under the sun, since dynamics is the eternal opposite of status, the survival value of the idea of progress as a way of thinking seems established beyond question, unless forsooth the historical chain of the ages should be suddenly broken by strange interpositions utterly beyond all previous human experience.

Bury was also well aware that many other thorny questions were entangled in the idea of progress. He was no cheerful optimist ready to applaud every statistical return indicating more bundles and bales of commodities, every change in the institutions acquired from the past, every movement of population on the face of the earth. He was never subdued to the Western tendency to measure everything by objective standards. He saw clearly that the idea of progress had to be more than a cold and mathematical description of the stream of history as fact. In his essay on "Darwinism and History," he said bluntly and positively: "Progress involves a judgment of value, which is not involved in the conception of history as a genetic process. It is also an idea distinct from evolution."

In the idea of progress, accordingly, there is inevitably an ethical element. It implies that the stream of history flows in a desirable direction, on the whole; and at once we are plunged in the middle of ethics. Immediately a fixed point of reference, bench mark, must be set up from which to determine whether the movement of history is in a desirable direction and, in the living present, what choices are to be made to accelerate the march toward the good. In other words some standard must be planted in the universal flux to furnish a guide for determining directions. A man on a steamer cannot tell by looking at the deck whether he is going east or west; he must look at the sun or the stars.

Although Bury does not enter into the debate thus raised between absolute ethics and relative ethics, those who seek to pass judgment on his book must face the issues involved.* On the one side they will encounter thinkers who believe "that ethical values have an objective status independent of all human cogitation or emotion—or of the existence of human beings as such." In this view ethical values have the same philosophical status as mathematical and logical truths. For instance, propositions such as "A breach of confidence is revolting" and "To gloat over others' misfortunes is contemptible" are eternally valid, are akin to the statement that two plus two equals four. On the other hand, a naturalistic conception of ethics calls for "the equilibration of interests and their rational adjustment to environment."

In both doctrines there are immense difficulties to be overcome and an excursion into them here would take us too far afield.

For the present it is sufficient to say that in itself the idea of progress cannot be regarded as "a law of social evolution" or an inevitable interpretation of historical development. While it is unescapable that, measured by any intellectual and physical standards, there has been an immense improvement in the lot of mankind since primitive days in many respects, historical researches do not "prove" that there will be a steady upward movement in the distant future in a desirable direction as tested by an ethical standard. At the end the idea of progress

---

* For this issue see Sydney Hook, "A Critique of Ethical Realism," in *The International Journal of Ethics*, January, 1930.

remains a reasoned conviction, a hope that may be realized, is indeed in process of realization.

Whatever may be the merits of the controversy over its philosophic soundness, the idea of progress, even when vaguely understood, has exerted a powerful influence on the development of civilization in the United States. Here a number of circumstances early conspired to make it the leading principle of society. In its economic note there was a special appeal. Although many of the original settlers fled to this continent in search of religious liberty, the motive with the overwhelming majority was the improvement of their economic status.

In such a motive they saw nothing to be ashamed of. Nor was there any reason why they should conceal or deny it. The kings and queens, lords and ladies, merchants and priests of the Old World had never been unmindful of increasing their patrimonies or raising their standards of living. Catholic Spain and Protestant England operated consistently on the principle that commerce and colonies were to be exploited for the advantage of the beneficiaries in the metropolis. Only a few ascetics in Europe were really willing to be hungry when they might be fed, cold when they could be warm, sick when health was at hand, and poor when the means of well-being could be had at the price of labor and ingenuity. On the rational and rationalist assumption that the material resources of the earth should be exploited in the interest of a comfortable life, immigrants came from the Old World to the New, founded the English colonies, and developed the United States. If many carried the idea to extremes and sought wealth for its own sake, piling up riches

and luxuries in avarice, that did not invalidate the
fundamental correctness of the general judgment.

If the simple economic motive, so striking in the
founding of the American colonies, had not been
sufficient to assure a progressive society, other conditions would have furnished the dynamics. For a
number of reasons it was impossible to establish
here a static system of land tenure, such as had
characterized the old régime in Europe. The In-
dians who inhabited the area settled by the British
could not be subdued to slavery and it was impossible to secure, for the Northern colonies at least,
a large body of immigrants who would accept a
permanently servile status. The very abundance of
land and natural resources made the reproduction
of any rigid order of tenure out of the question.
Attempts to establish a system of great estates tilled
by laborers bound to the task failed, save in the
planting sections of the South and temporarily in
certain small regions of the North.

Thus it turned out that the land was settled
mainly by small freeholders, mechanics, and laborers, with class lines loosely drawn, with possibilities
of improving economic status abundant, and with
opportunities for the ambitious open on every hand.
On such a large scale, this was a novel state of
affairs. In rigid societies, like those of feudal
Europe, progress was feasible, of course, but it was
hampered on all sides by the legal barriers of caste.
By landed aristocrats, merchants were held in contempt, mechanics were assigned to a low rank, and
tillers of the soil treated almost as a part of the
agricultural equipment. There were exceptions to
be sure, but the distinguishing characteristic of
America lay in the fact that what was deemed un-

usual in Europe became the rule here, especially after the abolition of Negro slavery.

Naturally the abundance of land and resources in a primitive state appealed to men and women of action—peasants, merchants, and artisans primarily concerned with making a realistic use of their opportunities for industrial enterprise. In this the British colonists differed fundamentally from the Europeans who occupied Latin America. The latter were mainly soldiers who conquered and settled down upon a subject population, encouraging priests to apply religious and social discipline. The major portion of the British colonists, on the other hand, were continuously engaged in practical economic affairs. They cut down forests, sailed the seas, hunted the whale under the frozen skies of two arctic regions, pioneered, plowed, planted, and reaped, eagerly making use of every instrument that invention could furnish to enlarge their powers and increase their wealth. Even the planting aristocracy of the South, while it spoke of merchants with contempt, was as zealous as any other class in augmenting its holdings and revenues. Outside New England, the clergy was nowhere supreme, and even there theocratic despotism was soon disintegrated by rational criticism, eventuating in Unitarianism and the thin transcendentalism of Emerson. It is not surprising, therefore, to find that the philosophers of progress in France, especially Saint-Simon, who fought under Washington in the American Revolution, looked upon the United States as the best possible theater in which to carry the new idea to full fruition.*

Two other conditions favorable to the flowering

* Beard, *Rise of American Civilization*, Vol. I, pp. 443ff.

of the idea of progress, to which Bury calls attention (p. 66), were especially prominent in the United States, namely emancipation from the rigors of classical education and preoccupation with scientific affairs. "So long as men believed that the Greeks and Romans had attained, in the best days of their civilization, to an intellectual plane which posterity could never hope to reach, so long as the authority of their thinkers was set up as unimpeachable, a theory of degeneration held the field, which excluded a theory of progress."

At no time in the history of education in America did this classical concept have a complete monopoly over intellectual life. Classical education there was, of course, in the early colleges, but those institutions were small in number in colonial times and the range of their influence over social life was extremely limited. The mass of the people and their leaders were not subdued to the classical discipline, nor were they dominated by an intellectual caste which paid excessive tribute to that type of education. When the great development of higher learning appeared, especially in the new state universities, the secular, realistic, and practical spirit became dominant, with the classics at best as a side line. Hence one form of intellectual tyranny was escaped, not without some loss to offset immense gains.

Founded on a realistic view of life, business enterprise, accompanied by its armies of inventors and explorers, therefore, made steady headway and at last established its supremacy. It could only attain its primary end—the accumulation of profits —by developing natural resources, stimulating popular demands, augmenting wealth, and encouraging applied science. Under the auspices of the state and federal governments, colleges and institutions for the advancement of technology were multiplied, and applications to every branch of economy were encouraged. Public grants were supplemented later by huge endowments from private purses as technical schools and universities widened the range of their interests. If no Saint-Pierres, Comtes, and Spencers appeared in the United States to give theoretical formulation to what was taking place, there was no doubt about the course of events. Immense energies, physical, intellectual, and moral, were being applied to the conquest of the earth, with a view to raising the standard of life, decreasing the death rate, overcoming illiteracy, eliminating physical suffering, and providing the comforts of a rational living.

With a society secular in motive, dynamic in economy, scientific in intellectual interest, it was inevitable that its political institutions should reflect these dominant drives. Legal rigidity, such as the French monarchy sought to maintain in the old régime, was impossible in social fluidity. Although it is the fashion in some quarters to treat the Constitution of the United States as a kind of straitjacket law, it in fact accepts the fundamental postulate of progress in human affairs. In the preamble it announces that the new government is founded "to form a more perfect union, establish justice, insure domestic tranquillity, provide for the common defense, promote the general welfare, and secure the blessings of liberty to ourselves and our posterity."

Nowhere does it assume perfection and completeness. Its language, deliberately made general in several parts, leaves room for wide and various interpretations, according to time and circumstance, thus assuring flexibility for ages to come. Indeed its adaptability to the succeeding purposes of the nation has been one of its supreme claims to excellence.

Well aware that when they had done their best to provide for the contingencies of the future, their work was not final, the framers of the Constitution incorporated in their document a separate article describing the process by which amendments were to be effected. While Washington admitted that the document as drafted was "not free from imperfection," he called attention, in urging ratification, to the fact that "a constitutional door is opened for future amendments and alterations." In other words, the Fathers were not trying to place the country in a straitjacket, but were providing for unity, stability, and development. And the history of more than a century and a half has borne witness to the wisdom of their discretion.

American social philosophy also took on the color of the main intellectual currents. Monarchy and feudalism were out of the question. So in due time the spirit of democracy, dramatized by Jefferson, swept over the United States. It is easy, no doubt, to speak lightly of his "glittering generalities" and to point out glaring discrepancies between practice and the perfection of the faith, but the fruits of his teachings are reflected in an insistence on equality before the law, in magnificent efforts at universal and secular education, in numerous institutions of beneficence, and in widespread attempts to level barriers in the way of opportunity, coming at last to a quest for a minimum of security for all.

Into the mood of the American people thus expressed the idea of progress fitted with extraordinary precision. Since political democracy evidently did not at once provide Utopia, it was apparent that important work remained to be done in the interest of human betterment, by increments, not by some final stroke of state. Hence the concept of continual progress furnished inspiration to countless thousands who knew little or nothing about its origins and are nameless in the narrow records of history. Change became the rule of American life. In the swift expansion of tiny settlements into a continental nation, transformations and alterations were obvious and bewilderingly rapid; so the thought that change as such called for defense seldom occurred to the participants in the drama. Although many things that were ugly and cruel occurred in the process, drawing a continuous fire of criticism, the idea of steady improvement in the lot of the masses was never lost to sight and it culminated in the opening years of the twentieth century in the belief that undeserved poverty could be utterly extirpated and a reasonable well-being assured to all. Violent differences of opinion over ways and means could not obliterate the conviction. Nor could economic depression destroy it. It remains, and will remain, a fundamental tenet of American society, and while vigor is left in the race it will operate with all the force of a dynamic idea rooted in purpose, will, and opportunity.

Although no scholar has searched American history for materials bearing on the idea of progress and no statesman has formulated them into a logical theory of statecraft, our records are rich in supporting data. The idea was explicit in the writings of Benjamin Franklin. Likewise in the rich

and varied mind of Jefferson it took manifold forms
—in his assumption that government exists for the
welfare of the governed rather than for the benefit
of governors, in his projects for the advancement
of science which flowered in the University of Virginia, in his schemes for universal education, and
in his legislation designed to secure religious liberty.
With regard to political aspects, the Virginia bill
of rights of 1776 summarized the whole creed:
"Government is, or ought to be, instituted for the
common benefit, protection and security of the people, nation, or community; of all the various modes
and forms of government, that is best which is
capable of producing the greatest degree of happiness and safety, and is most effectively secured
against the dangers of maladministration; and
when a government shall be found inadequate or
contrary to these purposes, a majority of the community hath an indubitable, unalienable, and inde-
feasible right to reform, alter or abolish it, in such
a manner as shall be judged most conducive to the
public weal." While anyone can pick flaws in this
declaration and find inconsistencies in practice, the
doctrine lies at the basis of American social thinking and has deeply influenced the course of its
development and application.

If we turn from American social theory to philosophy in general we encounter Emerson at once.
Here was a thinker equipped with wide learning
for his day, acquainted through travel with many
other lands, and severely critical in dealing with
the shallowness and crassness evident in American
life; nevertheless his belief in America as "a land
of opportunity" indicated a belief in the possibility
of progress. Although he could assail evils with

sharp pen and tongue, he did not look upon history as a huge mistake, or regard the events taking place around him as evidence of total depravity and unreason. On the contrary he said flatly in his essay on "Progress of Culture": "Who would live in the stone age or the bronze or the iron or the lacustrine? Who does not prefer the age of steel, of gold, of coal, petroleum, cotton, steam, electricity, and the spectroscope? . . . Consider, at this time, what variety of issues, of enterprises public and private, what genius of science, what of administration, what of practical skill, what masters, each in his separate province, the railroad, the telegraph, the mines, the inland and marine explorations, the novel and powerful philanthropies, as well as agriculture, the foreign trade and the home trade (whose circuits in this country are as spacious as the foreign), manufactures, the very inventions, all on a national scale, too, have evoked!" There were dark clouds in the picture, no doubt, and Emerson was always aware of them, but underneath his thinking lay a faith in the future of his native land, its inner strength, and its potentialities.

Coming down to a contemporary philosopher of outstanding leadership, John Dewey, we find a similar emphasis on the social aspects of the subject. With Dewey, philosophy is not a world of abstractions apart from the world of fact evolving under the impulses of science and economic interest. On the contrary he is always drawing the worlds of thought and fact into living relations, seeking to make philosophy an instrument of aid in bringing about a more ideal social order. He does not look upon the world as completed; nor does he expect to find perfection in an overnight adoption of some rigid Utopia. In his view the continuous improvement of social relations is possible, especially with the help of natural science, and the business of philosophy is to supply interpretation and guidance. Closed systems of thought, characterized by apparently logical perfection, seem to him interesting but largely irrelevant to the transformations of matter and mind that are continuously going on around us. Hence he is content with less than omniscience while he can see thought at work effecting an ever more harmonious and beautiful adjustment of social arrangements and relationships. If a prejudice in favor of the idea of progress does not lie at the base of his philosophy, the concept is certainly made manifest in the practical upshot of his thinking.

From what has been said in the preceding pages it is evident that the idea of progress is both an interpretation of history and a philosophy of action. Whether the evolution of mankind is at bottom a progressive revelation of the spirit of God, an unfolding of the Idea, as Hegel taught, or a continuous adaptation to changing material circumstances, as Marx emphasized, it is essentially movement. And defenders of progress must assume that on the whole it is in a desirable direction. If in final analysis the concept of progress is untenable as explanation, it may yet become the dominant note during an enormous future to be explored. Conceding for the sake of argument that the past has been chaos, without order or design, we are still haunted by the shadowing thought that by immense efforts of will and intelligence, employing natural science as the supreme instrumentality of power, mankind may rise above necessity into the kingdom of freedom. subduing material things to humane and rational purposes.

THE IDEA OF PROGRESS

INTRODUCTION

WHEN we say that ideas rule the world, or exercise a decisive power in history, we are generally thinking of those ideas which express human aims and depend for their realisation on the human will, such as liberty, toleration, equality of opportunity, socialism. Some of these have been partly realised, and there is no reason why any of them should not be fully realised, in a society or in the world, if it were the united purpose of a society or of the world to realise it. They are approved or condemned because they are held to be good or bad, not because they are true or false. But there is another order of ideas that play a great part in determining and directing the course of man's conduct but do not depend on his will—ideas which bear upon the mystery of life, such as Fate, Providence, or personal immortality. Such ideas may operate in important ways on the forms of social action, but they involve a question of fact and they are accepted or rejected not because they are believed to be useful or injurious, but because they are believed to be true or false.

The idea of the progress of humanity is an idea of this kind, and it is important to be quite clear on the point. We now take it so much for granted,

we are so conscious of constantly progressing in
knowledge, arts, organising capacity, utilities of all
sorts, that it is easy to look upon Progress as an
aim, like liberty or a world-federation, which it only
depends on our own efforts and good-will to achieve.
But though all increases of power and knowledge
depend on human effort, the idea of the Progress of
humanity, from which all these particular progresses
derive their value, raises a definite question of fact,
which man's wishes or labours cannot affect any
more than his wishes or labours can prolong life
beyond the grave.

This idea means that civilisation has moved, is
moving, and will move in a desirable direction.
But in order to judge that we are moving in a
desirable direction we should have to know precisely what the destination is.   To the minds of
most people the desirable outcome of human development would be a condition of society in which
all the inhabitants of the planet would enjoy a
perfectly happy existence.   But it is impossible to
be sure that civilisation is moving in the right
direction to realise this aim.   Certain features of
our "progress" may be urged as presumptions in

its favour, but there are always offsets, and it has
always been easy to make out a case that, from the
point of view of increasing happiness, the tendencies
of our progressive civilisation are far from desirable.
In short, it cannot be proved that the unknown
destination towards which man is advancing is
desirable.   The movement may be Progress, or it
may be in an undesirable direction and therefore
not Progress.   This is a question of fact, and one
which is at present as insoluble as the question of

personal immortality. It is a problem which bears on the mystery of life.

Moreover, even if it is admitted to be probable that the course of civilisation has so far been in a desirable direction, and such as would lead to general felicity if the direction were followed far enough, it cannot be proved that ultimate attainment depends entirely on the human will. For the advance might at some point be arrested by an insuperable wall. Take the particular case of knowledge, as to which it is generally taken for granted that the continuity of progress in the future depends altogether on the continuity of human effort (assuming that human brains do not degenerate). This assumption is based on a strictly limited experience. Science has been advancing without interruption during the last three or four hundred years; every new discovery has led to new problems and new methods of solution, and opened up new fields for exploration. Hitherto men of science have not been compelled to halt, they have always found means to advance further. But what assurance have we that they will not one day come up against impassable barriers? The experience of four hundred years, in which the surface of nature has been successfully tapped, can hardly be said to warrant conclusions as to the prospect of operations extending over four hundred or four thousand centuries. Take biology or astronomy. How can we be sure that some day progress may not come to a dead pause, not because knowledge is exhausted, but because our resources for investigation are exhausted—because, for instance, scientific instruments have reached the limit of perfection beyond which it is demonstrably impossible to improve them, or because (in the case of astronomy) we come into the presence of forces of which, unlike gravitation, we have no terrestrial experience? It is an assumption, which cannot be verified, that we shall not soon reach a point in our knowledge of nature beyond which the human intellect is unqualified to pass.

But it is just this assumption which is the light and inspiration of man's scientific research. For if the assumption is not true, it means that he can never come within sight of the goal which is, in the case of physical science, if not a complete knowledge of the cosmos and the processes of nature, at least an immeasurably larger and deeper knowledge than we at present possess.

Thus continuous progress in man's knowledge of his environment, which is one of the chief conditions of general Progress, is a hypothesis which may or may not be true. And if it is true, there remains the further hypothesis of man's moral and social "perfectibility," which rests on much less impressive evidence. There is nothing to show that he may not reach, in his psychical and social development, a stage at which the conditions of his life will be still far from satisfactory, and beyond which he will find it impossible to progress. This is a question of fact which no willing on man's part can alter. It is a question bearing on the mystery of life.

Enough has been said to show that the Progress of humanity belongs to the same order of ideas as Providence or personal immortality. It is true or it is false, and like them it cannot be proved either true or false. Belief in it is an act of faith.

The idea of human Progress then is a theory
which involves a synthesis of the past and a
prophecy of the future. It is based on an interpretation of history which regards men as slowly
advancing—*pedetemtim progredientes*—in a definite
and desirable direction, and infers that this progress
will continue indefinitely. And it implies that, as

The issue of the earth's great business,

a condition of general happiness will ultimately be
enjoyed, which will justify the whole process of
civilisation ; for otherwise the direction would not
be desirable. There is also a further implication.
The process must be the necessary outcome of the
psychical and social nature of man ; it must not be
at the mercy of any external will ; otherwise there
would be no guarantee of its continuance and its
issue, and the idea of Progress would lapse into the
idea of Providence.

As time is the very condition of the possibility of
Progress, it is obvious that the idea would be value-
less if there were any cogent reasons for supposing
that the time at the disposal of humanity is likely
to reach a limit in the near future. If there were
good cause for believing that the earth would be
uninhabitable in A.D. 2000 or 2100 the doctrine
of Progress would lose its meaning and would
automatically disappear. It would be a delicate
question to decide what is the minimum period of
time which must be assured to man for his future
development, in order that Progress should possess
value and appeal to the emotions. The recorded
history of civilisation covers 6000 years or so, and

if we take this as a measure of our conceptions of time-distances, we might assume that if we were sure of a period ten times as long ahead of us the idea of Progress would not lose its power of appeal. Sixty thousand years of *historical* time, when we survey the changes which have come to pass in six thousand, opens to the imagination a range vast enough to seem almost endless.

This psychological question, however, need not be decided. For science assures us that the stability of the present conditions of the solar system is certified for many myriads of years to come. Whatever gradual modifications of climate there may be, the planet will not cease to support life for a period which transcends and flouts all efforts of imagination. In short, the *possibility* of Progress is guaranteed by the high probability, based on astro-physical science, of an immense time to progress in.

It may surprise many to be told that the notion of Progress, which now seems so easy to apprehend, is of comparatively recent origin. It has indeed been claimed that various thinkers, both ancient (for instance, Seneca) and medieval (for instance, Friar Bacon), had long ago conceived it. But sporadic observations—such as man's gradual rise from primitive and savage conditions to a certain level of civilisation by a series of inventions, or the possibility of some future additions to his knowledge of nature—which were inevitable at a certain stage of human reflection, do not amount to an anticipation of the idea. The value of such observations was determined, and must be estimated, by the whole context of ideas in which they occurred. It is from its bearings on the future that Progress derives its

value, its interest, and its power. You may conceive civilisation as having gradually advanced in the
past, but you have not got the idea of Progress
until you go on to conceive that it is destined to
advance indefinitely in the future. Ideas have their
intellectual climates, and I propose to show briefly
in this Introduction that the intellectual climates of
classical antiquity and the ensuing ages were not
propitious to the birth of the doctrine of Progress.
It is not till the sixteenth century that the obstacles
to its appearance definitely begin to be transcended
and a favourable atmosphere to be gradually
prepared.

I

It may, in particular, seem surprising that the
Greeks, who were so fertile in their speculations on
human life, did not hit upon an idea which seems
so simple and obvious to us as the idea of Progress.
But if we try to realise their experience and the
general character of their thought we shall cease
to wonder. Their recorded history did not go back
far, and so far as it did go there had been no
impressive series of new discoveries suggesting
either an indefinite increase of knowledge or a
growing mastery of the forces of nature. In the
period in which their most brilliant minds were
busied with the problems of the universe men
might improve the building of ships, or invent new
geometrical demonstrations, but their science did
little or nothing to transform the conditions of life
or to open any vista into the future. They were

in the presence of no facts strong enough to counteract that profound veneration of antiquity which seems natural to mankind, and the Athenians of the age of Pericles or of Plato, though they were thoroughly, obviously "modern" compared with the Homeric Greeks, were never self-consciously "modern" as we are.

I

The indications that human civilisation was a gradual growth, and that man had painfully worked his way forward from a low and savage state, could not, indeed, escape the sharp vision of the Greeks. For instance, Aeschylus represents men as originally living at hazard in sunless caves, and raised from that condition by Prometheus, who taught them the arts of life.   In Euripides we find a similar recognition of the ascent of mankind to a civilised state, from primitive barbarism, some god or other playing the part of Prometheus.   In such passages as these we have, it may be said, the idea that man has progressed; and it may fairly be suggested that belief in a natural progress lay, for Aeschylus as well as for Euripides, behind the poetical fiction of supernatural intervention.   But these recognitions of a progress were not incompatible with the widely-spread belief in an initial degeneration of the human race; nor did it usually appear as a rival doctrine.   The old legend of a "golden age" of simplicity, from which man had fallen away, was generally accepted as truth, and leading thinkers combined it with the doctrine of a gradual sequence of social and material improve-

ments[1] during the subsequent period of decline.
We find the two views thus combined, for instance,
in Plato's *Laws*, and in the earliest reasoned history
of civilisation written by Dicaearchus, a pupil of
Aristotle.[2] But the simple life of the first age, in
which men were not worn with toil, and war and
disease were unknown, was regarded as the ideal
state to which man would be only too fortunate if
he could return. He had indeed at a remote time
in the past succeeded in ameliorating some of the
conditions of his lot, but such ancient discoveries as
fire or ploughing or navigation or law-giving did not
suggest the guess that new inventions might lead
ultimately to conditions in which life would be more
complex but as happy as the simple life of the
primitive world.

But, if some relative progress might be admitted,
the general view of Greek philosophers was that
they were living in a period of inevitable degeneration and decay—inevitable because it was prescribed
by the nature of the universe. We have only an
imperfect knowledge of the influential speculations
of Heraclitus, Pythagoras, and Empedocles, but we
may take Plato's tentative philosophy of history to
illustrate the trend and the prejudices of Greek
thought on this subject. The world was created
and set going by the Deity, and, as his work, it
was perfect; but it was not immortal and had in it

---

[1] In the masterly survey of early Greek history which Thucydides prefixed
to his work, he traces the social progress of the Greeks in historical times,
and finds the key to it in the increase of wealth.

[2] Aristotle's own view is not very clear. He thinks that all arts, sciences,
and institutions have been repeatedly, or rather an infinite number of
times (ἀπειράκις) discovered in the past and again lost. *Metaphysics*, xi. 8
ad fin.; *Politics*, iv. 10, cp. ii. 2. An infinite number of times seems to
imply the doctrine of cycles.

the seeds of decay.   The period of its duration is
72,000 solar years.   During the first half of this
period the original uniformity and order, which
were impressed upon it by the Creator, are maintained under his guidance ; but then it reaches a
point from which it begins, as it were, to roll back ;
the Deity has loosened his grip of the machine, the
order is disturbed, and the second 36,000 years are
a period of gradual decay and degeneration.   At
the end of this time, the world left to itself would
dissolve into chaos, but the Deity again seizes the
helm and restores the original conditions, and the
whole process begins anew.   The first half of such
a world-cycle corresponds to the Golden Age of
legend in which men lived happily and simply ; we
have now unfortunately reached some point in the
period of decadence.

Plato applies the theory of degradation in his
study of political communities.   He conceives his
own utopian aristocracy as having existed somewhere towards the beginning of the period of the
world's relapse, when things were not so bad,[1] and
exhibits its gradual deterioration, through the successive stages of timocracy, oligarchy, democracy,
and despotism.   He explains this deterioration as
primarily caused by a degeneration of the race, due
to laxity and errors in the State regulation of
marriages, and the consequent birth of biologically
inferior individuals.

The theories of Plato are only the most illustrious

[1] Similarly he places the ideal society which he describes in the *Critias*
9000 years before Solon.   The state which he plans in the *Laws* is indeed
imagined as a practicable project in his own day, but then it is only a second-
best.   The ideal state of which Aristotle sketched an outline (*Politics*, iv. v.)
is not set either in time or in place.

example of the tendency characteristic of Greek philosophical thinkers to idealise the immutable as possessing a higher value than that which varies. This affected all their social speculations. They believed in the ideal of an absolute order in society, from which, when it is once established, any deviation must be for the worse. Aristotle, considering the subject from a practical point of view, laid down that changes in an established social order are undesirable, and should be as few and slight as possible.[1] This prejudice against change excluded the apprehension of civilisation as a progressive movement. It did not occur to Plato or any one else that a perfect order might be attainable by a long series of changes and adaptations. Such an order, being an embodiment of reason, could be created only by a deliberate and immediate act of a planning mind. It might be devised by the wisdom of a philosopher or revealed by the Deity. Hence the salvation of a community must lie in preserving intact, so far as possible, the institutions imposed by the enlightened lawgiver, since change meant corruption and disaster. These *a priori* principles account for the admiration of the Spartan state entertained by many Greek philosophers, because it was supposed to have preserved unchanged for an unusually long period a system established by an inspired legislator.

2

Thus time was regarded as the enemy of humanity. Horace's verse,

Damnosa quid non imminuit dies ?

---

[1] *Politics*, ii. 5.

"time depreciates the value of the world," expresses the pessimistic axiom accepted in most systems of ancient thought.

The theory of world-cycles was so widely current that it may almost be described as the orthodox theory of cosmic time among the Greeks, and it passed from them to the Romans. According to some of the Pythagoreans each cycle repeated to the minutest particular the course and events of the preceding. If the universe dissolves into the original chaos, there appeared to them to be no reason why the second chaos should produce a world differing in the least respect from its predecessor. The nth cycle would be indeed numerically distinct from the first, but otherwise would be identical with it, and no man could possibly discover the number of the cycle in which he was living. As no end seems to have been assigned to the whole process, the course of the world's history would contain an endless number of Trojan Wars, for instance ; an endless number of Platos would write an endless number of *Republics*. Virgil uses this idea in his Fourth Eclogue, where he meditates a return of the Golden Age :

> Alter erit tum Tiphys, et altera quae uehat Argo
> Delectos heroas ; erunt etiam altera bella,
> Atque iterum ad Troiam magnus mittetur Achilles.

The periodic theory might be held in forms in which this uncanny doctrine of absolute identity was avoided ; but at the best it meant an endless monotonous iteration, which was singularly unlikely to stimulate speculative interest in the future. It must be remembered that no thinker had any means of knowing how near to the end of his cycle the present hour might be. The most influential school of the later Greek age, the Stoics, adopted the theory of cycles, and the natural psychological effect of the theory is vividly reflected in Marcus Aurelius, who frequently dwells on it in his *Meditations*. "The rational soul," he says, "wanders round the whole world and through the encompassing void, and gazes into infinite time, and considers the periodic destructions and rebirths of the universe, and reflects that our posterity will see nothing new, and that our ancestors saw nothing greater than we have seen. A man of forty years, possessing the most moderate intelligence, may be said to have seen all that is past and all that is to come ; so uniform is the world."[1]

3

And yet one Stoic philosopher saw clearly, and declared emphatically, that increases in knowledge must be expected in the future.

"There are many peoples to-day," Seneca wrote, "who are ignorant of the cause of eclipses of the moon, and it has only recently been demonstrated among ourselves. The day will come when time and human diligence will clear up problems which are now obscure. We divide the few years of our lives unequally between study and vice, and it will therefore be the work of many generations to explain such phenomena as comets. One day our posterity will marvel at our ignorance of causes so clear to them.

[1] xi. 1. The cyclical theory was curiously revived in the nineteenth century by Nietzsche, and it is interesting to note his avowal that it took him a long time to overcome the feeling of pessimism which the doctrine inspired.

" How many new animals have we first come to know in the present age? In time to come men will know much that is unknown to us. Many discoveries are reserved for future ages, when our memory will have faded from men's minds. We imagine ourselves initiated in the secrets of nature; we are standing on the threshold of her temple."

But these predictions are far from showing that Seneca had the least inkling of a doctrine of the Progress of humanity. Such a doctrine is sharply excluded by the principles of his philosophy and his profoundly pessimistic view of human affairs. Immediately after the passage which I have quoted he goes on to enlarge on the progress of vice. " Are you surprised to be told that human knowledge has not yet completed its whole task? Why, human wickedness has not yet fully developed."

Yet, at least, it may be said, Seneca believed in a progress of knowledge and recognised its value. Yes, but the value which he attributed to it did not lie in any advantages which it would bring to the general community of mankind. He did not expect from it any improvement of the world. The value of natural science, from his point of view, was this, that it opened to the philosopher a divine region, in which, "wandering among the stars," he could laugh at the earth and all its riches, and his mind "delivered as it were from prison could return to its original home." In other words, its value lay not in its results, but simply in the intellectual activity; and therefore it concerned not mankind at large but a few chosen individuals who, doomed to live in a miserable world, could thus deliver their souls from slavery.

For Seneca's belief in the theory of degeneration and the hopeless corruption of the race is uncompromising. Human life on the earth is periodically destroyed, alternately by fire and flood; and each period begins with a golden age in which men live in rude simplicity, innocent because they are ignorant not because they are wise. When they degenerate from this state, arts and inventions promote deterioration by ministering to luxury and vice.

Interesting, then, as Seneca's observations on the prospect of some future scientific discoveries are, and they are unique in ancient literature,[1] they were far from adumbrating a doctrine of the Progress of man. For him, as for Plato and the older philosophers, time is the enemy of man.

4

There was however a school of philosophical speculation, which might have led to the foundation of a theory of Progress, if the historical outlook of the Greeks had been larger and if their temper had been different. The Atomic theory of Democritus seems to us now, in many ways, the most wonderful achievement of Greek thought, but it had a small range of influence in Greece, and would have had less if it had not convinced the brilliant mind of Epicurus. The Epicureans developed it, and it may be that the views which they put forward as to the history of the human race are mainly their own superstructure. These philosophers rejected

[1] They are general and definite. This distinguishes them, for instance, from Plato's incidental hint in the *Republic* as to the prospect of the future development of solid geometry.

entirely the doctrine of a Golden Age and a subsequent degeneration, which was manifestly incompatible with their theory that the world was mechanically formed from atoms without the intervention of a Deity. For them, the earliest condition of men resembled that of the beasts, and from this primitive and miserable condition they laboriously reached the existing state of civilisation, not by external guidance or as a consequence of some initial design, but simply by the exercise of human intelligence throughout a long period.[1] The gradual amelioration of their existence was marked by the discovery of fire and the use of metals, the invention of language, the invention of weaving, the growth of arts and industries, navigation, the development of family life, the establishment of social order by means of kings, magistrates, laws, the foundation of cities. The last great step in the amelioration of life, according to Lucretius, was the illuminating philosophy of Epicurus, who dispelled the fear of invisible powers and guided man from intellectual darkness to light.

But Lucretius and the school to which he belonged did not look forward to a steady and continuous process of further amelioration in the future. They believed that a time would come when the universe would fall into ruins,[2] but the intervening period did not interest them. Like

---

[1] Lucretius v. 1448 *sqq.* (where the word *progress* is pronounced):

> Usus et impigrae simul experientia mentis
> Paulatim docuit pedetemtim *progredientis.*
> Sic unum quicquid paulatim protrahit aetas
> In medium ratioque in luminis erigit oras.
> Namque alid ex alio clarescere et ordine debet
> Artibus, ad summum donec uenere cacumen.

[2] *Ib.* 95.

many other philosophers, they thought that their own philosophy was the final word on the universe, and they did not contemplate the possibility that important advances in knowledge might be achieved by subsequent generations. And, in any case, their scope was entirely individualistic; all their speculations were subsidiary to the aim of rendering the life of the individual as tolerable as possible here and now. Their philosophy, like Stoicism, was a philosophy of resignation; it was thoroughly pessimistic and therefore incompatible with the idea of Progress. Lucretius himself allows an underlying feeling of scepticism as to the value of civilisation occasionally to escape.[1]

Indeed, it might be said that in the mentality of the ancient Greeks there was a strain which would have rendered them indisposed to take such an idea seriously, if it had been propounded. No period of their history could be described as an age of optimism. They were never, by their achievements in art or literature, in mathematics or philosophy, exalted into self-complacency or lured into setting high hopes on human capacity. Man has resourcefulness to meet everything—ἄπορος ἐπ' οὐδὲν ἔρχεται, —they did not go further than that.

This instinctive pessimism of the Greeks had a religious tinge which perhaps even the Epicureans found it hard entirely to expunge. They always felt that they were in the presence of unknown incalculable powers, and that subtle dangers lurked in human achievements and gains. Horace has taken this feeling as the *motif* of a criticism on

---

[1] His *eadem sunt omnia semper* (iii. 945) is the constant refrain of Marcus Aurelius.

man's inventive powers.   A voyage of Virgil
suggests the reflection that his friend's life would
not be exposed to hazards on the high seas if the
art of navigation had never been discovered—if
man had submissively respected the limits imposed
by nature.   But man is audacious :

> *Nequiquam deus abscidit*
> *Prudens oceano dissociabili*
> *Terras.*
> In vain a wise god sever'd lands
> By the dissociating sea.

Daedalus violated the air, as Hercules invaded
hell.   The discovery of fire put us in possession of
a forbidden secret.   Is this unnatural conquest of
nature safe or wise ?   *Nil mortalibus ardui est* :

> Man finds no feat too hard or high ;
> Heaven is not safe from man's desire.
> Our rash designs move Jove to ire,
> He dares not lay his thunder by.

The thought of this ode [1] roughly expresses what
would have been the instinctive sense of thoughtful
Greeks if the idea of Progress had been presented
to them.   It would have struck them as audacious,
the theory of men unduly elated and perilously
at ease in the presence of unknown incalculable
powers.

This feeling or attitude was connected with the
idea of Moira.   If we were to name any single idea
as generally controlling or pervading Greek thought
from Homer to the Stoics,[2] it would perhaps be
Moira, for which we have no equivalent.   The

---

[1] i. 3.
[2] The Stoics identified Moira with *Pronoia*, in accordance with their
theory that the universe is permeated by thought.

common rendering "fate" is misleading. Moira meant a fixed order in the universe; but as a fact to which men must bow, it had enough in common with fatality to demand a philosophy of resignation and to hinder the creation of an optimistic atmosphere of hope. It was this order which kept things in their places, assigned to each its proper sphere and function, and drew a definite line, for instance, between men and gods. Human progress towards perfection—towards an ideal of omniscience, or an ideal of happiness, would have been a breaking down of the bars which divide the human from the divine. Human nature does not alter; it is fixed by Moira.

5

We can see now how it was that speculative Greek minds never hit on the idea of Progress. In the first place, their limited historical experience did not easily suggest such a synthesis; and in the second place, the axioms of their thought, their suspiciousness of change, their theories of Moira, of degeneration and cycles, suggested a view of the world which was the very antithesis of progressive development. Epicurean philosophers made indeed what might have been an important step in the direction of the doctrine of Progress, by discarding the theory of degeneration, and recognising that civilisation had been created by a series of successive improvements achieved by the effort of man alone. But here they stopped short. For they had their eyes fixed on the lot of the individual here and now, and their study of the history of humanity was strictly subordinate to this personal interest. The value of their recognition of human progress in the past is conditioned by the general tenor and purpose of their theory of life. It was simply one item in their demonstration that man owed nothing to supernatural intervention and had nothing to fear from supernatural powers. It is however no accident that the school of thought which struck on a path that might have led to the idea of Progress was the most uncompromising enemy of superstition that Greece produced.

It might be thought that the establishment of Roman rule and order in a large part of the known world, and the civilising of barbarian peoples, could not fail to have opened to the imagination of some of those who reflected on it in the days of Virgil or of Seneca, a vista into the future. But there was no change in the conditions of life likely to suggest a brighter view of human existence. With the loss of freedom pessimism increased, and the Greek philosophies of resignation were needed more than ever. Those whom they could not satisfy turned their thoughts to new mystical philosophies and religions, which were little interested in the earthly destinies of human society.

II

I

The idea of the universe which prevailed throughout the Middle Ages, and the general orientation of men's thoughts were incompatible with some of the fundamental assumptions which are required by

the idea of Progress. According to the Christian
theory which was worked out by the Fathers, and
especially by St. Augustine, the whole movement
of history has the purpose of securing the happiness
of a small portion of the human race in another
world; it does not postulate a further development
of human history on earth. For Augustine, as for
any medieval believer, the course of history would
be satisfactorily complete if the world came to an
end in his own lifetime. He was not interested in
the question whether any gradual amelioration of
society or increase of knowledge would mark the
period of time which might still remain to run
before the day of Judgment. In Augustine's system
the Christian era introduced the last period of
history, the old age of humanity, which would
endure only so long as to enable the Deity to
gather in the predestined number of saved people.
This theory might be combined with the widely-
spread belief in a millennium on earth, but the
conception of such a dispensation does not render
it a theory of Progress.

Again, the medieval doctrine apprehends history
not as a natural development but as a series of
events ordered by divine intervention and revela-
tions. If humanity had been left to go its own
way it would have drifted to a highly undesirable
port, and all men would have incurred the fate of
everlasting misery from which supernatural interference rescued the minority. A belief in Providence might indeed, and in a future age would,
be held along with a belief in Progress, in the
same mind; but the fundamental assumptions were
incongruous, and so long as the doctrine of

Providence was undisputedly in the ascendant, a doctrine of Progress could not arise. And the doctrine of Providence, as it was developed in Augustine's *City of God*, controlled the thought of the Middle Ages.

There was, moreover, the doctrine of original sin, an insuperable obstacle to the moral amelioration of the race by any gradual process of development. For since, so long as the human species endures on earth, every child will be born naturally evil and worthy of punishment, a moral advance of humanity to perfection is plainly impossible.

2

But there are certain features in the medieval theory of which we must not ignore the significance. In the first place, while it maintained the belief in degeneration, endorsed by Hebrew mythology, it definitely abandoned the Greek theory of cycles. The history of the earth was recognised as a unique phenomenon in time ; it would never occur again, or anything resembling it. More important than all is the fact that Christian theology constructed a synthesis which for the first time attempted to give a definite meaning to the whole course of human events, a synthesis which represents the past as leading up to a definite and desirable goal in the future. Once this belief had been generally adopted and prevailed for centuries men might discard it along with the doctrine of Providence on which it rested, but they could not be content to return again to such views as satisfied the ancients, for whom human history, apprehended as a whole, was a tale of little meaning.[1] They must seek for some new synthesis to replace it.

Another feature of the medieval theory, pertinent to our inquiry, was an idea which Christianity took over from Greek and Roman thinkers. In the later period of Greek history, which began with the conquests of Alexander the Great, there had emerged the conception of the whole inhabited world as a unity and totality, the idea of the whole human race as one. We may conveniently call it the ecumenical idea—the principle of the *ecumene* or inhabited world, as opposed to the principle of the *polis* or city. Promoted by the vast extension of the geographical limits of the Greek world resulting from Alexander's conquests, and by his policy of breaking down the barriers between Greek and barbarian, the idea was reflected in the Stoic doctrine that all men are brothers, and that a man's true country is not his own particular city, but the *ecumene*.[2] It soon became familiar, popularised by the most popular of the later philosophies of Greece ; and just as it had been implied in the imperial aspiration and polity of Alexander, so it was implied, still more clearly, in the imperial theory of Rome. The idea of the

[1] It may be observed that Augustine (*De Civ. Dei*, x. 14) compares the teaching (*recta eruditio*) of the people of God, in the gradual process of history, to the education of an individual. Prudentius has a similar comparison for a different purpose (*c. Symmachum*, ii. 315 *sqq.*) :

Tardis semper processibus aucta
Crescit vita hominis et longo proficit usu.
Sic aevi mortalis habet se mobilis ordo,
Sic variat natura vices, infantia repit, etc.

Florus (*Epitome, ad init.*) had already divided Roman history into four periods corresponding to infancy, adolescence, manhood, and old age.

[2] Plutarch long ago saw the connection between the policy of Alexander and the cosmopolitan teaching of Zeno. *De Alexandri Magni virtute*, i. § 6.

Roman Empire, its theoretical justification, might
be described as the realisation of the unity of the
world by the establishment of a common order, the
unification of mankind in a single world-embracing
political organism. The term "world," *orbis* (*ter-
rarum*), which imperial poets use freely in speaking
of the Empire, is more than a mere poetical or
patriotic exaggeration ; it expresses the idea, the
unrealised ideal of the Empire. There is a stone
from Halicarnassus in the British Museum, on
which the idea is formally expressed from another
point of view. The inscription is of the time of
Augustus, and the Emperor is designated as
"saviour of the community of mankind." There
we have the notion of the human race apprehended
as a whole, the ecumenical idea, imposing upon
Rome the task described by Virgil as *regere imperio
populos*, and more humanely by Pliny as the
creation of a single fatherland for all the peoples
of the world.

   This idea, which in the Roman Empire and in
the Middle Ages took the form of a universal State
and a universal Church, passed afterwards into the
conception of the intercohesion of peoples as contributors to a common pool of civilisation — a
principle which, when the idea of Progress at last
made its appearance in the world, was to be one of
the elements in its growth.

3

   One remarkable man, the Franciscan friar Roger
Bacon,[1] who stands on an isolated pinnacle of his

---

[1] *c.* A.D. 1210–92.

own in the Middle Ages, deserves particular consideration. It has been claimed for him that he announced the idea of Progress; he has even been compared to Condorcet or Comte. Such claims are based on passages taken out of their context and indulgently interpreted in the light of later theories. They are not borne out by an examination of his general conception of the universe and the aim of his writings.

His aim was to reform higher education and introduce into the universities a wide, liberal, and scientific programme of secular studies. His chief work, the *Opus Majus*, was written for this purpose, to which his exposition of his own discoveries was subordinate. It was addressed and sent to Pope Clement IV., who had asked Bacon to give him an account of his researches, and was designed to persuade the Pontiff of the utility of science from an ecclesiastical point of view, and to induce him to sanction an intellectual reform, which without the approbation of the Church would at that time have been impossible. With great ingenuity and resourcefulness he sought to show that the studies to which he was devoted—mathematics, astronomy, physics, chemistry—were indispensable to an intelligent study of theology and Scripture. Though some of his arguments may have been urged simply to capture the Pope's good-will, there can be no question that Bacon was absolutely sincere in his view that theology was the mistress (*dominatrix*) of the sciences and that their supreme value lay in being necessary to it.

It was, indeed, on this principle of the close interconnection of all branches of knowledge that

Bacon based his plea and his scheme of reform. And the idea of the "solidarity" of the sciences, in which he anticipated a later age, is one of his two chief claims to be remembered. It is the motif of the *Opus Majus*, and it would have been more fully elaborated if he had lived to complete the encyclopaedic work, *Scriptum Principale*, which he had only begun before his death. His other title to fame is well-known. He realised, as no man had done before him, the importance of the experimental method in investigating the secrets of nature, and was an almost solitary pioneer in the paths to which his greater namesake, more than three hundred years later, was to invite the attention of the world.

But, although Roger Bacon was inspired by these enlightened ideas, although he cast off many of the prejudices of his time and boldly revolted against the tyranny of the prevailing scholastic philosophy, he was nevertheless in other respects a child of his age and could not disencumber himself of the current medieval conception of the universe. His general view of the course of human history was not materially different from that of St. Augustine. When he says that the practical object of all knowledge is to assure the safety of the human race, he explains this to mean "things which lead to felicity in the next life."

It is pertinent to observe that he not only shared in the belief in astrology, which was then universal, but considered it one of the most important parts of "mathematics." It was looked upon with disfavour by the Church as a dangerous study ; Bacon defended its use in the interests of the Church itself. He maintained, like Thomas Aquinas, the physiological influence of the celestial bodies, and regarded the planets as signs telling us what God has decreed from eternity to come to pass either by natural processes or by acts of human will or directly at his own good pleasure. Deluges, plagues, and earthquakes were capable of being predicted; political and religious revolutions were set in the starry rubric. The existence of six principal re- ligions was determined by the combinations of Jupiter with the other six planets. Bacon seriously expected the extinction of the Mohammedan religion before the end of the thirteenth century, on the ground of a prediction by an Arab astrologer.

One of the greatest advantages that the study of astrological lore will bring to humanity is that by its means the date of the coming of Anti-Christ may be fixed with certainty, and the Church may be prepared to face the perils and trials of that terrible time. Now the arrival of Anti-Christ meant the end of the world, and Bacon accepted the view, which he says was held by all wise men, that "we are not far from the times of Anti-Christ." Thus the intellectual reforms which he urged would have the effect, and no more, of preparing Christendom to resist more successfully the corruption in which the rule of Anti-Christ would involve the world. "Truth will prevail," by which he meant science will make advances, "though with difficulty, until Anti-Christ and his forerunners appear;" and on his own showing the interval would probably be short.

The frequency with which Bacon recurs to this subject, and the emphasis he lays on it, show that the appearance of Anti-Christ was a fixed point in his mental horizon. When he looked forward into the future, the vision which confronted him was a scene of corruption, tyranny, and struggle under the reign of a barbarous enemy of Christendom ; and after that, the end of the world.   It is from this point of view that we must appreciate the observations which he made on the advancement of knowledge.   " It is our duty," he says, " to supply what the ancients have left incomplete, because we have entered into their labours, which, unless we are asses, can stimulate us to achieve better results "; Aristotle corrected the errors of earlier thinkers ; Avicenna and Averroes have corrected Aristotle in some matters and have added much that is new ; and so it will go on till the end of the world.   And Bacon quotes passages from Seneca's *Physical Inquiries* to show that the acquisition of knowledge is gradual.   Attention has been already called to those passages, and it was shown how perverse it is, on the strength of such remarks, to claim Seneca as a teacher of the doctrine of Progress.   The same claim has been made for Bacon with greater confidence, and it is no less perverse.   The idea of Progress is glaringly incongruous with his vision of the world.   If his programme of revolutionising secular learning had been accepted—it fell completely dead, and his work was forgotten for many ages,— he would have been the author of a progressive reform ; but how many reformers have there been before and after Bacon on whose minds the idea of Progress never dawned ?

4

Thus Friar Bacon's theories of scientific reform, so far from amounting to an anticipation of the idea

of Progress, illustrate how impossible it was that
this idea could appear in the Middle Ages.   The
whole spirit of medieval Christianity excluded it.
The conceptions which were entertained of the
working of divine Providence, the belief that the
world, surprised like a sleeping household by a
thief in the night, might at any moment come to
a sudden end, had the same effect as the Greek
theories of the nature of change and of recurring
cycles of the world.   Or rather, they had a more
powerful effect, because they were not reasoned
conclusions, but dogmas guaranteed by divine
authority.   And medieval pessimism as to man's
mundane condition was darker and sterner than the
pessimism of the Greeks.   There was the prospect
of happiness in another sphere to compensate, but
this, engrossing the imagination, only rendered it
less likely that any one should think of speculating
about man's destinies on earth.

III

I

The civilised countries of Europe spent about
three hundred years in passing from the mental
atmosphere of the Middle Ages into the mental
atmosphere of the modern world.   These centuries
were one of the conspicuously progressive periods
in history, but the conditions were not favourable
to the appearance of an idea of Progress, though
the intellectual *milieu* was being prepared in which
that idea could be born.

This progressive period, which is conveniently
called the Renaissance, lasted from the fourteenth
into the seventeenth century. The great results,
significant for our present purpose, which the
human mind achieved at this stage of its development were two. Self-confidence was restored to
human reason, and life on this planet was recognised as possessing a value independent of any
hopes or fears connected with a life beyond the
grave.

But in discarding medieval *naïveté* and superstition, in assuming a freer attitude towards theological
authority, and in developing a new conception of the
value of individual personality, men looked to the
guidance of Greek and Roman thinkers, and called
up the spirit of the ancient world to exorcise the
ghosts of the dark ages. Their minds were thus
directed backwards to a past civilisation which, in
the ardour of new discovery, and in the reaction
against medievalism, they enthroned as ideal; and
a new authority was set up, the authority of ancient
writers. In general speculation the men of the
Renaissance followed the tendencies and adopted
many of the prejudices of Greek philosophy.
Although some great discoveries, with far-reaching,
revolutionary consequences, were made in this
period, most active minds were engaged in
rediscovering, elaborating, criticising, and imitating
what was old. It was not till the closing years of
the Renaissance that speculation began to seek and
feel its way towards new points of departure. It
was not till then that a serious reaction set in
against the deeper influences of medieval thought.

2

To illustrate the limitations of this period let us take Machiavelli, one of the most original thinkers that Italy ever produced.

There are certain fundamental principles underlying Machiavelli's science of politics, which he has indicated incidentally in his unsystematic way, but which are essential to the comprehension of his doctrines. The first is that at all times the world of human beings has been the same, varying indeed from land to land, but always presenting the same aspect of some societies advancing towards prosperity, and others declining. Those which are on the upward grade will always reach a point beyond which they cannot rise further, but they will not remain permanently on this level, they will begin to decline; for human things are always in motion and therefore must go up or down. Similarly, declining states will ultimately touch bottom and then begin to ascend. Thus a good constitution or social organisation can last only for a short time.

It is obvious that in this view of history Machiavelli was inspired and instructed by the ancients. And it followed from his premises that the study of the past is of the highest value because it enables men to see what is to come; since to all social events at any period there are correspondences in ancient times. "For these events are due to men, who have and always had the same passions, and therefore of necessity the effects must be the same."

Again, Machiavelli follows his ancient masters

in assuming as evident that a good organisation of society can be effected only by the deliberate design of a wise legislator. Forms of government and religions are the personal creations of a single brain; and the only chance for a satisfactory constitution or for a religion to maintain itself for any length of time is constantly to repress any tendencies to depart from the original conceptions of its creator.

It is evident that these two assumptions are logically connected. The lawgiver builds on the immutability of human nature; what is good for one generation must be good for another. For Machiavelli, as for Plato, change meant corruption. Thus his fundamental theory excluded any conception of a satisfactory social order gradually emerging by the impersonal work of successive generations, adapting their institutions to their own changing needs and aspirations. It is characteristic, and another point of resemblance with ancient thinkers, that he sought the ideal state in the past —republican Rome.

These doctrines, the sameness of human nature and the omnipotent lawgiver, left no room for anything resembling a theory of Progress. If not held afterwards in the uncompromising form in which Machiavelli presented them, yet it has well been pointed out that they lay at the root of some of the most famous speculations of the eighteenth century.

3

Machiavelli's sameness of human nature meant that man would always have the same passions and desires, weaknesses and vices. This assumption was compatible with the widely prevailing view that man had degenerated in the course of the last fifteen hundred years. From the exaltation of Greek and Roman antiquity to a position of unattainable superiority, especially in the field of knowledge, the degeneration of humanity was an easy and natural inference. If the Greeks in philosophy and science were authoritative guides, if in art and literature they were unapproachable, if the Roman republic, as Machiavelli thought, was an ideal state, it would seem that the powers of Nature had declined, and she could no longer produce the same quality of brain. So long as this paralysing theory prevailed, it is manifest that the idea of Progress could not appear.

But in the course of the sixteenth century men began here and there, somewhat timidly and tentatively, to rebel against the tyranny of antiquity, or rather to prepare the way for the open rebellion which was to break out in the seventeenth. Breaches were made in the proud citadel of ancient learning. Copernicus undermined the authority of Ptolemy and his predecessors; the anatomical researches of Vesalius injured the prestige of Galen; and Aristotle was attacked on many sides by men like Telesio, Cardan, Ramus, and Bruno. In particular branches of science an innovation was beginning which heralded a radical revolution in the study of natural phenomena, though the general significance of the prospect which these researches opened was but vaguely understood at the time. The thinkers and men of science were living in an intellectual twilight. It was the twilight of dawn. At one extremity we have

mysticism which culminated in the speculations of
Bruno and Campanella; at the other we have the
scepticism of Montaigne, Charron, and Sanchez.
The bewildered condition of knowledge is indicated
by the fact that while Bruno and Campanella
accepted the Copernican astronomy, it was rejected by one who in many other respects may
claim to be reckoned as a modern—I mean Francis
Bacon.

But the growing tendency to challenge the
authority of the ancients does not sever this period
from the spirit which informed the Renaissance.
For it is subordinate or incidental to a more general
and important interest. To rehabilitate the natural
man, to claim that he should be the pilot of his own
course, to assert his freedom in the fields of art
and literature had been the work of the early
Renaissance. It was the problem of the later
Renaissance to complete this emancipation in the
sphere of philosophical thought. The bold metaphysics of Bruno, for which he atoned by a fiery
death, offered the solution which was most un-
orthodox and complete. His deification of nature
and of man as part of nature involved the liberation
of humanity from external authority. But other
speculative minds of the age, though less audacious,
were equally inspired by the idea of freely inter-
rogating nature, and were all engaged in accomplishing the programme of the Renaissance—the
vindication of this world as possessing a value for
man independent of its relations to any super-
mundane sphere. The raptures of Giordano
Bruno and the sobrieties of Francis Bacon are here
on common ground. The whole movement was a

necessary prelude to a new age of which science was to be the mistress.

It is to be noted that there was a general feeling of complacency as to the condition of learning and intellectual pursuits. This optimism is expressed by Rabelais. Gargantua, in a letter to Pantagruel, studying at Paris, enlarges to his son on the vast improvements in learning and education which had recently, he says, been brought about. "All the world is full of savants, learned teachers, large libraries ; and I am of opinion that neither in the time of Plato nor of Cicero nor of Papinian were there such facilities for study as one sees now." It is indeed the study of the ancient languages and literatures that Gargantua considers in a liberal education, but the satisfaction at the present diffusion of learning, with the suggestion that here at least contemporaries have an advantage over the ancients, is the significant point. This satisfaction shines through the observation of Ramus that " in one century we have seen a greater progress in men and works of learning than our ancestors had seen in the whole course of the previous fourteen centuries." [1]

In this last stage of the Renaissance, which includes the first quarter of the seventeenth

---

[1] Guillaume Postel observed in his *De magistratibus Atheniensium liber* (1541) that the ages are always progressing (*secula semper proficere*), and every day additions are made to human knowledge, and that this process would only cease if Providence by war, or plague, or some catastrophe were to destroy all the accumulated stores of knowledge which have been transmitted from antiquity in books (*Praef.*, B verso). What is known of the life of this almost forgotten scholar has been collected by G. Weill (*De Gulielmi Postelli vita et indole*, 1892). He visited the East, brought back oriental MSS., and was more than once imprisoned on charges of heresy. He dreamed of converting the Mohammedans, and of uniting the whole world under the empire of France.

century, soil was being prepared in which the idea of Progress could germinate, and our history of its origin definitely begins with the work of two men who belong to this age, Bodin, who is hardly known except to special students of political science, and Bacon, who is known to all the world. Both had a more general grasp of the significance of their own time than any of their contemporaries, and though neither of them discovered a theory of Progress, they both made contributions to thought which directly contributed to its subsequent appearance.

CHAPTER I

SOME INTERPRETATIONS OF UNIVERSAL HISTORY:
BODIN AND LE ROY

I

IT is a long descent from the genius of Machiavelli
to the French historian, Jean Bodin, who published
his introduction to historical studies[1] about forty
years after Machiavelli's death.   His views and his
method differ widely from those of that great
pioneer, whom he attacks.   His readers were not
arrested by startling novelties or immoral doctrine;
he is safe, and dull.

But Bodin had a much wider range of thought
than Machiavelli, whose mind was entirely concentrated on the theory of politics; and his
importance for us lies not in the political speculations by which he sought to prove that monarchy
is the best form of government,[2] but in his attempt
to substitute a new theory of universal history for
that which prevailed in the Middle Ages.   He
rejected the popular conception of a golden age
and a subsequent degeneration of mankind; and
he refuted the view, generally current among
medieval theologians, and based on the prophecies

[1] *Methodus ad facilem historiarum cognitionem,* 1566.
[2] *Les six livres de la République,* 1576.

of Daniel, which divided the course of history into four periods corresponding to the Babylonian, Persian, Macedonian, and Roman monarchies, the last of which was to endure till the day of Judgement. Bodin suggests a division into three great periods : the first, of about two thousand years, in which the South-Eastern peoples were predominant ; the second, of the same duration, in which those whom he calls the Middle (Mediterranean) peoples came to the front ; the third, in which the Northern nations who overthrew Rome became the leaders in civilisation. Each period is stamped by the psychological character of the three racial groups. The note of the first is religion, of the second practical sagacity, of the third warfare and inventive skill. This division actually anticipates the synthesis of Hegel.[1] But the interesting point is that it is based on anthropological considerations, in which climate and geography are taken into account ; and, notwithstanding the crudeness of the whole exposition and the intrusion of astrological arguments, it is a new step in the study of universal history.

I have said that Bodin rejected the theory of the degeneration of man, along with the tradition of a previous age of virtue and felicity. The reason which he alleged against it is important. The powers of nature have always been uniform. It is illegitimate to suppose that she could at one time produce the men and conditions postulated by the theory of the golden age, and not produce them at another. In other words, Bodin asserts the

---

[1] Hegel's division is (1) the Oriental, (2) *a*, the Greek, *b*, the Roman, and (3) the Germanic worlds.

principle of the permanent and undiminishing capacities of nature, and, as we shall see in the sequel, this principle was significant. It is not to be confounded with the doctrine of the immutability of human things assumed by Machiavelli. The human scene has vastly changed since the primitive age of man ; " if that so-called golden age could be revoked and compared with our own, we should consider it iron." [1]   For history largely depends on the will of men, which is always changing ; every day new laws, new customs, new institutions, both secular and religious, come into being, and new errors.[2]

But in this changing scene we can observe a certain regularity, a law of oscillation. Rise is followed by fall, and fall by rise ; it is a mistake to think that the human race is always deteriorating.[3] If that were so, we should long ago have reached the lowest stage of vice and iniquity. On the contrary, there has been, through the series of oscillations, a gradual ascent. In the ages which have been foolishly designated as gold and silver men lived like the wild beasts ; and from that state they have slowly reached the humanity of manners and the social order which prevail to-day.[4]

Thus Bodin recognises a general progress in the past. That is nothing new ; it was the view, for instance, of the Epicureans. But much had passed in the world since the philosophy of

[1] *Methodus*, cap. VII. p. 353.
[2] *Ib.* cap. I. p. 12.
[3] *Ib.* cap. VII. p. 361 : "cum aeterna quadam lege naturae conversio rerum omnium velut in orbem redire videatur, ut aeque vitia virtutibus, ignoratio scientiae, turpe honesto consequens sit, atque tenebrae luci, fallunt qui genus hominum semper deterius seipso evadere putant."
[4] *Ib.* p. 356.

Epicurus was alive, and Bodin had to consider twelve hundred years of new vicissitudes. Could the Epicurean theory be brought up to date ?

2

Bodin deals with the question almost entirely in respect to human knowledge. In definitely denying the degeneration of man, Bodin was only expressing what many thinkers of the sixteenth century had been coming to feel, though timidly and obscurely. The philosophers and men of science, who criticised the ancients in special departments, did not formulate any general view on the privileged position of antiquity. Bodin was the first to do so.

Knowledge, letters, and arts have their vicissitudes, he says; they rise, increase, and flourish, and then languish and die. After the decay of Rome there was a long fallow period; but this was followed by a splendid revival of knowledge and an intellectual productivity which no other age has exceeded. The scientific discoveries of the ancients deserve high praise; but the moderns have not only thrown new light on phenomena which they had incompletely explained, they have made new discoveries of equal or indeed greater importance. Take, for instance, the mariner's compass which has made possible the circumnavigation of the earth and a universal commerce, whereby the world has been changed, as it were, into a single state.[1] Take

[1] Cardan had already signalised the compass, printing, and gunpowder as three modern inventions, to which "the whole of antiquity has nothing equal to show." He adds, "I pass over the other inventions of this age which, though wonderful, form rather a development of ancient arts than surpass the intellects of our ancestors." *De subtilitate*, lib. 3 *ad init.* (*Opera*, iii. p. 609).

the advances we have made in geography and
astronomy; the invention of gunpowder; the
development of the woollen and other industries.
The invention of printing alone can be set against
anything that the ancients achieved.[1]

An inference from all this, obvious to a modern
reader, would be that in the future there will be
similar oscillations, and new inventions and discoveries as remarkable as any that have been
made in the past. But Bodin does not draw this
inference. He confines himself to the past and
present, and has no word to say about the vicissitudes of the future. But he is not haunted by any
vision of the end of the world, or the coming
of Antichrist; three centuries of humanism lay
between him and Roger Bacon.

3

And yet the influence of medievalism, which it
had been the work of those three centuries to
overcome, was still pervasively there. Still more
the authority of the Greeks and Romans, which
had been set up by the revival of learning, was,
without their realising it, heavy even upon thinkers
like Bodin, who did not scruple freely to criticise
ancient authors. And so, in his thoughtful attempt
to find a clew to universal history, he was hampered
by theological and cosmic theories, the legacy of
the past. It is significant of the trend of his mind
that when he is discussing the periodic decline of
science and letters, he suggests that it may be due

[1] *Methodus*, cap. VII., pp. 359-61. Bodin also points out that there was
an improvement, in some respects, in manners and morals since the early
Roman Empire; for instance, in the abolition of gladiatorial spectacles
(p. 359).

to the direct action of God, punishing those who misapplied useful sciences to the destruction of men.

But his speculations were particularly compromised by his belief in astrology, which, notwithstanding the efforts of humanists like Petrarch, Aeneas Sylvius, and Pico to discredit it, retained its hold over the minds of many eminent, otherwise emancipated, thinkers throughout the period of the Renaissance. Here Bodin is in the company of Machiavelli and Lord Bacon. But not content with the doctrine of astral influence on human events, he sought another key to historical changes in the influence of numbers, reviving the ideas of Pythagoras and Plato, but working them out in a way of his own. He enumerates the durations of the lives of many famous men, to show that they can be expressed by powers of 7 and 9, or the product of these numbers. Other numbers which have special virtues are the powers of 12, the perfect number[1] 496, and various others. He gives many examples to prove that these mystic numbers determine the durations of empires and underlie historical chronology. For instance, the duration of the oriental monarchies from Ninus to the Conquest of Persia by Alexander the Great was 1728 ($= 12^3$) years. He gives the Roman republic from the foundation of Rome to the battle of Actium 729 ($= 9^3$) years.

4

From a believer in such a theory, which illustrates the limitations of men's outlook on the world in the Renaissance period, we could perhaps

---

[1] *I.e.* a number equal to the sum of all its factors.

hardly expect a vision of Progress. The best that can be said for it is that, both here and in his astrological creed, Bodin is crudely attempting to bring human history into close connection with the rest of the universe, and to establish the view that the whole world is built on a divine plan by which all the parts are intimately interrelated. He is careful, however, to avoid fatalism. He asserts, as we have seen, that history depends largely on the will of men. And he comes nearer to the idea of Progress than any one before him; he is on the threshold.

For if we eliminate his astrological and Pythagorean speculations, and various theological parentheses which do not disturb his argument, his work announces a new view of history which is optimistic regarding man's career on earth, without any reference to his destinies in a future life. And in this optimistic view there are three particular points to note, which were essential to the subsequent growth of the idea of Progress. In the first place, the decisive rejection of the theory of degeneration, which had been a perpetual obstacle to the apprehension of that idea. Secondly, the unreserved claim that his own age was fully equal, and in some respects superior, to the age of classical antiquity, in respect of science and the arts. He leaves the ancients reverently on their pedestal, but he erects another pedestal for the moderns, and it is rather higher. We shall see the import of this when we come to consider the intellectual movement in which the idea of Progress was afterwards to emerge. In the third place, he had a conception of the common interest of all the peoples of the earth, a conception which corresponded to the old ecumenical idea of the Greeks and Romans,[1] but had now a new significance through the discoveries of modern navigators.   He speaks repeatedly of the world as a universal state, and suggests that the various races, by their peculiar aptitudes and qualities, contribute to the common good of the whole.   This idea of the "solidarity" of peoples was to be an important element in the growth of the doctrine of Progress.

These ideas were in the air.   Another Frenchman, the classical scholar, Louis Le Roy, translator of Plato and Aristotle, put forward similar views in a work of less celebrity, *On the Vicissitude or Variety of the Things in the Universe*.[2]   It contains a survey of great periods in which particular peoples attained an exceptional state of dominion and prosperity, and it anticipates later histories of civilisation by dwelling but slightly on political events and bringing into prominence human achievements in science, philosophy, and the arts.   Beginning with the advance of man from primitive rudeness to ordered society—a sketch based on the conjectures of Plato in the *Protagoras*—Le Roy reviews the history, and estimates the merits, of the Egyptians, Assyrians and Persians, the Greeks, Romans and Saracens, and finally of the modern age.   The facts, he thinks, establish the proposition that the art of warfare, eloquence, philosophy, mathematics, and the fine arts, generally flourish and decline together.

---

[1] See above, p. 23.

[2] *De la vicissitude ou variété des choses en l'univers*, 1577, 2nd ed. (which I have used), 1584.

But they do decline. Human things are not perpetual; all pass through the same cycle—beginning, progress, perfection, corruption, end. This, however, does not explain the succession of empires in the world, the changes of the scene of prosperity from one people or set of peoples to another. Le Roy finds the cause in providential design. God, he believes, cares for all parts of the universe and has distributed excellence in arms and letters now to Asia, now to Europe, again to Africa, letting virtue and vice, knowledge and ignorance travel from country to country, that all in their turn may share in good and bad fortune, and none become too proud through prolonged prosperity.

But what of the modern age in Western Europe? It is fully the equal, he assevers, of the most illustrious ages of the past, and in some respects it is superior. Almost all the liberal and mechanical arts of antiquity, which had been lost for about 1200 years, have been restored, and there have been new inventions, especially printing, and the mariner's compass, and " I would give the third place to gunnery but that it seems invented rather for the ruin than for the utility of the human race." In our knowledge of astronomy and cosmography we surpass the ancients. "We can affirm that the whole world is now known, and all the races of men; they can interchange all their commodities and mutually supply their needs, as inhabitants of the same city or world-state." And hence there has been a notable increase of wealth.

Vice and suffering, indeed, are as grave as ever, and we are afflicted by the trouble of heresies; but this does not prove a general deterioration of morals. If that inveterate complaint, the refrain chanted by old men in every age, were true, the world would already have reached the extreme limit of wickedness, and integrity would have disappeared utterly. Seneca long ago made the right criticism. *Hoc maiores nostri questi sunt, hoc nos querimur, hoc posteri nostri querentur, eversos esse mores. . . . At ista stant loco eodem.* Perhaps Le Roy was thinking particularly of that curious book the *Apology for Herodotus*, in which the eminent Greek scholar, Henri Estienne, exposed with Calvinistic prejudice the iniquities of modern times and the corruption of the Roman Church.[1]

But if we are to judge by past experience, does it not follow that this modern age must go the same way as the great ages of the past which it rivals or even surpasses? Our civilisation, too, having reached perfection, will inevitably decline and pass away : is not this the clear lesson of history? Le Roy does not shirk the issue; it is the point to which his whole exposition has led and he puts it vividly.

" If the memory of the past is the instruction of the present and the premonition of the future, it is to be feared that having reached so great excellence, power, wisdom, studies, books, industries will decline, as has happened in the past, and disappear —confusion succeeding to the order and perfection of to-day, rudeness to civilisation, ignorance to knowledge. I already foresee in imagination

---

[1] *L'Introduction au traité de la conformité des merveilles anciennes avec les modernes, ou traité préparatif à l'Apologie pour Hérodote*, ed. Ristelhuber, 2 vols., 1879. The book was published in 1566.

nations, strange in form, complexion, and costume, overwhelming Europe — like the Goths, Huns, Vandals, Lombards, Saracens of old—destroying our cities and palaces, burning our libraries, devastating all that is beautiful. I foresee in all countries wars, domestic and foreign, factions and heresies which will profane all things human and divine ; famines, plagues, and floods ; the universe approaching an end, world-wide confusion, and the return of things to their original chaos." [1]

But having conducted us to this pessimistic conclusion Le Roy finds it repugnant, and is unwilling to acquiesce in it. Like an embarrassed dramatist he escapes from the knot which he has tied by introducing the *deus ex machina*.

" However much these things proceed according to the fatal law of the world, and have their natural causes, yet events depend principally on Divine Providence which is superior to nature and alone knows the predetermined times of events." That is to say, it depends, after all, on Providence whether the argument from past experience is valid. Who knows whether the modern age may not prove the exception to the law which has hitherto prevailed ? Let us act as if it would.

This is the practical moral that Le Roy enforces in the last book of his dissertation. We must not allow ourselves to be paralysed or dismayed by the destinies of past civilisations, but must work hard to transmit to posterity all that has been achieved, and augment the discoveries of the past by new

---

[1] It is characteristic of the age that in the last sentence the author goes beyond the issue and contemplates the possibility which still haunted men's minds that the end of the world might not be far off.

researches. For knowledge is inexhaustible. "Let us not be so simple as to believe that the ancients have known and said everything and left nothing to their successors. Or that nature gave them all her favours in order to remain sterile ever after." Here Le Roy lays down Bodin's principle which was to be asserted more urgently in the following century —the permanence of natural forces. Nature is the same now as always, and can produce as great intellects as ever. The elements have the same power, the constellations keep their old order, men are made of the same material. There is nothing to hinder the birth in this age of men equal in brains to Plato, Aristotle, or Hippocrates.

Philosophically, Le Roy's conclusion is lame enough. We are asked to set aside the data of experience and act on an off-chance. But the determination of the optimist to escape from the logic of his own argument is significant. He has no conception of an increasing purpose or under-lying unity in the history of man, but he thinks that Providence — the old Providence of St. Augustine, who arranged the events of Roman history with a view to the coming of Christ—may, for some unknown reason, prolong indefinitely the modern age. He is obeying the instinct of optimism and confidence which was already beginning to create the appropriate atmosphere for the intel-lectual revolution of the coming century.

His book was translated into English, but neither in France nor in England had it the same influence as the speculations of Bodin. But it insinuated, as the reader will have observed, the same three views which Bodin taught, and must

have helped to propagate them : that the world
has not degenerated ; that the modern age is not
inferior to classical antiquity ; and that the races
of the earth form now a sort of "mundane
republic."

CHAPTER II

I

AMONG the great precursors of a new order of thought Francis Bacon occupies a unique position. He drew up a definite programme for a "great Renovation" of knowledge ; he is more clearly conscious than his contemporaries of the necessity of breaking with the past and making a completely new start ; and his whole method of thought seems intellectually nearer to us than the speculations of a Bruno or a Campanella. Hence it is easy to understand that he is often regarded, especially in his own country, as more than a precursor, as the first philosopher of the modern age, definitely within its precincts.

It is not indeed a matter of fundamental importance how we classify these men who stood on the border of two worlds, but it must be recognised that if in many respects Bacon is in advance of contemporaries who cannot be dissociated from the Renaissance, in other respects, such as belief in astrology and dreams, he stands on the same ground, and in one essential point—which might almost be taken as the test of mental progress at this period—

Bruno and Campanella have outstripped him. For him Copernicus, Kepler, and Galileo worked in vain ; he obstinately adhered to the old geocentric system.

It must also be remembered that the principle which he laid down in his ambitious programme for the reform of science—that experiment is the key for discovering the secrets of nature—was not a new revelation. We need not dwell on the fact that he had been anticipated by Roger Bacon ; for the ideas of that wonderful thinker had fallen dead in an age which was not ripe for them. But the direct interrogation of nature was already recognised both in practice and in theory in the sixteenth century. What Bacon did was to insist upon the principle more strongly and explicitly, and to formulate it more precisely. He clarified and explained the progressive ideas which inspired the scientific thought of the last period of the European Renaissance, from which he cannot, I think, be dissociated.

But in clearing up and defining these progressive ideas, he made a contribution to the development of human thought which had far-reaching importance and has a special significance for our present subject. In the hopes of a steady increase of knowledge, based on the application of new methods, he had been anticipated by Roger Bacon, and further back by Seneca. But with Francis Bacon this idea of the augmentation of knowledge has an entirely new value. For Seneca the exploration of nature was a means of escaping from the sordid miseries of life. For the friar of Oxford the principal use of increasing knowledge was to prepare for the coming of Antichrist. Francis Bacon sounded the modern note ; for him the end of knowledge is utility.

2

The principle that the proper aim of knowledge
is the amelioration of human life, to increase men's
happiness and mitigate their sufferings—*commodis
humanis inservire*—was the guiding star of Bacon in
all his intellectual labour.   He declared the advancement of "the happiness of mankind" to be the
direct purpose of the works he had written or
designed.   He considered that all his predecessors
had gone wrong because they did not apprehend
that the *finis scientiarum*, the real and legitimate
goal of the sciences, is "the endowment of human life
with new inventions and riches"; and he made this
the test for defining the comparative values of the
various branches of knowledge.

The true object, therefore, of the investigation
of nature is not, as the Greek philosophers held,
speculative satisfaction, but to establish the reign of
man over nature; and this Bacon judged to be
attainable, provided new methods of attacking the
problems were introduced.   Whatever may be
thought of his daring act in bringing natural science
down from the clouds and assigning to her the
function of ministering to the material convenience
and comfort of man, we may criticise Bacon for his
doctrine that every branch of science should be
pursued with a single eye towards practical use.
Mathematics, he thought, should conduct herself
as a humble, if necessary, handmaid, without any
aspirations of her own.   But it is not thus that the
great progress in man's command over nature since
Bacon's age has been effected.   Many of the most
valuable and surprising things which science has

succeeded in doing for civilisation would never have
been performed if each branch of knowledge were
not guided by its own independent ideal of speculative completeness.[1] But this does not invalidate
Bacon's pragmatic principle, or diminish the importance of the fact that in laying down the utilitarian
view of knowledge he contributed to the creation of
a new mental atmosphere in which the theory of
Progress was afterwards to develop.

3

Bacon's respect for the ancients and his familiarity
with their writings are apparent on almost every
page he wrote. Yet it was one of his principal
endeavours to shake off the yoke of their authority,
which he recognised to be a fatal obstacle to the
advancement of science. "Truth is not to be
sought in the good fortune of any particular con-
juncture of time"; its attainment depends on
experience, and how limited was theirs. In their
age "the knowledge both of time and of the world
was confined and meagre; they had not a thousand
years of history worthy of that name, but mere fables
and ancient traditions; they were not acquainted
with but a small portion of the regions and countries
of the world." In all their systems and scientific
speculation "there is hardly one single experiment
that has a tendency to assist mankind." Their
theories were founded on opinion, and therefore
science has remained stationary for the last two
thousand years; whereas mechanical arts, which are
founded on nature and experience, grow and increase.

[1] This was to be well explained by Fontenelle, Préface sur l'utilité des
mathématiques, in Œuvres (ed. 1729), iii. 1 sqq.

In this connection, Bacon points out that the word "antiquity" is misleading, and makes a remark which will frequently recur in writers of the following generations. *Antiquitas seculi iuventus mundi*; what we call antiquity and are accustomed to revere as such was the youth of the world. But it is the old age and increasing years of the world—the time in which we are now living—that deserves in truth to be called antiquity. We are really the ancients, the Greeks and Romans were younger than we, in respect to the age of the world. And as we look to an old man for greater knowledge of the world than from a young man, so we have good reason to expect far greater things from our own age than from antiquity, because in the meantime the stock of knowledge has been increased by an endless number of observations and experiments. Time is the great discoverer, and truth is the daughter of time, not of authority.

Take the three inventions which were unknown to the ancients—printing, gunpowder, and the compass. These "have changed the appearance and state of the whole world ; first in literature, then in warfare, and lastly in navigation ; and innumerable changes have been thence derived, so that no empire, sect, or star appears to have exercised a greater power or influence on human affairs than these mechanical discoveries."[1] It was perhaps the results of navigation and the exploration of unknown lands that impressed Bacon more than all, as they had impressed Bodin. Let me quote one passage.

---

[1] *Nov. Org.* 129. We have seen that these three inventions had already been classed together as outstanding by Cardan and Le Roy. They also appear in Campanella. Bodin, as we saw, included them in a longer list.

" It may truly be affirmed to the honour of these times, and in a virtuous emulation with antiquity, that this great building of the world had never through-lights made in it till the age of us and our fathers.   For although they [the ancients] had knowledge of the antipodes . . . yet that mought be by demonstration, and not in fact ; and if by travel, it requireth the voyage but of half the earth.   But to circle the earth, as the heavenly bodies do, was not done nor enterprised till these later times : and therefore these times may justly bear in their word . . . *plus ultra* in precedence of the ancient *non ultra.* . . . And this proficience in navigation and discoveries may plant also an expectation of the further proficience and augmentation of all sciences, because it may seem that they are ordained by God to be coevals, that is, to meet in one age.   For so the prophet Daniel, speaking of the latter times foretelleth, *Plurimi pertransibunt, et multiplex erit scientia* : as if the openness and through-passage of the world and the increase of knowledge were appointed to be in the same ages ; as we see it is already performed in great part : the learning of these later times not much giving place to the former two periods or returns of learning, the one of the Grecians, the other of the Romans."

In all this we have a definite recognition of the fact that knowledge progresses.   Bacon did not come into close quarters with the history of civilisa-tion, but he has thrown out some observations which amount to a rough synthesis.   Like Bodin, he divided history into three periods—(1) the antiquities of the world ; (2) the middle part of time which comprised two sections, the Greek and the Roman ;

(3) "modern history," which included what we now call the Middle Ages. In this sequence three particular epochs stand out as fertile in science and favourable to progress—the Greek, the Roman, and our own—"and scarcely two centuries can with justice be assigned to each." The other periods of time are deserts, so far as philosophy and science are concerned. Rome and Greece are "two exemplar States of the world for arms, learning, moral virtue, policy, and laws." But even in those two great epochs little progress was made in natural philosophy. For in Greece moral and political speculation absorbed men's minds; in Rome, meditation and labour were wasted on moral philosophy, and the greatest intellects were devoted to civil affairs. Afterwards, in the third period, the study of theology was the chief occupation of the Western European nations. It was actually in the earliest period that the most useful discoveries for the comfort of human life were made, "so that, to say the truth, when contemplation and doctrinal science began, the discovery of useful works ceased."

So much for the past history of mankind, during which many things conspired to make progress in the subjugation of nature slow, fitful, and fortuitous. What of the future? Bacon's answer is: if the errors of the past are understood and avoided there is every hope of steady progress in the modern age.

But it might be asked, Is there not something in the constitution of things which determines epochs of stagnation and vigour, some force against which man's understanding and will are impotent? Is it not true that in the revolutions of ages there are floods and ebbs of the sciences, which flourish now and then decline, and that when they have reached a certain point they can proceed no further? This doctrine of Returns or *ricorsi*[1] is denounced by Bacon as the greatest obstacle to the advancement of knowledge, creating, as it does, diffidence or despair. He does not formally refute it, but he marshals the reasons for an optimistic view, and these reasons supply the disproof. The facts on which the fatalistic doctrine of Returns is based can be explained without resorting to any mysterious law. Progress has not been steady or continuous on account of the prejudices and errors which hindered men from setting to work in the right way. The difficulties in advancing did not arise from things which are not in our power ; they were due to the human understanding, which wasted time and labour on improper objects. " In proportion as the errors which have been committed impeded the past, so do they afford reason to hope for the future."

4

But will the new period of advance, which Bacon expected and strove to secure, be of indefinite duration? He does not consider the question. His view that he lived in the old age of the world implies that he did not anticipate a vast tract of time before the end of mankind's career on earth. And an orthodox Christian of that time could hardly be expected to predict. The impression we get is that, in his sanguine enthusiasm, he imagined that a "prudent interrogation" of nature could extort

---

[1] Bodin's *conversiones.*

all her secrets in a few generations.   As a reformer he was so engaged in the immediate prospect of results that his imagination did not turn to the possibilities of a remoter future, though these would logically follow from his recognition of "the inseparable propriety of time which is ever more and more to disclose truth."   He hopes everything from his own age in which learning has made her third visitation to the world, a period which he is persuaded will far surpass that of Grecian and Roman learning.   If he could have revisited England in 1700 and surveyed what science had performed since his death his hopes might have been more than satisfied.

But, animated though he was with the pro-gressive spirit, as Leonardo da Vinci had been before him, all that he says of the prospects of an increase of knowledge fails to amount to the theory of Progress.   He prepares the way, he leads up to it ; but his conception of his own time as the old age of humanity excludes the conception of an indefinite advance in the future, which is essential if the theory is to have significance and value.   And in regard to progress in the past, though he is clearer and more emphatic than Bodin, he hardly adds anything to what Bodin had observed.   The novelty of his view lies not in his recognition of the advance of knowledge and its power to advance still further, but in the purpose which he assigned to it.   The end of the sciences is their usefulness to the human race. To increase knowledge is to extend the dominion of man over nature, and so to increase his comfort and happiness, so far as these depend on external circum-stances.   To Plato or Seneca, or to a Christian dreaming of the City of God, this doctrine would seem material and trivial ; and its announcement was revolutionary : for it implied that happiness on earth was an end to be pursued for its own sake, and to be secured by co-operation for mankind at large. This idea is an axiom which any general doctrine of Progress must presuppose ; and it forms Bacon's great contribution to the group of ideas which rendered possible the subsequent rise of that doctrine.

Finally, we must remember that by Bacon, as by most of his Elizabethan contemporaries, the doctrine of an active intervening Providence, the Providence of Augustine, was taken as a matter of course, and governed more or less their conceptions of the history of civilisation. But, I think, we may say that Bacon, while he formally acknowledged it, did not press it or emphasise it.

5

Bacon illustrated his view of the social importance of science in his sketch of an ideal state, the *New Atlantis*. He completed only a part of the work, and the fragment was published after his death.[1] It is evident that the predominating interest that moved his imagination was different from that

---

[1] In 1627. It was composed about 1623. It seems almost certain that he was acquainted with the *Christianopolis* of Johann Valentin Andreae (1586–1654), which had appeared in Latin in 1614, and contained a plan for a scientific college to reform the civilised world. Andreae, who was acquainted both with More and with Campanella, placed his ideal society in an island which he called Caphar Salama (the name of a village in Palestine). Andreae's work had also a direct influence on the *Nova Solyma* of Samuel Gott (1648). See the Introduction of F. E. Held to his edition of *Christianopolis* (1916). In Macaria, another imaginary state of the seventeenth century (*A description of the famous Kingdome of Macaria*, 1641, by Hartlib), the pursuit of science is not a feature.

which guided Plato.   While Plato aimed at securing
a permanent solid order founded on immutable
principles, the design of Bacon was to enable his
imaginary community to achieve dominion over
nature by progressive discoveries. The heads of
Plato's city are metaphysicians, who regulate the
welfare of the people by abstract doctrines established once for all ; while the most important feature
in the *New Atlantis* is the college of scientific
investigators, who are always discovering new truths
which may alter the conditions of life.   Here,
though only in a restricted field, an idea of progressive improvement, which is the note of the
modern age, comes in to modify the idea of a
fixed order which exclusively prevailed in ancient
speculation.

On the other hand, we must not ignore the fact
that Bacon's ideal society is established by the same
kind of agency as the ideal societies of Plato and
Aristotle.   It has not developed ; it was framed by
the wisdom of an original legislator Solamona.   In
this it resembles the other imaginary commonwealths
of the sixteenth and seventeenth centuries.   The
organisation of More's *Utopia* is fixed initially once
for all by the lawgiver Utopus.   The origin of
Campanella's *Civitas Solis* is not expressly stated,
but there can be no doubt that he conceived its
institutions as created by the fiat of a single lawgiver.   Harrington, in his *Oceana*, argues with
Machiavelli that a commonwealth, to be well
turned, must be the work of one man, like a book or
a building.

What measure of liberty Bacon would have
granted to the people of his perfect state we cannot

say ; his work breaks off before he comes to describe their condition.   But we receive the impression that the government he conceived was strictly paternal, though perhaps less rigorous than the theocratic despotism which Campanella, under Plato's influence, set up in the City of the Sun.   But even Campanella has this in common with More—and we may be sure that Bacon's conception would have agreed here—that there are no hard-and-fast lines between the classes, and the welfare and happiness of all the inhabitants is impartially considered, in contrast with Plato's scheme in the *Laws*, where the artisans and manual labourers were an inferior caste existing less for their own sake than for the sake of the community as a whole.[1]

It may finally be pointed out that these three imaginary commonwealths stand together as a group, marked by a humaner temper than the ancient, and also by another common characteristic which distinguishes them, on one hand, from the ideal states of Plato and, on the other, from modern sketches of desirable societies.   Plato and Aristotle conceived their constructions within the geographical limits of Hellas, either in the past or in the present.   More, Bacon, and Campanella placed theirs in distant seas, and this remoteness in space helped to create a certain illusion of reality.   The modern plan is to project the perfect society into a period of future time.   The device of More and his successors was suggested by the maritime explorations of the fifteenth and sixteenth centuries ; the later method was a result of the rise of the idea of Progress.

[1] This however does not apply to the *Republic*, as is so commonly asserted. See the just criticisms of A. A. Trever, *A History of Greek Economic Thought* (Chicago, 1916), 49 *sqq.*

6

A word or two more may be said about the City of the Sun. Campanella was as earnest a believer in the interrogation of nature as Bacon, and the place which science and learning hold in his state (although research is not so prominent as in the *New Atlantis*), and the scientific training of all the citizens, are a capital feature. The progress in inventions, to which science may look forward, is suggested. The men of the City of the Sun " have already discovered the one art which the world seemed to lack—the art of flying ; and they expect soon to invent ocular instruments which will enable them to see the invisible stars and auricular instruments for hearing the harmony of the spheres." Campanella's view of the present conditions and prospects of knowledge is hardly less sanguine than that of Bacon, and characteristically he confirms his optimism by astrological data. "If you only knew what their astrologers say about the coming age. Our times, they assert, have more history in a hundred years than the whole world in four thousand. More books have been published in this century than in five thousand years before. They dwell on the wonderful inventions of printing, of artillery, and of the use of the magnet,—clear signs of the times —and also instruments for the assembling of the inhabitants of the world into one fold," and show that these discoveries were conditioned by stellar influences.

But Campanella is not very sure or clear about the future. Astrology and theology cause him to hesitate. Like Bacon, he dreams of a great Renova-

tion and sees that the conditions are propitious, but
his faith is not secure. The astronomers of his
imaginary state scrutinise the stars to discover
whether the world will perish or not, and they
believe in the oracular saying of Jesus that the end
will come like a thief in the night. Therefore they
expect a new age, and perhaps also the end of the
world.

The new age of knowledge was about to begin.
Campanella, Bruno, and Bacon stand, as it were, on
the brink of the dividing stream, *tenduntque manus
ripae ulterioris amore.*

CHAPTER III

CARTESIANISM

If we are to draw any useful lines of demarcation in the continuous flux of history we must neglect anticipations and announcements, and we need not scruple to say that, in the realm of knowledge and thought, modern history begins in the seventeenth century. Ubiquitous rebellion against tradition, a new standard of clear and precise thought which affects even literary expression, a flow of mathematical and physical discoveries so rapid that ten years added more to the sum of knowledge than all that had been added since the days of Archimedes, the introduction of organised co-operation to increase knowledge by the institution of the Royal Society at London, the Academy of Sciences at Paris, Observatories — realising Bacon's Atlantic dream—characterise the opening of a new era.

For the ideas with which we are concerned, the seventeenth century centres round Descartes, whom an English admirer described as "the grand secretary of Nature."[1] Though his brilliant mathematical discoveries were the sole permanent contribution he made to knowledge, though his metaphysical and physical systems are only of

[1] Joseph Glanvill, *Vanity of Dogmatising*, p. 211.

historical interest, his genius exercised a more extensive and transforming influence on the future development of thought than any other man of his century.

Cartesianism affirmed the two positive axioms of the supremacy of reason, and the invariability of the laws of nature; and its instrument was a new rigorous analytical method, which was applicable to history as well as to physical knowledge. The axioms had destructive corollaries. The immutability of the processes of nature collided with the theory of an active Providence. The supremacy of reason shook the thrones from which authority and tradition had tyrannised over the brains of men. Cartesianism was equivalent to a declaration of the Independence of Man.

It was in the atmosphere of the Cartesian spirit that a theory of Progress was to take shape.

I

Let us look back. We saw that all the remarks of philosophers prior to the seventeenth century, which have been claimed as enunciations of the idea of Progress, amount merely to recognitions of the obvious fact that in the course of the past history of men there have been advances and improvements in knowledge and arts, or that we may look for some improvements in the future. There is not one of them that adumbrates a theory that can be called a theory of Progress. We have seen several reasons why the idea could not emerge in the ancient or in the Middle Ages. Nor could it have easily appeared in the period of the

Renaissance. Certain preliminary conditions were required, and these were not fulfilled till the seventeenth century.

So long as men believed that the Greeks and Romans had attained, in the best days of their civilisation, to an intellectual plane which posterity could never hope to reach, so long as the authority of their thinkers was set up as unimpeachable, a theory of degeneration held the field, which excluded a theory of Progress. It was the work of Bacon and Descartes to liberate science and philosophy from the yoke of that authority; and at the same time, as we shall see, the rebellion began to spread to other fields.

Another condition for the organisation of a theory of Progress was a frank recognition of the value of mundane life and the subservience of knowledge to human needs. The secular spirit of the Renaissance prepared the world for this new valuation, which was formulated by Bacon, and has developed into modern utilitarianism.

There was yet a third preliminary condition. There can be no certainty that knowledge will continually progress until science has been placed on sure foundations. And science does not rest for us on sure foundations unless the invariability of the laws of nature is admitted. If we do not accept this hypothesis, if we consider it possible that the uniformities of the natural world may be changed from time to time, we have no guarantee that science can progress indefinitely. The philosophy of Descartes established this principle, which is the palladium of science; and thus the third preliminary condition was fulfilled.

2

During the Renaissance period the authority of the Greeks and Romans had been supreme in the realm of thought, and in the interest of further free development it was necessary that this authority should be weakened.   Bacon and others had begun the movement to break down this tyranny, but the influence of Descartes was weightier and more decisive, and his attitude was more uncompromising. He had none of Bacon's reverence for classical literature ; he was proud of having forgotten the Greek which he had learned as a boy.   The inspiration of his work was the idea of breaking sharply and completely with the past, and constructing a system which borrows nothing from the dead. He looked forward to an advancement of knowledge in the future, on the basis of his own method and his own discoveries,[1] and he conceived that this intellectual advance would have far-reaching effects on the condition of mankind.   The first title he had proposed to give to his *Discourse on Method* was "The Project of a Universal Science which can elevate our Nature to its highest degree of Perfection."   He regarded moral and material improvement as depending on philosophy and science.

The justification of an independent attitude towards antiquity, on the ground that the world is now older and more mature, was becoming a current view.   Descartes expressed it like Bacon, and it was taken up and repeated by many whom

---

[1] Cp. for instance his remarks on medicine, at the end of the *Discours de la méthode*.

Descartes influenced.   Pascal, who till 1654 was a man of science and a convert to Cartesian ideas, put it in a striking way.   The whole sequence of men (he says) during so many centuries should be considered as a single man, continually existing and continually learning.   At each stage of his life this universal man profited by the knowledge he had acquired in the preceding stages, and he is now in his old age.   This is a fuller, and probably an independent, development of the comparison of the race to an individual which we found in Bacon.   It occurs in a fragment which remained unpublished for more than a hundred years, and is often quoted as a recognition, not of a general progress of man, but of a progress in human knowledge.

To those who reproached Descartes with disrespect towards ancient thinkers he might have replied that, in repudiating their authority, he was really paying them the compliment of imitation and acting far more in their own spirit than those who slavishly followed them.   Pascal saw this point. "What can be more unjust," he wrote, "than to treat our ancients with greater consideration than they showed towards their own predecessors, and to have for them this incredible respect which they deserve from us only because they entertained no such regard for those who had the same advantage (of antiquity) over them?"

At the same time Pascal recognised that we are indebted to the ancients for our very superiority to them in the extent of our knowledge.   "They reached a certain point, and the slightest effort enables us to mount higher; so that we find ourselves on a loftier plane with less trouble and less glory." The attitude of Descartes was very different. Aspiring to begin *ab integro* and reform the foundations of knowledge, he ignored or made little of what had been achieved in the past. He attempted to cut the threads of continuity as with the shears of Atropos. This illusion [1] hindered him from stating a doctrine of the progress of knowledge as otherwise he might have done. For any such doctrine must take account of the past as well as of the future.

But a theory of progress was to grow out of his philosophy, though he did not construct it. It was to be developed by men who were imbued with the Cartesian spirit.

3

The theological world in France was at first divided on the question whether the system of Descartes could be reconciled with orthodoxy or not. The Jesuits said no, the Fathers of the Oratory said yes. The Jansenists of Port Royal were enthusiastic Cartesians. Yet it was probably the influence of the great spiritual force of Jansenism that did most to check the immediate spread of Cartesian ideas. It was preponderant in France for fifty years. The date of the *Discourse of Method* is 1637. The *Augustinus* of Jansenius was published in 1640, and in 1643 Arnauld's *Frequent Communion* made Jansenism a popular power.

The Jansenist movement was in France in some measure what the Puritan movement was in England,

---

[1] He may be reproached himself with scholasticism in his metaphysical reasoning.

and it caught hold of serious minds in much the
same way. The Jesuits had undertaken the task of
making Christianity easy, of finding a compromise
between worldliness and religion, and they flooded

the world with a casuistic literature designed for
this purpose. *Ex opinionum varietate jugum
Christi suavius deportatur.* The doctrine of Jansenius was directed against this corruption of faith
and morals. He maintained that there can be
no compromise with the world; that casuistry is
incompatible with morality; that man is naturally
corrupt; and that in his most virtuous acts some
corruption is present.

Now the significance of these two forces—the
stern ideal of the Jansenists and the casuistry of
the Jesuit teachers—is that they both attempted to

meet, by opposed methods, the wave of libertine
thought and conduct which is a noticeable feature
in the history of French society from the reign of
Henry IV. to that of Louis XV. This libertinism
had its philosophy, a sort of philosophy of nature,
of which the most brilliant exponents were Rabelais
and Molière. The maxim, " Be true to nature,"
was evidently opposed sharply to the principles of
the Christian religion, and it was associated with
sceptical views which prevailed widely in France
from the early years of the seventeenth century.
The Jesuits sought to make terms by saying
virtually: "Our religious principles and your
philosophy of nature are not after all so incompatible in practice. When it comes to the application of principles, opinions differ. Theology is as
elastic as you like. Do not abandon your religion
on the ground that her yoke is hard." Jansenius

and his followers, on the other hand, fought uncompromisingly with the licentious spirit of the time, maintaining the austerest dogmas and denouncing any compromise or condescension. And their doctrine had a wonderful success, and penetrated everywhere. Few of the great literary men of the reign of Louis XIV. escaped it. Its influence can be traced in the *Maximes* of La Rochefoucauld and the *Caractères* of La Bruyère. It was through its influence that Molière found it difficult to get some of his plays staged. It explains the fact that the court of Louis XIV., however corrupt, was decorous compared with the courts of Henry IV. and Louis XV.; a severe standard was set up, if it was not observed.

The genius of Pascal made the fortunes of Jansenism. He outlived his Cartesianism and became its most influential spokesman. His *Provinciales* (1656) rendered abstruse questions of theology more or less intelligible, and invited the general public to pronounce an opinion on them. His lucid exposition interested every one in the abstruse problem, Is man's freedom such as not to render grace superfluous? But Pascal perceived that casuistry was not the only enemy that menaced the true spirit of religion for which Jansenism stood. He came to realise that Cartesianism, to which he was at first drawn, was profoundly opposed to the fundamental views of Christianity. His *Pensées* are the fragments of a work which he designed in defence of religion, and it is easy to see that this defence was to be specially directed against the ideas of Descartes.

Pascal was perfectly right about the Cartesian

conception of the Universe, though Descartes might pretend to mitigate its tendencies, and his fervent disciple, Malebranche, might attempt to prove that it was more or less reconcilable with orthodox doctrine. We need not trouble about the special metaphysical tenets of Descartes. The two axioms which he launched upon the world—the supremacy of reason, and the invariability of natural laws—struck directly at the foundations of orthodoxy. Pascal was attacking Cartesianism when he made his memorable attempt to discredit the authority of reason, by showing that it is feeble and deceptive. It was a natural consequence of his changed attitude that he should speak (in the *Pensées*) in a much less confident tone about the march of science than he had spoken in the passage which I quoted above. And it was natural that he should be pessimistic about social improvement, and that, keeping his eyes fixed on his central fact that Christianity is the goal of history, he should take only a slight and subsidiary interest in amelioration.

The preponderant influence of Jansenism only began to wane during the last twenty years of the seventeenth century, and till then it seems to have been successful in counteracting the diffusion of the Cartesian ideas. Cartesianism begins to become active and powerful when Jansenism is beginning to decline. And it is just then that the idea of Progress begins definitely to emerge. The atmosphere in France was favourable for its reception.

4

The Cartesian mechanical theory of the world and the doctrine of invariable law, carried to a logical conclusion, excluded the doctrine of Providence. This doctrine was already in serious danger. Perhaps no article of faith was more insistently attacked by sceptics in the seventeenth century, and none was more vital. The undermining of the theory of Providence is very intimately connected with our subject; for it was just the theory of an active Providence that the theory of Progress was to replace; and it was not till men felt independent of Providence that they could organise a theory of Progress.

Bossuet was convinced that the question of Providence was the most serious and pressing among all the questions of the day that were at issue between orthodox and heretical thinkers. Brunetière, his fervent admirer, has named him the theologian of Providence, and has shown that in all his writings this doctrine is a leading note. It is sounded in his early sermons in the fifties, and it is the theme of his most ambitious work, the *Discourse on Universal History*, which appeared in 1681. This book, which has received high praise from those who most heartily dissent from its conclusions, is in its main issue a restatement of the view of history which Augustine had worked out in his memorable book. The whole course of human experience has been guided by Providence for the sake of the Church; that is, for the sake of the Church to which Bossuet belonged. Regarded as a philosophy of history the *Discourse* may seem

little more than the theory of the *De Civitate Dei*
brought up to date ; but this is its least important
aspect. We shall fail to understand it unless we
recognise that it was a pragmatical, opportune work,
designed for the needs of the time, and with express
references to current tendencies of thought.

One main motive of Bossuet in his lifelong
concern for Providence was his conviction that the
doctrine was the most powerful check on immorality,
and that to deny it was to remove the strongest
restraint on the evil side of human nature. There
is no doubt that the free-living people of the time
welcomed the arguments which called Providence
in question, and Bossuet believed that to champion
Providence was the most efficient means of opposing
the libertine tendencies of his day. " Nothing," he
declared in one of his sermons (1662), " has appeared
more insufferable to the arrogance of libertines than
to see themselves continually under the observation
of this ever-watchful eye of Providence. They have
felt it as an importunate compulsion to recognise
that there is in Heaven a superior force which
governs all our movements and chastises our loose
actions with a severe authority. They have wished
to shake off the yoke of this Providence, in order to
maintain, in independence, an unteachable liberty
which moves them to live at their own fancy,
without fear, discipline, or restraint." Bossuet was
thus working in the same cause as the Jansenists.

He had himself come under the influence of
Descartes, whose work he always regarded with the
deepest respect. The cautiousness of the master
had done much to disguise the insidious dangers of
his thought, and it was in the hands of those

disciples who developed his system and sought to reconcile it at all points with orthodoxy that his ideas displayed their true nature. Malebranche's philosophy revealed the incompatibility of Providence — in the ordinary acceptation — with immutable natural laws. If the Deity acts upon the world, as Malebranche maintained, only by means of general laws, His freedom is abolished, His omnipotence is endangered, He is subject to a sort of fatality. What will become of the Christian belief in the value of prayers, if God cannot adapt or modify, on any given occasion, the general order of nature to the needs of human beings? These are some of the arguments which we find in a treatise composed by Fénelon, with the assistance of Bossuet, to demonstrate that the doctrine of Malebranche is inconsistent with piety and orthodox religion. They were right. Cartesianism was too strong a wine to be decanted into old bottles.

Malebranche's doctrine of what he calls divine Providence was closely connected with his philosophical optimism. It enabled him to maintain the perfection of the universe. Admitting the obvious truth that the world exhibits many imperfections, and allowing that the Creator could have produced a better result if he had employed other means, Malebranche argued that, in judging the world, we must take into account not only the result but the methods by which it has been produced. It is the best world, he asserts, that could be framed by general and simple methods; and general and simple methods are the most perfect, and alone worthy of the Creator. Therefore, if we take the methods and the result together, a more perfect world is impossible. The argument was ingenious, though full of assumptions, but it was one which could only satisfy a philosopher. It is little consolation to creatures suffering from the actual imperfections of the system into which they are born to be told that the world might have been free from those defects, only in that case they would not have the satisfaction of knowing that it was created and conducted on theoretically superior principles.

Though Malebranche's conception was only a metaphysical theory, metaphysical theories have usually their pragmatic aspects ; and the theory that the universe is as perfect as it could be marks a stage in the growth of intellectual optimism which we can trace from the sixteenth century. It was a view which could appeal to the educated public in France, for it harmonised with the general spirit of self-complacency and hopefulness which prevailed among the higher classes of society in the reign of Louis XIV. For them the conditions of life under the new despotism had become far more agreeable than in previous ages, and it was in a spirit of optimism that they devoted themselves to the enjoyment of luxury and elegance. The experience of what the royal authority could achieve encouraged men to imagine that one enlightened will, with a centralised administration at its command, might accomplish endless improvements in civilisation. There was no age had ever been more glorious, no age more agreeable to live in.

The world had begun to abandon the theory of corruption, degeneration, and decay.

Some years later the optimistic theory of the

perfection of the universe found an abler exponent in Leibnitz, whom Diderot calls the father of optimism. The Creator, before He acted, had considered all possible worlds, and had chosen the best. He might have chosen one in which humanity would have been better and happier, but that would not have been the best possible, for He had to consider the interests of the whole universe, of which the earth with humanity is only an insignificant part. The evils and imperfections of our small world are negligible in comparison with the happiness and perfection of the whole cosmos. Leibnitz, whose theory is deduced from the abstract proposition that the Creator is perfect, does not say that now or at any given moment the universe is as perfect as it could be; its merit lies in its potentialities; it will develop towards perfection throughout infinite time.

The optimism of Leibnitz therefore concerns the universe as a whole, not the earth, and would obviously be quite consistent with a pessimistic view of the destinies of humanity. He does indeed believe that it would be impossible to improve the universal order, " not only for the whole, but for ourselves in particular," and incidentally he notes the possibility that " in the course of time the human race may reach a greater perfection than we can imagine at present." But the significance of his speculation and that of Malebranche lies in the fact that the old theories of degeneration are definitely abandoned.

CHAPTER IV

THE DOCTRINE OF DEGENERATION :
THE ANCIENTS AND MODERNS

OUTSIDE the circle of systematic thinkers the prevalent theory of degeneration was being challenged
early in the seventeenth century. The challenge
led to a literary war, which was waged for about a
hundred years in France and England, over the
comparative merits of the ancients and the moderns.
It was in the matter of literature, and especially
poetry, that the quarrel was most acrimonious, and
that the interest of the public was most keenly
aroused, but the ablest disputants extended the
debate to the general field of knowledge. The
quarrel of the Ancients and Moderns used commonly to be dismissed as a curious and rather
ridiculous episode in the history of literature.[1]
Auguste Comte was, I think, one of the first to
call attention to some of its wider bearings.

The quarrel, indeed, has considerable significance
in the history of ideas. It was part of the rebellion
against the intellectual yoke of the Renaissance ;
the cause of the Moderns, who were the aggressors,
represented the liberation of criticism from the

---

[1] The best and fullest work on the subject is Rigault's *Histoire de la
querelle des Anciens et des Modernes* (1856).

authority of the dead ; and, notwithstanding the
perversities of taste of which they were guilty, their
polemic, even on the purely literary side, was distinctly important, as M. Brunetière has convincingly
shown,[1] in the development of French criticism.
But the form in which the critical questions were
raised forced the debate to touch upon a problem
of greater moment. The question, Can the men of
to-day contend on equal terms with the illustrious
ancients, or are they intellectually inferior ? implied
the larger issue, Has nature exhausted her powers ;
is she no longer capable of producing men equal in
brains and vigour to those whom she once produced ; is humanity played out, or are her forces
permanent and inexhaustible ?

The assertion of the permanence of the powers
of nature by the champions of the Moderns was the
direct contradiction of the theory of degeneration,
and they undoubtedly contributed much towards
bringing that theory into discredit. When we
grasp this it will not be surprising to find that the
first clear assertions of a doctrine of progress in
knowledge were provoked by the controversy about
the Ancients and Moderns.

I

Although the great scene of the controversy was
France, the question had been expressly raised by
an Italian, no less a person than Alessandro Tassoni,
the accomplished author of that famous ironical
poem, " La Secchia rapita," which caricatured the
epic poets of his day. He was bent on exposing

[1] See his *L'Évolution des genres dans l'histoire de la littérature.*

the prejudices of his time and uttering new doctrine, and he created great scandal in Italy by his attacks on Petrarch, as well as on Homer and Aristotle. The earliest comparison of the merits of the ancients and the moderns will be found in a volume of *Miscellaneous Thoughts* which he published in 1620.[1] He speaks of the question as a matter of current dispute,[2] on which he proposes to give an impartial decision by instituting a comprehensive comparison in all fields, theoretical, imaginative, and practical.

He begins by criticising the *a priori* argument that, as arts are brought to perfection by experience and long labour, the modern age must necessarily have the advantage. This reasoning, he says, is unsound, because the same arts and studies are not always uninterruptedly pursued by the most powerful intellects, but pass into inferior hands, and so decline or are even extinguished, as was the case in Italy in the decrepitude of the Roman Empire, when for many centuries the arts fell below mediocrity. Or, to phrase it otherwise, the argument would be admissible only if there were no breaches of continuity.[3]

In drawing his comparison Tassoni seeks to make good his claim that he is not an advocate.

---

[1] *Dieci libri di pensieri diversi* (Carpi, 1620). The first nine books had appeared in 1612. The tenth contains the comparison. Rigault was the first to connect this work with the history of the controversy.

[2] It was incidental to the controversy which arose over the merits of Tasso's *Jerusalem Delivered*. That the subject had been discussed long before may be inferred from a remark of Estienne in his *Apology for Herodotus*, that while some of his contemporaries carry their admiration of antiquity to the point of superstition, others depreciate and trample it underfoot.

[3] Tassoni argues that a decline in all pursuits is inevitable when a certain point of excellence has been reached, quoting Velleius Paterculus (i. 17):
difficilisque in perfecto mora est naturaliterque quod procedere non potest recedit.

But while he awards superiority here and there to
the ancients, the moderns on the whole have much
the best of it.   He takes a wide enough survey,
including the material side of civilisation, even
costume, in contrast with some of the later controversialists, who narrowed the field of debate to
literature and art.

Tassoni's *Thoughts* were translated into French,
and the book was probably known to Boisrobert,
a dramatist who is chiefly remembered for the part
he took in founding the Académie française.   He
delivered a discourse before that body immediately
after its institution (February 26, 1635), in which
he made a violent and apparently scurrilous attack
on Homer.   This discourse kindled the controversy
in France, and even struck a characteristic note.
Homer—already severely handled by Tassoni—
was to be the special target for the arrows of the
Moderns, who felt that, if they could succeed in
discrediting him, their cause would be won.

Thus the gauntlet was flung—and it is important
to note this—before the appearance of the *Discourse of Method* (1637); but the influence of
Descartes made itself felt throughout the controversy, and the most prominent moderns were men
who had assimilated Cartesian ideas.   This seems
to be true even of Desmarets de Saint Sorlin, who,
a good many years after the discourse of Boisrobert,
opened the campaign.   Saint Sorlin had become a
fanatical Christian; that was one reason for hating
the ancients.   He was also, like Boisrobert, a bad
poet; that was another.   His thesis was that the
history of Christianity offered subjects far more
inspiring to a poet than those which had been

treated by Homer and Sophocles, and that Christian poetry must bear off the palm from pagan. His own *Clovis* and *Mary Magdalene or the Triumph of Grace* were the demonstration of Homer's defeat. Few have ever heard of these productions; how many have read them? Curiously, about the same time an epic was being composed in England which might have given to the foolish contentions of Saint Sorlin some illusory plausibility.

But the literary dispute does not concern us here. What does concern us is that Saint Sorlin was aware of the wider aspects of the question, though he was not seriously interested in them. Antiquity, he says, was not so happy or so learned or so rich or so stately as the modern age, which is really the mature old age, and as it were the autumn of the world, possessing the fruits and the spoils of all the past centuries, with the power to judge of the inventions, experiences, and errors of predecessors, and to profit by all that. The ancient world was a spring which had only a few flowers. Nature indeed, in all ages, produces perfect works; but it is not so with the creations of man, which require correction; and the men who live latest must excel in happiness and knowledge. Here we have both the assertion of the permanence of the forces of nature and the idea, already expressed by Bacon and others, that the modern age has advantages over antiquity comparable to those of old age over childhood.

2

How seriously the question between the Moderns and the Ancients — on whose behalf

Boileau had come forward and crossed swords with
Saint Sorlin—was taken is shown by the fact that
Saint Sorlin, before his death, solemnly bequeathed
the championship of the Moderns to a younger man,
Charles Perrault.   We shall see how he fulfilled
the trust.   It is illustrated too by a book which
appeared in the seventies, *Les Entretiens d'Ariste
et Eugène*, by Bouhours, a mundane and popular
Jesuit Father.   In one of these dialogues the
question is raised, but with a curious caution and
evasiveness, which suggests that the author was
afraid to commit himself; he did not wish to make
enemies.[1]

The general atmosphere in France, in the reign
of Louis XIV., was propitious to the cause of the
Moderns.   Men felt that it was a great age, comparable to the age of Augustus, and few would
have preferred to have lived at any other time.
Their literary artists, Corneille, and then Racine
and Molière, appealed so strongly to their taste
that they could not assign to them any rank but
the first.   They were impatient of the claims to
unattainable excellence advanced for the Greeks
and Romans.   " The ancients," said Molière, "are
the ancients, we are the people of to-day."   This
might be the motto of Descartes, and it probably
expressed a very general feeling.

It was in 1687 that Charles Perrault—who is

---

[1] Rigault notes that he makes one contribution to the subject, the idea
that the torch of civilisation has passed from country to country, in different
ages, *e.g.* from Greece to Rome, and recently from Italy to France.   In the
last century the Italians were first in *doctrine* and *politesse*.   The present
century is for France what the last was for Italy : " We have all the *esprit*
and all the *science*, all other countries are barbarous in comparison " (p. 239,
ed. 1782, Amsterdam).   But, as we shall see, he had been anticipated by
Hakewill, whose work was unknown to Rigault.

better remembered for his collection of fairy-tales
than for the leading *rôle* which he played in this
controversy—published his poem on " The Age of
Louis the Great." The enlightenment of the
present age surpasses that of antiquity,—this is the
theme.

> La docte Antiquité dans toute sa durée
> A l'égal de nos jours ne fut point éclairée.

Perrault adopts a more polite attitude to " la belle
antiquité " than Saint Sorlin, but his criticism is
more insidious.   Greek and Roman men of genius,
he suggests, were all very well in their own times,
and might be considered divine by our ancestors.
But nowadays Plato is rather tiresome ; and the
" inimitable Homer " would have written a much
better epic if he had lived in the reign of Louis the
Great. The important passage, however, in the
poem is that in which the permanent power of
nature to produce men of equal talent in every age
is affirmed.

> À former les esprits comme à former les corps
> La Nature en tout temps fait les mesmes efforts ;
> Son être est immuable, et cette force aisée
> Dont elle produit tout ne s'est point épuisée ;
>
> .   .   .   .   .
>
> De cette mesme main les forces infinies
> Produisent en tout temps de semblables génies.

The " Age of Louis the Great " was a brief
declaration of faith. Perrault followed it up by a
comprehensive work, his Comparison of the Ancients
and the Moderns (*Parallèle des Anciens et des
Modernes*), which appeared in four parts during the
following years (1688–1696). Art, eloquence, poetry,
the sciences, and their practical applications are all

discussed at length ; and the discussion is thrown into the form of conversations between an enthusiastic champion of the modern age, who conducts the debate, and a devotee of antiquity, who finds it difficult not to admit the arguments of his opponent, yet obstinately persists in his own views.

Perrault bases his thesis on those general considerations which we have met incidentally in earlier writers, and which were now almost commonplaces among those who paid any attention to the matter. Knowledge advances with time and experience ; perfection is not necessarily associated with antiquity; the latest comers have inherited from their predecessors and added new acquisitions of their own. But Perrault has thought out the subject methodically, and he draws conclusions which have only to be extended to amount to a definite theory of the progress of knowledge.

A particular difficulty had done much to hinder a general admission of progressive improvement in the past. The proposition that the posterior is better and the late comers have the advantage seemed to be incompatible with an obvious historical fact. We are superior to the men of the dark ages in knowledge and arts. Granted. But will you say that the men of the tenth century were superior to the Greeks and Romans? To this question—on which Tassoni had already touched—Perrault replies: Certainly not. There are breaches of continuity. The sciences and arts are like rivers, which flow for part of their course underground, and then, finding an opening, spring forth as abundant as when they plunged beneath the earth. Long wars, for instance, may force peoples to neglect studies and throw all their vigour into the more urgent needs of self-preservation ; a period of ignorance may ensue ; but with peace and felicity knowledge and inventions will begin again and make further advances.

It is to be observed that he does not claim any superiority in talents or brain power for the moderns. On the contrary, he takes his stand on the principle which he had asserted in the "Age of Louis the Great," that nature is immutable. She still produces as great men as ever, but she does not produce greater. The lions of the deserts of Africa in our days do not differ in fierceness from those of the days of Alexander the Great, and the best men of all times are equal in vigour. It is their work and productions that are unequal, and, given equally favourable conditions, the latest must be the best. For science and the arts depend upon the accumulation of knowledge, and knowledge necessarily increases as time goes on.

But could this argument be applied to poetry and literary art, the field of battle in which the belligerents, including Perrault himself, were most deeply interested ? It might prove that the modern age was capable of producing poets and men of letters no less excellent than the ancient masters, but did it prove that their works must be superior? The objection did not escape Perrault, and he answers it ingeniously. It is the function of poetry and eloquence to please the human heart, and in order to please it we must know it. Is it easier to penetrate the secrets of the human heart than the secrets of nature, or will it take less time? We are always making new discoveries about its passions and desires. To take only the tragedies of Corneille, you will find there finer and more delicate reflections on ambition, vengeance, and jealousy than in all the books of antiquity.   At the close of his *Parallel*, however, Perrault, while he declares the general superiority of the moderns, makes a reservation in regard to poetry and eloquence "for the sake of peace."

The discussion of Perrault falls far short of embodying a full idea of Progress.   Not only is he exclusively concerned with progress in knowledge—though he implies, indeed, without developing, the doctrine that happiness depends on knowledge—but he has no eyes for the future, and no interest in it.   He is so impressed with the advance of know-ledge in the recent past that he is almost incapable of imagining further progression.   " Read the journals of France and England," he says, " and glance at the publications of the Academies of these great kingdoms, and you will be convinced that within the last twenty or thirty years more dis-coveries have been made in natural science than throughout the period of learned antiquity.   I own that I consider myself fortunate to know the happiness we enjoy ; it is a great pleasure to survey all the past ages in which I can see the birth and the progress of all things, but nothing which has not received a new increase and lustre in our own times.   Our age has, in some sort, arrived at the summit of perfection.   And since for some years the rate of the progress is much slower and appears almost insensible — as the days seem to cease lengthening when the solstice is near—it is pleasant to think that probably there are not many things for which we need envy future generations."

Indifference to the future, or even a certain scepticism about it, is the note of this passage, and accords with the view that the world has reached its old age. The idea of the progress of knowledge, which Perrault expounds, is still incomplete.

3

Independently of this development in France, the doctrine of degeneration had been attacked, and the comparison of the ancients with the moderns incidentally raised, in England.

A divine named George Hakewill published in 1627 a folio of six hundred pages to confute "the common error touching Nature's perpetual and universal decay."[1] He and his pedantic book, which breathes the atmosphere of the sixteenth century, are completely forgotten; and though it ran to three editions, it can hardly have attracted the attention of many except theologians. The writer's object is to prove that the power and providence of God in the government of the world are not consistent with the current view that the physical universe, the heavens and the elements, are undergoing a process of decay, and that man is degenerating physically, mentally, and morally. His arguments in general are futile as well as tedious. But he has profited by reading Bodin and Bacon, whose ideas, it would appear, were already agitating theological minds.

A comparison between the ancients and the moderns arises in a general refutation of the

---

[1] *An Apologie or Declaration of the Power and Providence of God in the Government of the World, consisting in an Examination and Censure of the common Errour, etc.* (1627, 1630, 1635).

doctrine of decay, as naturally as the question of the stability of the powers of nature arises in a comparison between the ancients and moderns. Hakewill protests against excessive admiration of antiquity, just because it encourages the opinion of the world's decay. He gives his argument a much wider scope than the French controversialists. For him the field of debate includes not only science, arts, and literature, but physical qualities and morals. He seeks to show that mentally and physically there has been no decay, and that the morals of modern Christendom are immensely superior to those of pagan times. There has been social progress, due to Christianity; and there has been an advance in arts and knowledge.

> Multa dies uariusque labor mutabilis aeui
> Rettulit in melius.

Hakewill, like Tassoni, surveys all the arts and sciences, and concludes that the moderns are equal to the ancients in poetry, and in almost all other things excel them.

One of the arguments which he urges against the theory of degeneration is pragmatic — its paralysing effect on human energy. "The opinion of the world's universal decay quails the hopes and blunts the edge of men's endeavours." And the effort to improve the world, he implies, is a duty we owe to posterity.

"Let not then the vain shadows of the world's fatal decay keep us either from looking backward to the imitation of our noble predecessors or forward in providing for posterity, but as our predecessors worthily provided for us, so let our posterity bless us in providing for them, it being still as uncertain to us what generations are still to ensue, as it was to our predecessors in their ages."

We note the suggestion that history may be conceived as a sequence of improvements in civilisation, but we note also that Hakewill here is faced by the obstacle which Christian theology offered to the logical expansion of the idea. It is uncertain what generations are still to ensue. Roger Bacon stood before the same dead wall. Hakewill thinks that he is living in the last age of the world; but how long it shall last is a question which cannot be resolved, "it being one of those secrets which the Almighty hath locked up in the cabinet of His own counsel." Yet he consoles himself and his readers with a consideration which suggests that the end is not yet very near. "It is agreed upon all sides by Divines that at least two signs forerunning the world's end remain unaccomplished—the subversion of Rome and the conversion of the Jews. And when they shall be accomplished God only knows, as yet in man's judgment there being little appearance of the one or the other."

It was well to be assured that nature is not decaying or man degenerating. But was the doctrine that the end of the world does not "depend upon the law of nature," and that the growth of human civilisation may be cut off at any moment by a fiat of the Deity, less calculated to "quail the hopes and blunt the edge of men's endeavours?" Hakewill asserted with confidence that the universe will be suddenly wrecked by fire. *Una dies dabit exitio.* Was the prospect of an arrest which might come the day after to-morrow likely to induce men to exert themselves to make provision for posterity?

The significance of Hakewill lies in the fact that he made the current theory of degeneration, which stood in the way of all possible theories of progress, the object of a special inquiry. And his book illustrates the close connection between that theory and the dispute over the Ancients and Moderns. It cannot be said that he has added anything valuable to what may be found in Bodin and Bacon on the development of civilisation. The general synthesis of history which he attempts is equivalent to theirs. He describes the history of knowledge and arts, and all things besides, as exhibiting "a kind of circular progress," by which he means that they have a birth, growth, flourishing, failing and fading, and then within a while after a resurrection and reflourishing. In this method of progress the lamp of learning passed from one people to another. It passed from the Orientals (Chaldeans and Egyptians) to the Greeks; when it was nearly extinguished in Greece it began to shine afresh among the Romans; and having been put out by the barbarians for the space of a thousand years it was relit by Petrarch and his contemporaries. In stating this view of "circular progress," Hakewill comes perilously near to the doctrine of Ricorsi or Returns which had been severely denounced by Bacon.

In one point indeed Hakewill goes far beyond Bodin. It was suggested, as we saw, by the French thinker that in some respects the modern age is superior in conduct and morals to antiquity, but he said little on the matter. Hakewill develops the suggestion at great length into a severe and partial impeachment of ancient manners and morals.   Unjust and unconvincing though his arguments are, and inspired by theological motives, his thesis nevertheless deserves to be noted as an assertion of the progress of man in social morality. Bacon, and the thinkers of the seventeenth century generally, confined their views of progress in the past to the intellectual field.   Hakewill, though he overshot the mark and said nothing actually worth remembering, nevertheless anticipated the larger problem of social progress which was to come to the front in the eighteenth century.

4

During the forty years that followed the appearance of Hakewill's book much had happened in the world of ideas, and when we take up Glanvill's *Plus ultra, or the Progress and Advancement of Knowledge since the days of Aristotle*,[1] we breathe a different atmosphere.   It was published in 1668, and its purpose was to defend the recently founded Royal Society which was attacked on the ground that it was inimical to the interests of religion and sound learning.   For the Aristotelian tradition was still strongly entrenched in the English Church and Universities, notwithstanding the influence of Bacon ; and the Royal Society, which realised "the romantic model" of Bacon's society of experimenters, repudiated the scholastic principles and methods associated with Aristotle's name.

Glanvill was one of those latitudinarian clergy-

---

[1] The title is evidently suggested by a passage in Bacon quoted above, p. 55.

men, so common in the Anglican Church in the
seventeenth century, who were convinced that
religious faith must accord with reason, and were
unwilling to abate in its favour any of reason's
claims. He was under the influence of Bacon,
Descartes, and the Cambridge Platonists, and no
one was more enthusiastic than he in following the
new scientific discoveries of his time. Unfortunately for his reputation he had a weak side.
Enlightened though he was, he was a firm believer
in witchcraft, and he is chiefly remembered not as
an admirer of Descartes and Bacon, and a champion
of the Royal Society, but as the author of *Sadu-
cismus Triumphatus*, a monument of superstition,
which probably contributed to check the gradual
growth of disbelief in witches and apparitions.

His *Plus ultra* is a review of modern improvements of useful knowledge. It is confined to
mathematics and science, in accordance with its
purpose of justifying the Royal Society; and the
discoveries of the past sixty years enable the author
to present a far more imposing picture of modern
scientific progress than was possible for Bodin or
Bacon.[1] He had absorbed Bacon's doctrine of
utility. His spirit is displayed in the remark that
more gratitude is due to the unknown inventor of
the mariners' compass

"than to a thousand Alexanders and Caesars, or to
ten times the number of Aristotles. And he really did
more for the increase of knowledge and the advantage of

---

[1] Bacon indeed could have made out a more impressive picture of the
new age if he had studied mathematics and taken the pains to master the
evidence which was revolutionising astronomy. Glanvill had the advantage
of comprehending the importance of mathematics for the advance of physical
science.

the world by this one experiment than the numerous subtle disputers that have lived ever since the erection of the school of talking."

Glanvill, however, in his complacency with what has already been accomplished, is not misled into over-estimating its importance. He knows that it is indeed little compared with the ideal of attainable knowledge. The human design, to which it is the function of the Royal Society to contribute, is laid as low, he says, as the profoundest depths of nature, and reaches as high as the uppermost storey of the universe, extends to all the varieties of the great world, and aims at the benefit of universal mankind. Such a work can only proceed slowly, by insensible degrees. It is an undertaking wherein all the generations of men are concerned, and our own age can hope to do little more than to remove useless rubbish, lay in materials, and put things in order for the building. "We must seek and gather, observe and examine, and lay up in bank for the ages that come after."

These lines on "the vastness of the work" suggest to the reader that a vast future will be needed for its accomplishment. Glanvill does not dwell on this, but he implies it. He is evidently unembarrassed by the theological considerations which weighed so heavily on Hakewill. He does not trouble himself with the question whether Anti-Christ has still to appear. The difference in general outlook between these two clergymen is an indication how the world had travelled in the course of forty years.

Another point in Glanvill's little book deserves

attention.   He takes into his prospect the inhabitants of the Transatlantic world; they, too, are to share in the benefits which shall result from the subjugation of nature.

"By the gaining that mighty continent and the numerous fruitful isles beyond the Atlantic, we have obtained a larger field of nature, and have thereby an advantage for more phenomena, and more helps both for knowledge and for life, which 'tis very like that future ages will make better use of to such purposes than those hitherto have done ; and that science also may at last travel into those parts and enrich Peru with a more precious treasure than that of its golden mines, is not improbable."

Sprat, the Bishop of Rochester, in his interesting *History of the Royal Society*, so sensible and liberal—published shortly before Glanvill's book,—also contemplates the extension of science over the world.   Speaking of the prospect of future discoveries, he thinks it will partiy depend on the enlargement of the field of western civilisation "if this mechanic genius which now prevails in these parts of Christendom shall happen to spread wide amongst ourselves and other civil nations, or if by some good fate it shall pass farther on to other countries that were yet never fully civilised."

This then being imagin'd, that there may some lucky tide of civility flow into those lands which are yet salvage, then will a double improvement thence arise both in respect of ourselves and them.   For even the present skilful parts of mankind will be thereby made more skilful, and the other will not only increase those arts which we shall bestow upon them, but will also venture on new searches themselves.

He expects much from the new converts, on the ground that nations which have been taught have proved more capable than their teachers, appealing to the case of the Greeks who outdid their eastern masters, and to that of the peoples of modern Europe who received their light from the Romans but have "well nigh doubled the ancient stock of trades delivered to their keeping."

5

The establishment of the Royal Society in 1660 and the Academy of Sciences in 1666 made physical science fashionable in London and Paris. Macaulay, in his characteristic way, describes how "dreams of perfect forms of government made way for dreams of wings with which men were to fly from the Tower to the Abbey, and of double-keeled ships which were never to founder in the fiercest storm. All classes were hurried along by the prevailing sentiment. Cavalier and Round-head, Churchman and Puritan were for once allied. Divines, jurists, statesmen, nobles, princes, swelled the triumph of the Baconian philosophy." The seeds sown by Bacon had at last begun to ripen, and full credit was given to him by those who founded and acclaimed the Royal Society. The ode which Cowley addressed to that institution might have been entitled an ode in honour of Bacon, or still better—for the poet seized the essential point of Bacon's labours—a hymn on the liberation of the human mind from the yoke of Authority.

Bacon has broke that scar-crow Deity.

Dryden himself, in the *Annus Mirabilis*, had turned aside from his subject, the defeat of the Dutch and England's mastery of the seas, to pay a compliment to the Society, and to prophesy man's mastery of the universe.

> Instructed ships shall sail to rich commerce,
>   By which remotest regions are allied ;
> Which makes one city of the universe,
>   Where some may gain and all may be supplied.
>
> Then we upon our globe's last verge shall go,
>   And view the ocean leaning on the sky,
> From thence our rolling neighbours we shall know,
>   And on the lunar world securely pry.

Men did not look far into the future ; they did not dream of what the world might be a thousand or ten thousand years hence. They seem to have expected quick results. Even Sprat thinks that "the absolute perfection of the true philosophy" is not far off, seeing that "this first great and necessary preparation for its coming"—the institution of scientific co-operation—has been accomplished. Superficial and transient though the popular enthusiasm was, it was a sign that an age of intellectual optimism had begun, in which the science of nature would play a leading *rôle*.

CHAPTER V

I

Nine months before the first part of Perrault's work appeared a younger and more brilliant man had formulated, in a short tract, the essential points of the doctrine of the progress of knowledge. It was Fontenelle.

Fontenelle was an *anima naturaliter moderna:* Trained in the principles of Descartes, he was one of those who, though like Descartes himself, too critical to swear by a master, appreciated unreservedly the value of the Cartesian method. Sometimes, he says, a great man gives the tone to his age ; and this is true of Descartes, who can claim the glory of having established a new art of reasoning. He sees the effects in literature. The best books on moral and political subjects are distinguished by an arrangement and precision which he traces to the *esprit géométrique* characteristic of Descartes.[1] Fontenelle himself had this "geometrical mind," which we see at its best in Descartes and Hobbes and Spinoza.

He had indeed a considerable aptitude for letters.

---

[1] *Sur l'utilite des mathématiques et de la physique* (*Œuvres,* iii. p. 6, ed. 1729).

He wrote poor verses, and could not distinguish good poetry from bad.   That perhaps was the defect of *l'esprit géométrique*.   But he wrote lucid prose. There was an ironical side to his temper, and he had an ingenious paradoxical wit, which he indulged, with no little felicity, in his early work, *Dialogues of the Dead*.   These conversations, though they show no dramatic power and are simply a vehicle for the author's satirical criticisms on life, are written with a light touch, and are full of surprises and unexpected turns.   The very choice of the interlocutors shows a curious fancy, which we do not associate with the geometrical intellect.   Descartes is confronted with the Third False Demetrius, and we wonder what the gourmet Apicius will find to say to Galileo.

2

In the *Dialogues of the Dead*, which appeared in 1683, the Ancient and Modern controversy is touched on more than once, and it is the subject of the conversation between Socrates and Montaigne. Socrates ironically professes to expect that the age of Montaigne will show a vast improvement on his own ; that men will have profited by the experience of many centuries ; and that the old age of the world will be wiser and better regulated than its youth. Montaigne assures him that it is not so, and that the vigorous types of antiquity, like Pericles, Aristides, and Socrates himself, are no longer to be found.   To this assertion Socrates opposes the doctrine of the permanence of the forces of Nature. Nature has not degenerated in her other works ; why should she cease to produce reasonable men ?

He goes on to observe that antiquity is enlarged
and exalted by distance : " In our own day we
esteemed our ancestors more than they deserved,
and now our posterity esteems us more than we
deserve. There is really no difference between
our ancestors, ourselves, and our posterity. *C'est
toujours la même chose.*" But, objects Montaigne,
I should have thought that things were always
changing ; that different ages had their different
characters. Are there not ages of learning and
ages of ignorance, rude ages and polite ? True,
replies Socrates, but these are only externalities.
The heart of man does not change with the fashions
of his life. The order of Nature remains constant
(*l'ordre général de la Nature a l'air bien constant*).

This conclusion harmonises with the general
spirit of the *Dialogues*. The permanence of the
forces of Nature is asserted, but for the purpose of
dismissing the whole controversy as rather futile.
Elsewhere modern discoveries, like the circulation
of the blood and the motions of the earth, are
criticised as useless ; adding nothing to the happiness
and pleasures of mankind. Men acquired, at an
early period, a certain amount of useful knowledge,
to which they have added nothing ; since then they
have been slowly discovering things that are unnecessary. Nature has not been so unjust as to
allow one age to enjoy more pleasures than another.
And what is the value of civilisation ? It moulds
our words, and embarrasses our actions ; it does not
affect our feelings.[1]

One might hardly have expected the author of

---

[1] See the dialogues of Harvey with Erasistratus (a Greek physician of the
third century B.C.) ; Galileo with Apicius ; Montezuma with Fernando Cortez.

these *Dialogues* to come forward a few years later
as a champion of the Moderns, even though, in the
dedicatory epistle to Lucian, he compared France to
Greece. But he was seriously interested in the
debated question, as an intellectual problem, and
in January 1688 he published his *Digression on
the Ancients and Moderns*, a short pamphlet, but
weightier and more suggestive than the large work
of his friend Perrault, which began to appear nine
months later.

3

The question of pre-eminence between the
Ancients and Moderns is reducible to another.
Were trees in ancient times greater than to-day?
If they were, then Homer, Plato, and Demosthenes
cannot be equalled in modern times; if they were
not, they can.

Fontenelle states the problem in this succinct
way at the beginning of the *Digression*. The
permanence of the forces of Nature had been
asserted by Saint Sorlin and Perrault; they had
offered no proof, and had used the principle rather
incidentally and by way of illustration. But the
whole inquiry hinged on it. If it can be shown
that man has not degenerated, the cause of the
Moderns is practically won. The issue of the
controversy must be decided not by rhetoric but by
physics. And Fontenelle offers what he regards
as a formal Cartesian proof of the permanence of
natural forces.

If the Ancients had better intellects than ours,
the brains of that age must have been better
arranged, formed of firmer or more delicate fibres,

fuller of "animal spirits." But if such a difference existed, Nature must have been more vigorous; and in that case the trees must have profited by that superior vigour and have been larger and finer. The truth is that Nature has in her hands a certain paste which is always the same, which she is ever turning over and over again in a thousand ways, and of which she forms men, animals, and plants. She has not formed Homer, Demosthenes, and Plato of a finer or better kneaded clay than our poets, orators, and philosophers. Do not object that minds are not material. They are connected by a material bond with the brain, and it is the quality of this material bond that determines intellectual differences.

But although natural processes do not change from age to age, they differ in their effects in different climates. "It is certain that as a result of the reciprocal dependence which exists between all parts of the material world, differences of climate, which so clearly affect the life of plants, must also produce some effect on human brains." May it not be said then that, in consequence of climatic conditions, ancient Greece and Rome produced men of mental qualities different from those which could be produced in France? Oranges grow easily in Italy; it is more difficult to cultivate them in France. Fontenelle replies that art and cultivation exert a much greater influence on human brains than on the soil; ideas can be transported more easily from one country to another than plants; and as a consequence of commerce and mutual influence, peoples do not retain the original mental peculiarities due to climate. This may not be true of the

extreme climates in the torrid and glacial zones, but
in the temperate zone we may discount entirely
climatic influence.   The climates of Greece and
Italy and that of France are too similar to cause
any sensible difference between the Greeks or
Latins and the French.

Saint Sorlin and Perrault had argued directly
from the permanence of vigour in lions or trees to
the permanence of vigour in man.   If trees are the
same as ever, brains must also be the same.   But
what about the minor premiss?   Who knows that
trees are precisely the same?   It is an indemon-
strable assumption that oaks and beeches in the
days of Socrates and Cicero were not slightly
better trees than the oaks and beeches of to-day.
Fontenelle saw the weakness of this reasoning.
He saw that it was necessary to prove that the
trees, no less than human brains, have not degenerated.   But his *a priori* proof is simply a
statement of the Cartesian principle of the stability
of natural processes, which he put in a thoroughly
unscientific form.   The stability of the laws of
nature is a necessary hypothesis, without which
science would be impossible.   But here it was put
to an illegitimate use.   For it means that, given
precisely the same conditions, the same physical
phenomena will occur.   Fontenelle therefore was
bound to show that conditions had not altered in
such a way as to cause changes in the quality of
nature's organic productions.   He did not do this.
He did not take into consideration, for instance, that
climatic conditions may vary from age to age as
well as from country to country.

4

Having established the natural equality of the Ancients and Moderns, Fontenelle inferred that whatever differences exist are due to external conditions—(1) time ; (2) political institutions and the state of affairs in general.

The ancients were prior in time to us, therefore they were the authors of the first inventions. For that, they cannot be regarded as our superiors. If we had been in their place we should have been the inventors, like them ; if they were in ours, they would add to those inventions, like us. There is no great mystery in that. We must impute equal merit to the early thinkers who showed the way and to the later thinkers who pursued it. If the ancient attempts to explain the universe have been recently replaced by the discovery of a simple system (the Cartesian), we must consider that the truth could only be reached by the elimination of false routes, and in this way the numbers of the Pythagoreans, the ideas of Plato, the qualities of Aristotle, all served indirectly to advance knowledge. "We are under an obligation to the ancients for having exhausted almost all the false theories that could be formed." Enlightened both by their true views and by their errors, it is not surprising that we should surpass them.

But all this applies only to scientific studies, like mathematics, physics, and medicine, which depend partly on correct reasoning and partly on experience. Methods of reasoning improve slowly, and the most important advance which has been

made in the present age is the method inaugurated
by Descartes. Before him reasoning was loose;
he introduced a more rigid and precise standard,
and its influence is not only manifest in our best
works on physics and philosophy, but is even
discernible in books on ethics and religion.

We must expect posterity to excel us as we excel
the Ancients, through improvement of method,
which is a science in itself—the most difficult and
least studied of all—and through increase of experience. Evidently the process is endless (*il est
évident que tout cela n'a point de fin*), and the latest
men of science must be the most competent.

But this does not apply to poetry or eloquence,
round which the controversy has most violently
raged. For poetry and eloquence do not depend on
correct reasoning. They depend principally on
vivacity of imagination, and "vivacity of imagination does not require a long course of experiments,
or a great multitude of rules, to attain all the
perfection of which it is capable." Such perfection
might be attained in a few centuries. If the
ancients did achieve perfection in imaginative
literature, it follows that they cannot be surpassed;
but we have no right to say, as their admirers are
fond of pretending, that they cannot be equalled.

5

Besides the mere nature of time, we have to
take into account external circumstances in considering this question.

If the forces of nature are permanent, how are
we to explain the fact that in the barbarous centuries
after the decline of Rome—the term Middle Ages

has not yet come into currency—ignorance was so dense and deep? This breach of continuity is one of the plausible arguments of the advocates of the Ancients. Those ages, they say, were ignorant and barbarous because the Greek and Latin writers had ceased to be read; as soon as the study of the classical models revived there was a renaissance of reason and good taste. That is true, but it proves nothing. Nature never forgot how to mould the head of Cicero or Livy. She produces in every age men who might be great men; but the age does not always allow them to exert their talents. Inundations of barbarians, universal wars, governments which discourage or do not favour science and art, prejudices which assume all variety of shapes —like the Chinese prejudice against dissecting corpses—may impose long periods of ignorance or bad taste.

But observe that, though the return to the study of the ancients revived, as at one stroke, the aesthetic ideals which they had created and the learning which they had accumulated, yet even if their works had not been preserved we should, though it would have cost us many long years of labour, have discovered for ourselves " ideas of the true and the beautiful." Where should we have found them? Where the ancients themselves found them, after much groping.

6

The comparison of the life of collective humanity to the life of a single man, which had been drawn by Bacon and Pascal, Saint Sorlin and Perrault, contains or illustrates an important truth which

bears on the whole question. Fontenelle puts it
thus. An educated mind is, as it were, composed of
all the minds of preceding ages; we might say that
a single mind was being educated throughout all
history. Thus this secular man, who has lived
since the beginning of the world, has had his infancy
in which he was absorbed by the most urgent needs
of life; his youth in which he succeeded pretty
well in things of imagination like poetry and eloquence, and even began to reason, but with more
courage than solidity. He is now in the age of
manhood, is more enlightened, and reasons better;
but he would have advanced further if the passion
for war had not distracted him and given him a
distaste for the sciences to which he has at last
returned.

Figures, if they are pressed, are dangerous;
they suggest unwarrantable conclusions. It may be
illuminative to liken the development of humanity
to the growth of an individual; but to infer that the
human race is now in its old age, merely on the
strength of the comparison, is obviously unjustifiable.
That is what Bacon and the others had done.
The fallacy was pointed out by Fontenelle.

From his point of view, an "old age" of
humanity, which if it meant anything meant decay
as well as the wisdom of experience, was contrary
to the principle of the permanence of natural forces.
Man, he asserts, will have no old age. He will
be always equally capable of achieving the successes
of his youth; and he will become more and more
expert in the things which become the age of
virility. Or "to drop metaphor, men will never
degenerate."

In ages to come we may be regarded—say in America—with the same excess of admiration with which we regard the ancients. We might push the prediction further. In still later ages the interval of time which divides us from the Greeks and Romans will appear so relatively small to posterity that they will classify us and the ancients as virtually contemporary; just in the same way as we group together the Greeks and Romans, though the Romans in their own day were moderns in relation to the Greeks. In that remote period men will be able to judge without prejudice the comparative merits of Sophocles and Corneille.

Unreasonable admiration for the ancients is one of the chief obstacles to progress (*le progrès des choses*). Philosophy not only did not advance, but even fell into an abyss of unintelligible ideas, because, through devotion to the authority of Aristotle, men sought truth in his enigmatic writings instead of seeking it in nature. If the authority of Descartes were ever to have the same fortune, the results would be no less disastrous.

7

This memorable brochure exhibits, without pedantry, perspicuous arrangement and the "geometrical" precision on which Fontenelle remarked as one of the notes of the new epoch introduced by Descartes. It displays too the author's open-mindedness, and his readiness to follow where the argument leads. He is able already to look beyond Cartesianism; he knows that it cannot be final. No man of his time was more open-minded and free from prejudice than Fontenelle. This quality

of mind helped him to turn his eyes to the future.
Perrault and his predecessors were absorbed in the
interest of the present and the past. Descartes
was too much engaged in his own original discoveries to do more than throw a passing glance at
posterity.

Now the prospect of the future was one of the
two elements which were still needed to fashion the
theory of the progress of knowledge. All the
conditions for such a theory were present. Bodin
and Bacon, Descartes and the champions of the
Moderns—the reaction against the Renaissance,
and the startling discoveries of science — had
prepared the way ; progress was established for the
past and present. But the theory of the progress
of knowledge includes and acquires its value by
including the indefinite future. This step was
taken by Fontenelle. The idea had been almost
excluded by Bacon's misleading metaphor of old
age, which Fontenelle expressly rejects. Man will
have no old age ; his intellect will never degenerate ;
and "the sound views of intellectual men in successive generations will continually add up."

But progress must not only be conceived as
extending indefinitely into the future ; it must also
be conceived as necessary and certain. This is the
second essential feature of the theory. The theory
would have little value or significance, if the
prospect of progress in the future depended on
chance or the unpredictable discretion of an external
will. Fontenelle asserts implicitly the certainty of
progress when he declares that the discoveries and
improvements of the modern age would have been
made by the ancients if they exchanged places with

the moderns; for this amounts to saying that science will progress and knowledge increase independently of particular individuals. If Descartes had not been born, some one else would have done his work; and there could have been no Descartes before the seventeenth century. For, as he says in a later work,[1] "there is an order which regulates our progress. Every science develops after a certain number of preceding sciences have developed, and only then; it has to await its turn to burst its shell."

Fontenelle, then, was the first to formulate the idea of the progress of knowledge as a complete doctrine. At the moment the import and far-reaching effects of the idea were not realised, either by himself or by others, and his pamphlet, which appeared in the company of a perverse theory of pastoral poetry, was acclaimed merely as an able defence of the Moderns.

8

If the theory of the indefinite progress of knowledge is true, it is one of those truths which were originally established by false reasoning. It was established on a principle which excluded degeneration, but equally excluded evolution; and the whole conception of nature which Fontenelle had learned from Descartes is long since dead and buried.

But it is more important to observe that this principle, which seemed to secure the indefinite progress of knowledge, disabled Fontenelle from suggesting a theory of the progress of society.

---

[1] *Préface des élémens de la géométrie de l'infini* (*Œuvres*, x. p. 40, ed. 1790).

The invariability of nature, as he conceived it, was true of the emotions and the will, as well as of the intellect. It implied that man himself would be psychically always the same—unalterable, incurable. *L'ordre général de la Nature a l'air bien constant.* His opinion of the human race was expressed in the *Dialogues of the Dead,*[1] and it never seems to have varied. The world consists of a multitude of fools, and a mere handful of reasonable men. Men's passions will always be the same and will produce wars in the future as in the past. Civilisation makes no difference; it is little more than a veneer.

Even if theory had not stood in his way, Fontenelle was the last man who was likely to dream dreams of social improvement. He was temperamentally an Epicurean, of the same refined stamp as Epicurus himself, and he enjoyed throughout his long life—he lived to the age of a hundred —the tranquillity which was the true Epicurean ideal. He was never troubled by domestic cares, and his own modest ambition was satisfied when, at the age of forty, he was appointed permanent Secretary of the Academy of Sciences. He was not the man to let his mind dwell on the woes and evils of the world; and the follies and perversities which cause them interested him only so far as they provided material for his wit.

It remains, however, noteworthy that the author of the theory of the progress of knowledge, which was afterwards to expand into a general theory of human Progress, would not have allowed that this extension was legitimate; though it was through

[1] It may be seen too in the *Plurality of Worlds.*

this extension that Fontenelle's idea acquired human value and interest and became a force in the world.

9

Fontenelle did a good deal more than formulate the idea. He reinforced it by showing that the prospect of a steady and rapid increase of knowledge in the future was certified.

The postulate of the immutability of the laws of nature, which has been the indispensable basis for the advance of modern science, is fundamental with Descartes. But Descartes did not explicitly insist on it, and it was Fontenelle, perhaps more than any one else, who made it current coin. That was a service performed by the disciple; but he seems to have been original in introducing the fruitful idea of the sciences as confederate and intimately interconnected [1]; not forming a number of isolated domains, as hitherto, but constituting a system in which the advance of one will contribute to the advance of the others. He exposed with masterly ability the reciprocal relations of physics and mathematics. No man of his day had a more comprehensive view of all the sciences, though he made no original contributions to any. His curiosity was universal, and as Secretary of the Academy he was obliged, according to his own high standard of his duty, to keep abreast of all that was being done in every branch of knowledge. That was possible then; it would be impossible now.

In the famous series of obituary discourses which he delivered on savants who were members

---

[1] Roger Bacon, as we saw, had a glimpse of this principle.

of the Academy, Fontenelle probably thought that
he was contributing to the realisation of this ideal
of "solidarity," for they amounted to a chronicle of
scientific progress in every department.   They are
free from technicalities and extraordinarily lucid,
and they appealed not only to men of science, but
to those of the educated public who possessed some
scientific curiosity.   This brings us to another
important *rôle* of Fontenelle—the *rôle* of interpreter of the world of science to the world outside.
It is closely related to our subject.

For the popularisation of science, which was to
be one of the features of the nineteenth century,
was in fact a condition of the success of the idea
of Progress.   That idea could not insinuate itself
into the public mind and become a living force
in civilised societies until the meaning and value
of science had been generally grasped, and the
results of scientific discovery had been more
or less diffused.   The achievements of physical
science did more than anything else to convert
the imaginations of men to the general doctrine
of Progress.

Before the later part of the seventeenth century,
the remarkable physical discoveries of recent date
had hardly escaped beyond academic circles.   But
an interest in these subjects began to become the
fashion in the later years of Louis XIV.   Science
was talked in the salons; ladies studied mechanics
and anatomy.   Molière's play, *Les Femmes savantes*,
which appeared in 1672, is one of the first indications.   In 1686 Fontenelle published his *Conversations on the Plurality of Worlds*, in which a savant
explains the new astronomy to a lady in the park of

a country house. It is the first book—at least the first that has any claim to be remembered—in the literature of popular science, and it is one of the most striking. It met with the success which it deserved. It was reprinted again and again, and it was almost immediately translated into English.

The significance of the *Plurality of Worlds* is indeed much greater than that of a pioneer work in popularisation and a model in the art of making technical subjects interesting. We must remember that at this time the belief that the sun revolves round the earth still prevailed. Only the few knew better. The cosmic revolution which is associated with the names of Copernicus, Kepler, and Galileo was slow in producing its effects. It was rejected by Bacon; and the condemnation of Galileo by the Church made Descartes, who dreaded nothing so much as a collision with the ecclesiastical authorities, unwilling to insist on it.[1] Milton's Raphael, in the Eighth Book of *Paradise Lost* (published 1667), does not venture to affirm the Copernican system; he explains it sympathetically, but leaves the question open.[2] Fontenelle's book was an event. It disclosed to the general public a new picture of the universe, to which men would have to accustom their imaginations.

We may perhaps best conceive all that this change meant by supposing what a difference it

[1] Cp. Bouillier, *Histoire de la philosophie cartésienne*, i. p. 42-3.
[2] Masson (*Milton's Poetical Works*, vol. 2) observes that Milton's life (1608-74) "coincides with the period of the struggle between the two systems" (p. 90). Milton's friends, the Smectymnians, in answer to Bishop Hall's *Humble Remonstrance* (1641), "had cited the Copernican doctrine as an unquestionable instance of a supreme absurdity." Masson has some apposite remarks on the influence of the Ptolemaic system "upon the thinkings and imaginations of mankind everywhere on all subjects whatsoever till about two hundred years ago."

would make to us if it were suddenly discovered that
the old system which Copernicus upset was true
after all, and that we had to think ourselves back
into a strictly limited universe of which the earth is
the centre.   The loss of its privileged position by
our own planet ; its degradation, from a cosmic point
of view, to insignificance ; the necessity of admitting
the probability that there may be many other
inhabited worlds—all this had consequences ranging
beyond the field of astronomy.   It was as if a man
who dreamed that he was living in Paris or London
should awake to discover that he was really in an
obscure island in the Pacific Ocean, and that the
Pacific Ocean was immeasurably vaster than he had
imagined.   The Marquise, in the *Plurality of
Worlds*, reacts to the startling illumination : " Voila
l'univers si grand que je m'y perds, je ne sais plus
où je suis ; je ne suis plus rien.—La terre est si
effroyablement petite ! "

Such a revolution in cosmic values could not fail
to exert a penetrating influence on human thought.
The privileged position of the earth had been a capital
feature of the whole doctrine, as to the universe and
man's destinies, which had been taught by the
Church, and it had made that doctrine more specious
than it might otherwise have seemed.   Though the
Churches could reform their teaching to meet the
new situation, the fact remained that the Christian
scheme sounded less plausible when the central importance of the human race was shown to be an
illusion.   Would man, stripped of his cosmic pre-
tensions, and finding himself lost in the immensities
of space, invent a more modest theory of his
destinies confined to his own little earth — *si*

effroyablement petite? The eighteenth century answered this question by the theory of Progress.

10

Fontenelle is one of the most representative thinkers of that period—we have no distinguishing name for it—which lies between the characteristic thinkers of the seventeenth century and the characteristic thinkers of the eighteenth. It is a period of over sixty years, beginning about 1680; for though Montesquieu and Voltaire were writing long before 1740, the great influential works of the "age of illumination" begin with the *Esprit des lois* in 1748. The intellectual task of this intervening period was to turn to account the ideas provided by the philosophy of Descartes, and use them as solvents of the ideas handed down from the Middle Ages. We might almost call it the Cartesian period; for, though Descartes was dead, it was in these years that Cartesianism performed its task and transformed human thought.

When we speak of Cartesianism we do not mean the metaphysical system of the master, or any of his particular views such as that of innate ideas. We mean the general principles, which were to leave an abiding impression on the texture of thought : the supremacy of reason over authority, the stability of the laws of Nature, rigorous standards of proof. Fontenelle was far from accepting all the views of Descartes, whom he does not scruple to criticise ; but he was a true Cartesian in the sense that he was deeply imbued with these principles, which generated, to use an expression of his own "des espèces de rebelles, qui conspiraient contre l'ignorance et les préjugés dominants."[1] And of all these rebels against ruling prejudices he probably did more than any single man to exhibit the consequences of the Cartesian ideas and drive them home.

The *Plurality of Worlds* was a contribution to the task of transforming thought and abolishing ancient error ; but the *History of Oracles* which appeared in the following year was more characteristic. It was a free adaptation of an unreadable Latin treatise by a Dutchman, which in Fontenelle's skilful hands becomes a vehicle for applying Cartesian solvents to theological authority. The thesis is that the Greek oracles were a sacerdotal imposture, and not, as ecclesiastical tradition said, the work of evil spirits, who were stricken silent at the death of Jesus Christ. The effect was to discredit the authority of the early Fathers of the Church, though the writer has the discretion to repudiate such an intention. For the publication was risky ; and twenty years later a Jesuit Father wrote a treatise to confute it, and exposed the secret poison, with consequences which might have been disastrous for Fontenelle if he had not had powerful friends among the Jesuits themselves. Fontenelle had none of the impetuosity of Voltaire, and after the publication of the *History of Oracles* he confined his criticism of tradition to the field of science. He was convinced that "les choses fort établies ne peuvent être attaquées que par degrez."[2]

The secret poison, of which Fontenelle prepared this remarkable dose with a touch which reminds us

---

[1] *Éloge de M. Lémery.*   [2] *Éloge de M. Lémery.*

of Voltaire, was being administered in the same Cartesian period, and with similar precautions, by Bayle. Like Fontenelle, this great sceptic, "the father of modern incredulity" as he was called by Joseph de Maistre, stood between the two centuries and belonged to both. Like Fontenelle, he took a gloomy view of humanity; he had no faith in that goodness of human nature which was to be a characteristic dogma of the age of illumination. But he was untouched by the discoveries of science; he took no interest in Galileo or Newton; and while the most important work of Fontenelle was the interpretation of the positive advances of knowledge, Bayle's was entirely subversive.

The principle of unchangeable laws in nature is intimately connected with the growth of Deism which is a note of this period. The function of the Deity was virtually confined to originating the machine of nature, which, once regulated, was set beyond any further interference on His part, though His existence might be necessary for its conservation. A view so sharply opposed to the current belief could not have made way as it did without a penetrating criticism of the current theology. Such criticism was performed by Bayle. His works were a school for rationalism for about seventy years. He supplied to the thinkers of the eighteenth century, English as well as French, a magazine of subversive arguments, and he helped to emancipate morality both from theology and from metaphysics.

This intellectual revolutionary movement, which was propagated in *salons* as well as by books, shook the doctrine of Providence which Bossuet had so eloquently expounded. It meant the en-

thronement of reason—Cartesian reason—before
whose severe tribunal history as well as opinions
were tried. New rules of criticism were introduced,
new standards of proof. When Fontenelle observed
that the existence of Alexander the Great could not
be strictly demonstrated and was ·no more than
highly probable,[1] it was an undesigned warning
that tradition would receive short shrift at the hands
of men trained in analytical Cartesian methods.

II

That the issue between the claims of antiquity
and the modern age should have been debated
independently in England and France indicates
that the controversy was an inevitable incident in
the liberation of the human spirit from the authority
of the ancients. Towards the end of the century
the debate in France aroused attention in England
and led to a literary quarrel, less important but not
less acrimonious than that which raged in France.
Sir William Temple's *Essay*, Wotton's *Reflexions*,
and Swift's satire the *Battle of the Books* are the
three outstanding works in the episode, which is
however chiefly remembered on account of its
connection with Bentley's masterly exposure of the
fabricated letters of Phalaris.

The literary debate in France, indeed, could not
have failed to reverberate across the Channel; for
never perhaps did the literary world in England
follow with more interest, or appreciate more
keenly the productions of the great French writers
of the time. In describing Will's coffee-house,

---

[1] *Pluralité des mondes*, sixième soir.

which was frequented by Dryden and all who pretended to be interested in polite letters, Macaulay says, "there was a faction for Perrault and the moderns, a faction for Boileau and the ancients." In the discussions on this subject a remarkable Frenchman who had long lived in England as an exile, M. de Saint Évremond, must have constantly taken part. The disjointed pieces of which Saint Évremond's writings consist are tedious and superficial, but they reveal a mind of much cultivation and considerable common sense. His judgement on Perrault's *Parallel* is that the author "has discovered the defects of the ancients better than he has made out the advantage of the moderns; his book is good and capable of curing us of abundance of errors." He was not a partisan. But his friend, Sir William Temple, excited by the French depreciations of antiquity, rushed into the lists with greater courage than discretion.

Temple was ill equipped for the controversy, though his *Essay on Ancient and Modern Learning* (1690) is far from deserving the disdain of Macaulay, who describes its matter as "ludicrous and contemptible to the last degree."[1] And it must be confessed that the most useful result of the *Essay* was the answer which it provoked from

[1] The only point in it which need be noted here is that the author questioned the cogency of Fontenelle's argument, that the forces of nature being permanent human ability is in all ages the same. "May there not," he asks, "many circumstances concur to one production that do not to any other in one or many ages?" Fontenelle speaks of trees. It is conceivable that various conditions and accidents "may produce an oak, a fig, or a plane-tree, that shall deserve to be renowned in story, and shall not perhaps be paralleled in other countries or times. May not the same have happened in the production, growth, and size of wit and genius in the world, or in some parts or ages of it, and from many more circumstances that contributed towards it than what may concur to the stupendous growth of a tree or animal?"

Wotton. For Wotton had a far wider range of knowledge, and a more judicious mind, than any of the other controversialists, with the exception of Fontenelle ; and in knowledge of antiquity he was Fontenelle's superior. His inquiry stands out as the most sensible and unprejudiced contribution to the whole debate. He accepts as just the reasoning of Fontenelle "as to the comparative force of the geniuses of men in the several ages of the world and of the equal force of men's understandings absolutely considered in all times since learning first began to be cultivated amongst mankind." But this is not incompatible with the thesis that in some branches the ancients excelled all who came after them. For it is not necessary to explain such excellence by the hypothesis that there was a particular force of genius evidently discernible in former ages, but extinct long since, and that nature is now worn out and spent. There is an alternative explanation. There may have been special circumstances "which might suit with those ages which did exceed ours, and with those things wherein they did exceed us, and with no other age nor thing besides."

But we must begin our inquiry by sharply distinguishing two fields of mental activity—the field of art, including poetry, oratory, architecture, painting, and statuary ; and the field of knowledge, including mathematics, natural science, physiology, with all their dependencies. In the case of the first group there is room for variety of opinion ; but the superiority of the Greeks and Romans in poetry and literary style may be admitted without prejudice to the mental equality of the moderns, for it may be explained partly by the genius of their languages and partly by political circumstances—for example, in the case of oratory,[1] by the practical necessity of eloquence. But as regards the other group, knowledge is not a matter of opinion or taste, and a definite judgement is possible. Wotton then proceeds to review systematically the field of science, and easily shows, with more completeness and precision than Perrault, the superiority of modern methods and the enormous strides which had been made.

As to the future, Wotton expresses himself cautiously. It is not easy to say whether knowledge will advance in the next age proportionally to its advancé in this. He has some fears that there may be a falling away, because ancient learning has still too great a hold over modern books, and physical and mathematical studies tend to be neglected. But he ends his *Reflexions* by the speculation that "some future age, though perhaps not the next, and in a country now possibly little thought of, may do that which our great men would be glad to see done ; that is to say, may raise real knowledge, upon foundations laid in this age, to the utmost possible perfection to which it may be brought by mortal men in this imperfect state."

The distinction, on which Wotton insisted, between the sciences which require ages for their development and the imaginative arts which may reach perfection in a short time had been recognised by Fontenelle, whose argument on this point differs from that of his friend Perrault. For Perrault contended that in literature and art, as well as in

---

[1] This had been noted by Fontenelle in his *Digression.*

science, later generations can, through the advantage
of time and longer experience, attain to a higher
excellence than their predecessors. Fontenelle, on
the other hand, held that poetry and eloquence
have a restricted field, and that therefore there
must be a time at which they reach a point of
excellence which cannot be exceeded. It was his
personal opinion that eloquence and history actually
reached the highest possible perfection in Cicero
and Livy.

But neither Fontenelle nor Wotton came into
close quarters with the problem which was raised—
not very clearly, it is true—by Perrault. Is there
development in the various species of literature and
art? Do they profit and enrich themselves by the
general advance of civilisation? Perrault, as we
have seen, threw out the suggestion that increased
experience and psychological study enabled the
moderns to penetrate more deeply into the recesses
of the human soul, and therefore to bring to a
higher perfection the treatment of the character,
motives, and passions of men. This suggestion
admits of being extended. In the Introduction to
his *Revolt of Islam*, Shelley, describing his own
intellectual and aesthetic experiences, writes:

The poetry of ancient Greece and Rome, and
modern Italy, and our own country, has been to me like
external nature, a passion and an enjoyment. . . . I have
considered poetry in its most comprehensive sense; and
have read the poets and the historians and the metaphysicians whose writings have been accessible to me—
and have looked upon the beautiful and majestic scenery
of the earth—as common sources of those elements which
it is the province of the Poet to embody and combine.

And he appends a note :

In this sense there may be such a thing as perfectibility in works of fiction, notwithstanding the concession
often made by the advocates of human improvement,
that perfectibility is a term applicable only to science.

In other words, all the increases of human
experience, from age to age, all the speculative
adventures of the intellect, provide the artist, in
each succeeding generation, with more abundant
sources for aesthetic treatment. As years go on,
life in its widest sense offers more and more
materials "which it is the province of the Poet to
embody and combine." This is evidently true;
and would it not seem to follow that literature is
not excluded from participating in the common
development of civilisation? One of the latest of
the champions of the Moderns, the Abbé Terrasson,
maintained that "to separate the general view of
the progress of the human mind in regard to
natural science, and in regard to *belles-lettres*,
would be a fitting expedient to a man who had
two souls, but it is useless to him who has only
one." He put the matter in too abstract a way to
carry conviction; but the nineteenth century was
to judge that he was not entirely wrong. For the
question was, as we shall see, raised anew by
Madame de Staël, and the theory was finally to
emerge that art and literature, like laws and institutions, are an expression of society and therefore
inextricably linked with the other elements of social
development—a theory, it may be observed, which
while it has discredited the habit of considering
works of art in a vacuum, dateless and detached,

as they were generally considered by critics of the
seventeenth century, leaves the aesthetic problem
much where it was.

Perrault's suggestion as to the enrichment of the
material of the artist by new acquisitions would
have served to bring literature and art into the
general field of human development, without
compromising the distinction on which Wotton
and others insisted between the natural sciences
and the aesthetic arts.   But that distinction, emphatically endorsed by Voltaire, had the effect of
excluding literature and art from the view of those
who in the eighteenth century recognised progress
in the other activities of man.

12

It is notable that in this literary controversy the
Moderns, even Fontenelle, seem curiously negligent
of the import of the theory which they were pro-
pounding of the intellectual progress of man.   They
treat it almost incidentally, as part of the case for the
defence, not as an immensely important conclusion.
Its bearings were more definitely realised by the
Abbé Terrasson, whom I have just named.   A
geometer and a Cartesian, he took part in the controversy in its latest stage, when La Motte and
Madame Dacier were the principal antagonists.
The human mind, he said, has had its infancy and
youth ; its maturity began in the age of Augustus ;
the barbarians arrested its course till the Renaissance ; in the seventeenth century, through the
illuminating philosophy of Descartes, it passed
beyond the stage which it had attained in the
Augustan age, and the eighteenth century should

surpass the seventeenth.   Cartesianism is not final ;
it has its place in a development.   It was made
possible by previous speculations, and it will be
succeeded by other systems.   We must not pursue
the analogy of humanity with an individual man
and anticipate a period of old age.   For unlike the
individual, humanity "being composed of all ages,"
is always gaining instead of losing.   The age of
maturity will last indefinitely, because it is a progressive, not a stationary, maturity.   Later generations will always be superior to the earlier, for
progress is "a natural and necessary effect of the
constitution of the human mind."

CHAPTER VI

THE GENERAL PROGRESS OF MAN:
ABBÉ DE SAINT-PIERRE

THE revolutionary speculations on the social and moral condition of man which were the outstanding feature of the eighteenth century in France, and began about 1750, were the development of the intellectual movement of the seventeenth, which had changed the outlook of speculative thought. It was one continuous rationalistic movement. In the days of Racine and Perrault men had been complacently conscious of the enlightenment of the age in which they were living, and as time went on, this consciousness became stronger and acuter; it is a note of the age of Voltaire. In the last years of Louis XIV., and in the years which followed, the contrast between this mental enlightenment and the dark background—the social evils and miseries of the kingdom, the gross misgovernment and oppression—began to insinuate itself into men's minds. What was the value of the achievements of science, and the improvement of the arts of life, if life itself could not be ameliorated? Was not some radical reconstruction possible in the social fabric, corresponding to the radical reconstruction inaugurated by Descartes in the principles of science and in the methods of thought? Year by year the obscurantism of the ruling powers became more glaring, and the most gifted thinkers, towards the middle of the century, began to concentrate their brains on the problems of social science and to turn the light of reason on the nature of man and the roots of society. They wrought with unscrupulous resolution and with far-reaching effects.

With the extension of rationalism into the social domain, it came about naturally that the idea of intellectual progress was enlarged into the idea of the general Progress of man. The transition was easy. If it could be proved that social evils were due neither to innate and incorrigible disabilities of the human being nor to the nature of things, but simply to ignorance and prejudices, then the improvement of his state, and ultimately the attainment of felicity, would be only a matter of illuminating ignorance and removing errors, of increasing knowledge and diffusing light. The growth of the "universal human reason"—a Cartesian phrase, which had figured in the philosophy of Malebranche—must assure a happy destiny to humanity.

Between 1690 and 1740 the conception of an indefinite progress of enlightenment had been making its way in French intellectual circles, and must often have been a topic of discussion in the *salons*, for instance, of Madame de Lambert, Madame de Tencin, and Madame Dupin, where Fontenelle was one of the most conspicuous guests. To the same circle belonged his friend the Abbé de Saint-Pierre, and it is in his writings that we first find the theory widened in its compass to embrace progress towards social perfection.[1]

---

[1] For his life and works the best book is J. Drouet's monograph, *L'Abbé*

I

He was brought up on Cartesian principles, and he idealised Descartes somewhat as Lucretius idealised Epicurus. But he had no aptitude for philosophy, and he prized physical science only as far as it directly administered to the happiness of men. He was a natural utilitarian, and perhaps no one was ever more consistent in making utility the criterion of all actions and theories. Applying this standard he obliterated from the roll of great men most of those whom common opinion places among the greatest. Alexander, Julius Caesar, Charlemagne receive short shrift from the Abbé de Saint-Pierre.[1] He was superficial in his knowledge both of history and of science, and his conception of utility was narrow and a little vulgar. Great theoretical dis-coverers like Newton and Leibnitz he sets in a lower rank than ingenious persons who used their scientific skill to fashion some small convenience of life. Monuments of art, like *Notre Dame*, possessed little value in his eyes compared with a road, a bridge, or a canal.

Like most of his distinguished contemporaries he was a Deist. On his deathbed he received the usual rites of the Church in the presence of his household, and then told the priest that he did not believe a word of all that. His real views are transparent in some of his works through the conventional dis-guises in which prudent writers of the time were

---

de Saint-Pierre : *l'homme et l'œuvre* (1912), but on some points Goumy's older study (1859) is still worth consulting. I have used the edition of his works in 12 volumes published during his lifetime at Rotterdam, 1733–37.

[1] Compare Voltaire, *Lettres sur les Anglais*, xii., where Newton is acclaimed as the greatest man who ever lived.

wont to wrap their assaults on orthodoxy. To attack Mohammedanism by arguments which are equally applicable to Christianity was a device for propagating rationalism in days when it was dangerous to propagate it openly. This is what the Abbé did in his *Discourse against Mohammedanism*. Again, in his *Physical Explanation of an Apparition* he remarks : "To diminish our fanatical proclivities, it would be useful if the Government were to establish an annual prize, to be awarded by the Academy of Sciences, for the best explanation, by natural laws, of the extraordinary effects of imagination, of the prodigies related in Greek and Latin literature, and of the pretended miracles told by Protestants, Schismatics, and Mohammedans." The author carefully keeps on the right side of the fence. No Catholic authorities could take exception to this. But no intelligent reader could fail to see that all miracles were attacked. The miracles accepted by the Protestants were also believed in by the Catholics.

He was one of the remarkable figures of his age. We might almost say that he was a new type—a nineteenth century humanitarian and pacifist in an eighteenth century environment. He was a born reformer, and he devoted his life to the construction of schemes for increasing human happiness. He introduced the word *bienfaisance* into the currency of the French language, and beneficence was in his eyes the sovran virtue. There were few departments of public affairs in which he did not point out the deficiencies and devise ingenious plans for improvement. Most of his numerous writings are *projets* — schemes of reform in government, economics, finance, education, all worked out in detail, and all aiming at the increase of pleasure and the diminution of pain. The Abbé's nimble intelligence had a weak side, which must have somewhat compromised his influence. He was so confident in the reasonableness of his projects that he always believed that if they were fairly considered the ruling powers could not fail to adopt them in their own interests. It is the nature of a reformer to be sanguine, but the optimism of Saint-Pierre touched *naïveté*. Thousands might have agreed with his view that the celibacy of the Catholic clergy was an unwholesome institution, but when he drew up a proposal for its abolition and imagined that the Pope, unable to resist his arguments, would immediately adopt it, they might be excused for putting him down as a crank who could hardly be taken seriously. The form in which he put forward his memorable scheme for the abolition of war exhibits the same sanguine simplicity. All his plans, Rousseau observed, showed a clear vision of what their effects would be, "but he judged like a child of means to bring them about." But his abilities were great, and his actual influence was considerable. It would have been greater if he had possessed the gift of style.

2

He was not the first to plan a definite scheme for establishing a perpetual peace. Long ago Émeric Cruce had given to the world a proposal for a universal league, including not only the Christian nations of Europe, but the Turks, Persians, and Tartars, which by means of a court of arbitration sitting at Venice should ensure the settlement of all disputes by peaceful means.[1] The consequence of universal peace, he said, will be the arrival of "that beautiful century which the ancient theologians promise after there have rolled by six thousand years. For they say that then the world will live happily and in repose. Now it happens that that time has nearly expired, and even if it is not, it depends only on the Princes to give beforehand this happiness to their peoples." Later in the century, others had ventilated similar projects in obscure publications, but the Abbé does not refer to any of his predecessors.

He was not blinded by the superficial brilliancy of the reign of Louis XIV. to the general misery which the ambitious war-policy of that sovran brought both upon France and upon her enemies. His *Annales politiques* are a useful correction to the *Siècle de Louis Quatorze*. It was in the course of the great struggle of the Spanish Succession that he turned his attention to war and came to the conclusion that it is an unnecessary evil and even an absurdity. In 1712 he attended the congress at Utrecht in the capacity of secretary to Cardinal de Polignac, one of the French delegates. His experiences there confirmed his optimistic mind in the persuasion that perpetual peace was an aim which might readily be realised ; and in the following year he published the memoir which he had been preparing, in two volumes, to which he added a third four years later.

Though he appears not to have known the work of Cruce he did not claim originality. He sheltered

---

[1] *Le Nouveau Cynée* (Paris, 1623). It has recently been reprinted with an English translation by T. W. Balch, Philadelphia (1909).

his proposal under an august name, entitling it
*Project of Henry the Great to render Peace Perpetual,
explained by the Abbé de Saint-Pierre.* The reference is to the "great design" ascribed to Henry
IV. by Sully, and aimed at the abasement of the
power of Austria: a federation of the Christian States
of Europe arranged in groups and under a sovran
Diet, which would regulate international affairs and
arbitrate in all quarrels.[1]   Saint-Pierre, ignoring the
fact that Sully's object was to eliminate a rival
power, made it the text for his own scheme of a
perpetual alliance of all the sovrans of Europe to
guarantee to one another the preservation of their
states and to renounce war as a means of settling
their differences.   He drew up the terms of such
an alliance, and taking the European powers one
by one demonstrated that it was the plain interest
of each to sign the articles.   Once the articles
were signed the golden age would begin.

It is not to our present purpose to comment on
this plan which the author with his characteristic
simplicity seriously pressed upon the attention of
statesmen.   It is easy to criticise it in the light of
subsequent history, and to see that, if the impossible
had happened and the experiment had been tried
and succeeded, it might have caused more suffering
than all the wars from that day to this.   For it was
based on a perpetuation of the political *status quo* in
Europe.   It assumed that the existing political distribution of power was perfectly satisfactory and
conformable to the best interests of all the peoples
concerned.   It would have hindered the Partition of
Poland, but it would have maintained the Austrian

---

[1] It is described in Sully's *Mémoires*, Book XXX.

oppression of Italians. The project also secured to the sovrans the heritage of their authority and guarded against civil wars. This assumed that the various existing constitutions were fundamentally just. The realisation of the scheme would have perpetuated all the evils of autocratic governments. Its author did not perceive that the radical evil in France was irresponsible power. It needed the reign of Louis XV. and the failure of attempts at reform under his successor to bring this home. The Abbé even thought that an increase of the despotic authority of the government was desirable, provided this were accompanied by an increase in the enlightenment and virtue of its ministers.

In 1729 he published an abridgment of his scheme, and here he looks beyond its immediate results to its value for distant posterity. No one, he says, can imagine or foresee the advantages which such an alliance of European states will yield to Europe five hundred years after its establishment. Now we can see the first beginnings, but it is beyond the powers of the human mind to discern its infinite effects in the future. It may produce results more precious than anything hitherto experienced by man. He supports his argument by observing that our primitive ancestors could not foresee the improvements which the course of ages would bring in their rudimentary arrangements for securing social order.

3

It is characteristic that the Abbé de Saint-Pierre's ideas about Progress were a by-product of his particular schemes. In 1773 he published a *Project to Perfect the Government of States*, and here he

sketched his view of the progressive course of civilisation. The old legend of the golden age, when
men were perfectly happy, succeeded by the ages of
silver, bronze, and iron, exactly reverses the truth
of history. The age of iron came first, the infancy
of society, when men were poor and ignorant of the
arts ; it is the present condition of the savages of
Africa and America. The age of bronze ensued, in
which there was more security, better laws, and the
invention of the most necessary arts began. There
followed the age of silver, and Europe has not yet
emerged from it. Our reason has indeed reached
the point of considering how war may be abolished,
and is thus approaching the golden age of the future;
but the art of government and the general regulation
of society, notwithstanding all the improvements of
the past, is still in its infancy. Yet all that is needed
is a short series of wise reigns in our European
states to reach the age of gold or, in other words, a
paradise on earth.

A few wise reigns. The Abbé shared the illusion
of many that government is omnipotent and can
bestow happiness on men. The imperfections of
governments were, he was convinced, chiefly due to
the fact that hitherto the ablest intellects had not
been dedicated to the study of the science of governing. The most essential part of his project was the
formation of a Political Academy which should do
for politics what the Academy of Sciences did for the
study of nature, and should act as an advisory body
to ministers of state on all questions of the public
welfare. If this proposal and some others were
adopted, he believed that the golden age would not
long be delayed.

These observations—hardly more than *obiter dicta*—show that Saint-Pierre's general view of the world was moulded by a conception of civilisation progressing towards a goal of human happiness. In 1737 he published a special work to explain this conception : the *Observations on the Continuous Progress of Universal Reason.*

He recurs to the comparison of the life of collective humanity to that of an individual, and, like Fontenelle and Terrasson, accentuates the point where the analogy fails. We may regard our race as composed of all the nations that have been and will be—and assign to it different ages. For instance, when the race is ten thousand years old a century will be what a single year is in the life of a centenarian. But there is this prodigious difference. The mortal man grows old and loses his reason and happiness through the enfeeblement of his bodily machine ; whereas the human race, by the perpetual and infinite succession of generations, will find itself at the end of ten thousand years more capable of growing in wisdom and happiness than it was at the end of four thousand.

At present the race is apparently not more than seven or eight thousand years old, and is only " in the infancy of human reason," compared with what it will be five or six thousand years hence. And when that stage is reached, it will only have entered on what we may call its first youth, when we consider what it will be when it is a hundred thousand years older still, continually growing in reason and wisdom.

Here we have for the first time, expressed in definite terms, the vista of an immensely long progressive life in front of humanity. Civilisation is only in its infancy. Bacon, like Pascal, had conceived it to be in its old age. Fontenelle and Perrault seem to have regarded it as in its virility ; they set no term to its duration, but they did not dwell on future prospects. The Abbé was the first to fix his eye on the remote destinies of the race and name immense periods of time. It did not occur to him to consider that our destinies are bound up with those of the solar system, and that it is useless to operate with millennial periods of progress unless you are assured of a corresponding stability in the cosmic environment.

As a test of the progress which reason has already made, Saint-Pierre asserts that a comparison of the best English and French works on morals and politics with the best works of Plato and Aristotle proves that the human race has made a sensible advance. But that advance would have been infinitely greater were it not that three general obstacles retarded it and even, at some times and in some countries, caused a retrogression. These obstacles were wars, superstition, and the jealousy of rulers who feared that progress in the science of politics would be dangerous to themselves. In consequence of these impediments it was only in the time of Bodin and Bacon that the human race began to start anew from the point which it had reached in the days of Plato and Aristotle.

Since then the rate of progress has been accelerated, and this has been due to several causes. The expansion of sea commerce has produced more wealth, and wealth means greater leisure, and more writers and readers. In the second place, mathe-

matics and physics are more studied in colleges, and
their tendency is to liberate us from subjection to
the authority of the ancients.   Again, the foundation
of scientific Academies has given facilities both for
communicating and for correcting new discoveries ;
the art of printing provides a means for diffusing
them ; and, finally, the habit of writing in the vulgar
tongue makes them accessible.   The author might
also have referred to the modern efforts to popularise
science, in which his friend Fontenelle had been
one of the leaders.

He proceeds, in this connection, to lay down a
rather doubtful principle, that in any two countries
the difference in enlightenment between the lowest
classes will correspond to the difference between the
most highly educated classes.   At present, he says,
Paris and London are the places where human
wisdom has reached the most advanced stage.   It
is certain that the ten best men of the highest class
at Ispahan or Constantinople will be inferior in their
knowledge of politics and ethics to the ten most
distinguished sages of Paris or London.   And this
will be true in all classes.   The thirty most intelligent children of the age of fourteen at Paris
will be more enlightened than the thirty most intelligent children of the same age at Constantinople,
and the same proportional difference will be true of
the lowest classes of the two cities.

But while the progress of speculative reason has
been rapid, practical reason—the distinction is the
Abbé's—has made little advance.   In point of morals
and general happiness the world is apparently much
the same as ever.   Our mediocre savants know
twenty times as much as Socrates and Confucius,

but our most virtuous men are not more virtuous than they. The growth of science has added much to the arts and conveniences of life, and to the sum of pleasures, and will add more. The progress in physical science is part of the progress of the "universal human reason," whose aim is the augmentation of our happiness. But there are two other sciences which are much more important for the promotion of happiness—Ethics and Politics—and these, neglected by men of genius, have made little way in the course of two thousand years. It is a grave misfortune that Descartes and Newton did not devote themselves to perfecting these sciences, so incomparably more useful for mankind than those in which they made their great discoveries. They fell into a prevailing error as to the comparative values of the various domains of knowledge, an error to which we must also ascribe the fact that while Academies of Sciences and Belles-Lettres exist there are no such institutions for Politics or Ethics.

By these arguments he establishes to his own satisfaction that there are no irremovable obstacles to the Progress of the human race towards happiness, no hindrances that could not be overcome if governments only saw eye to eye with the Abbé de Saint-Pierre. Superstition is already on the decline; there would be no more wars if his simple scheme for permanent peace were adopted. Let the State immediately found Political and Ethical Academies; let the ablest men consecrate their talents to the science of government; and in a hundred years we shall make more progress than we should make in two thousand at the rate we are moving. If these things are done, human reason will have advanced so far in two or three millenniums that the wisest men of that age will be as far superior to the wisest of to-day as these are to the wisest African savages. This "perpetual and unlimited augmentation of reason" will one day produce an increase in human happiness which would astonish us more than our own civilisation would astonish the Kaffirs.

4

The Abbé de Saint-Pierre was indeed terribly at ease in confronting the deepest and most complex problems which challenge the intellect of man. He had no notion of their depth and complexity, and he lightly essayed them, treating human nature, as if it were an abstraction, by a method which he would doubtless have described as Cartesian. He was simply operating with the ideas which were all round him in a society saturated with Cartesianism, —supremacy of human reason, progressive enlightenment, the value of this life for its own sake, and the standard of utility. Given these ideas and the particular bias of his own mind, it required no great ingenuity to advance from the thought of the progress of science to the thought of progress in man's moral nature and his social conditions. The omnipotence of governments to mould the destinies of peoples, the possibility of the creation of enlightened governments, and the indefinite progress of enlightenment—all articles of his belief—were the terms of an argument of the sorites form, which it was a simple matter to develop in his brief treatise.

But we must not do him injustice. He was a much more considerable thinker than posterity for a

long time was willing to believe. It is easy to
ridicule some of his *projets*, and dismiss him as a
crank who was also somewhat of a bore. The
truth, however, is that many of his schemes were
sound and valuable. His economic ideas, which he
thought out for himself, were in advance of his time,
and he has even been described by a recent writer
as " un contemporain égaré au xviii⁰ siècle." Some
of his financial proposals were put into practice by
Turgot. But his significance in the development of
the revolutionary ideas which were to gain control
in the second half of the eighteenth century has
hardly been appreciated yet, and it was imperfectly
appreciated by his contemporaries.

It is easy to see why. His theories are buried in
his multitudinous *projets*. If, instead of working
out the details of endless particular reforms, he had
built up general theories of government and society,
economics and education, they might have had no
more intrinsic value, but he would have been
recognised as the precursor of the Encyclopaedists.

For his principles are theirs. The omnipotence
of government and laws to mould the morals of
peoples; the subordination of all knowledge to the
goddess of utility; the deification of human reason;
and the doctrine of Progress. His crude utilitarianism led him to depreciate the study of mathematical and physical sciences—notwithstanding his
veneration for Descartes—as comparatively useless,
and he despised the fine arts as waste of time and
toil which might be better spent. He had no
knowledge of natural science and he had no artistic
susceptibility. The philosophers of the Encyclopaedia did not go so far, but they tended in this

direction.   They were cold and indifferent towards
speculative science, and they were inclined to set
higher value on artisans than on artists.

In his religious ideas the Abbé differed from
Voltaire and the later social philosophers in one
important respect, but this very difference was a
consequence of his utilitarianism.   Like them he
was a Deist, as we saw ; he had imbibed the spirit
of Bayle and the doctrine of the English rationalists,
which were penetrating French society during the
later part of his life.   His God, however, was more
than the creator and organiser of the Encyclopaedists,
he was also the " Dieu vengeur et rémunérateur "
in whom Voltaire believed.   But here his faith was
larger than Voltaire's.   For while Voltaire referred
the punishments and rewards to this life, the Abbé
believed in the immortality of the soul, in heaven
and hell.   He acknowledged that immortality could
not be demonstrated, that it was only probable, but
he clung to it firmly and even intolerantly.   It is
clear from his writings that his affection for this
doctrine was due to its utility, as an auxiliary to
the magistrate and the tutor, and also to the consideration that Paradise would add to the total of
human happiness.

But though his religion had more articles, he
was as determined a foe of " superstition " as
Voltaire, Diderot, and the rest.   He did not go so
far as they in aggressive rationalism—he belonged
to an older generation—but his principles were the
same.

The Abbé de Saint-Pierre thus represents the
transition from the earlier Cartesianism, which was
occupied with purely intellectual problems, to the

later thought of the eighteenth century, which concentrated itself on social problems. He anticipated the "humanistic" spirit of the Encyclopaedists, who were to make man, in a new sense, the centre of the world. He originated, or at least was the first to proclaim, the new creed of man's destinies, indefinite social progress.

CHAPTER VII

NEW CONCEPTIONS OF HISTORY :
MONTESQUIEU, VOLTAIRE, TURGOT

THE theory of human Progress could not be durably established by abstract arguments, or on the slender foundations laid by the Abbé de Saint-Pierre. It must ultimately be judged by the evidence afforded by history, and it is not accidental that, contemporaneously with the advent of this idea, the study of history underwent a revolution. If Progress was to be more than the sanguine dream of an optimist it must be shown that man's career on earth had not been a chapter of accidents which might lead anywhere or nowhere, but is subject to discoverable laws which have determined its general route, and will secure his arrival at the desirable place. Hitherto a certain order and unity had been found in history by the Christian theory of providential design and final causes. New principles of order and unity were needed to replace the principles which rationalism had discredited. Just as the advance of science depended on the postulate that physical phenomena are subject to invariable laws, so if any conclusions were to be drawn from history some similar postulate as to social phenomena was required.

144

It was thus in harmony with the general movement of thought that about the middle of the
eighteenth century new lines of investigation were
opened leading to sociology, the history of civilisation, and the philosophy of history. Montesquieu's
De l'esprit des lois, which may claim to be the
parent work of modern social science, Voltaire's
Essai sur les mœurs, and Turgot's plan of a
Histoire universelle begin a new era in man's vision
of the past.

I

Montesquieu was not among the apostles of the
idea of Progress. It never secured any hold upon
his mind. But he had grown up in the same
intellectual climate in which that idea was produced; he had been nurtured both on the dissolving
dialectic of Bayle, and on the Cartesian enunciation
of natural law. And his work contributed to the
service, not of the doctrine of the past, but of the
doctrine of the future.

For he attempted to extend the Cartesian
theory to social facts. He laid down that political,
like physical, phenomena are subject to general
laws. He had already conceived this, his most
striking and important idea, when he wrote the
*Considerations on the Greatness and Decadence of
the Romans* (1734), in which he attempted to
apply it:

It is not Fortune who governs the world, as we see
from the history of the Romans. There are general
causes, moral or physical, which operate in every
monarchy, raise it, maintain it, or overthrow it; all that
occurs is subject to these causes; and if a particular

cause, like the accidental result of a battle, has ruined a state, there was a general cause which made the downfall of this state ensue from a single battle. In a word, the principal movement (*l'allure principale*) draws with it all the particular occurrences.

But if this excludes Fortune it also dispenses with Providence, design, and final causes; and one of the effects of the *Considerations* which Montesquieu cannot have overlooked was to discredit Bossuet's treatment of history.

The *Esprit des lois* appeared fourteen years later. Among books which have exercised a considerable influence on thought few are more disappointing to a modern reader. The author had not the gift of what might be called logical architecture, and his work produces the effect of a collection of ideas which he was unable to co-ordinate in the clarity of a system. A new principle, the operation of general causes, is enthroned; but, beyond the obvious distinction of physical and moral, they are not classified. We have no guarantee that the moral causes are fully enumerated, and those which are original are not distinguished from those which are derived. The general cause which Montesquieu impresses most clearly on the reader's mind is that of physical environment—geography and climate.

The influence of climate on civilisation was not a new idea. In modern times, as we have seen, it was noticed by Bodin and recognised by Fontenelle. The Abbé de Saint-Pierre applied it to explain the origin of the Mohammedan religion, and the Abbé Du Bos in his *Reflexions on Poetry and Painting* maintained that climate ·helps to determine the epochs of art and science. Chardin in his *Travels*, a book which Montesquieu studied, had also appreciated its importance. But Montesquieu drew general attention to it, and since he wrote, geographical conditions have been recognised by all inquirers as an influential factor in the development of human societies. His own discussion of the question did not result in any useful conclusions. He did not determine the limits of the action of physical conditions, and a reader hardly knows whether to regard them as fundamental or accessory, as determining the course of civilisation or only perturbing it. "Several things govern men," he says, "climate, religion, laws, precepts of government, historical examples, morals, and manners, whence is formed as their result a general mind (*esprit général*)." This co-ordination of climate with products of social life is characteristic of his unsystematic thought. But the remark which the author went on to make, that there is always a correlation between the laws of a people and its *esprit général*, was important. It pointed to the theory that all the products of social life are closely interrelated.

In Montesquieu's time people were under the illusion that legislation has an almost unlimited power to modify social conditions. We have seen this in the case of Saint-Pierre. Montesquieu's conception of general laws should have been an antidote to this belief. It had however less effect on his contemporaries than we might have expected, and they found more to their purpose in what he said of the influence of laws on manners. There may be something in Comte's suggestion

that he could not give his conception any real
consistency or vigour, just because he was himself
unconsciously under the influence of excessive faith
in the effects of legislative action.

A fundamental defect in Montesquieu's treatment of social phenomena is that he abstracted
them from their relations in time.   It was his merit
to attempt to explain the correlation of laws and
institutions with historical circumstances, but he
did not distinguish or connect stages of civilisation.
He was inclined to confound, as Sorel has observed,
all periods and constitutions.   Whatever be the
value of the idea of Progress, we may agree with
Comte that, if Montesquieu had grasped it, he
would have produced a more striking work.   His
book announces a revolution in the study of
political science, but in many ways belongs itself
to the pre-Montesquieu era.

2

In the same years in which Montesquieu was
busy on the composition of the *Esprit des lois*,
Voltaire was writing his *Age of Louis XIV.* and
his *Essay on the Manners and Mind of Nations, and
on the Principal Facts of History from Charlemagne
to the Death of Louis XIII.*   The former work,
which everybody reads still, appeared in 1751.
Parts of the *Essay*, which has long since fallen into
neglect, were published in the *Mercure de France*
between 1745 and 1751 ; it was issued complete
in 1756, along with the *Age of Louis XIV.*, which
was its continuation.   If we add the *Précis of the
Reign of Louis XV.* (1769), and observe that the

Introduction and first fourteen chapters of the *Essay* sketch the history of the world before Charlemagne, and that China, India, and America are included in the survey, Voltaire's work amounts to a complete survey of the civilisation of the world from the earliest times to his own. If Montesquieu founded social science, Voltaire created the history of civilisation, and the *Essay*, for all its limitations, stands out as one of the considerable books of the century.

In his *Age of Louis XIV.* he announced that his object was "to paint not the actions of a single man, but the mind of men (*l'esprit des hommes*) in the most enlightened age that had ever been," and that "the progress of the arts and sciences" was an essential part of his subject. In the same way he proposed in the *Essay* to trace "l'histoire de l'esprit humain," not the details of facts, and to show by what steps man advanced "from the barbarous rusticity" of the times of Charlemagne and his successors "to the politeness of our own." To do this, he said, was really to write the history of opinion, for all the great successive social and political changes which have transformed the world were due to changes of opinion. Prejudice succeeded prejudice, error followed error; "at last, with time men came to correct their ideas and learn to think."

The *motif* of the book is, briefly, that wars and religions have been the great obstacles to the progress of humanity, and that if they were abolished, with the prejudices which engender them, the world would rapidly improve.

"We may believe," he says, "that reason and

industry will always progress more and more ; that
the useful arts will be improved ; that of the evils
which have afflicted men, prejudices, which are not
their least scourge, will gradually disappear among
all those who govern nations, and that philosophy,
universally diffused, will give some consolation to
human nature for the calamities which it will
experience in all ages."

This indeed is not the tone of the Abbé de
Saint - Pierre.   Voltaire's optimism was always
tempered with cynicism.   But the idea of Progress
is there, though moderately conceived.   And it is
based on the same principle—universal reason
implanted in man, which "subsists in spite of all
the passions which make war on it, in spite of all
the tyrants who would drown it in blood, in spite
of the imposters who would annihilate it by superstition."   And this was certainly his considered
view.   His common sense prevented him from
indulging in Utopian speculations about the future ;
and his cynicism constantly led him to use the
language of a pessimist.   But at an early stage of
his career he had taken up arms for human nature
against that "sublime misanthrope" Pascal, who
"writes against human nature almost as he wrote
against the Jesuits" ; and he returned to the attack at
the end of his life.   Now Pascal's *Pensées* enshrined
a theory of life—the doctrine of original sin, the
idea that the object of life is to prepare for death—
which was sternly opposed to the spirit of Progress.
Voltaire instinctively felt that this was an enemy
that had to be dealt with.   In a lighter vein he
had maintained in a well-known poem, *Le Mondain*,[1]

[1] 1756.

the value of civilisation and all its effects, including luxury, against those who regretted the simplicity of ancient times, the golden age of Saturn.

> O le bon temps que ce siècle de fer !

Life in Paris, London, or Rome to-day is infinitely preferable to life in the garden of Eden.

> D'un bon vin frais ou la mousse ou la sève
> Ne gratta point le triste gosier d'Ève.
> La soie et l'or ne brillaient point chez eux.
> Admirez-vous pour cela nos aïeux ?
> Il leur manquait l'industrie et l'aisance :
> Est-ce vertu ? c'était pure ignorance.

To return to the *Essay*, it flung down the gage of battle to that conception of the history of the world which had been brilliantly represented by Bossuet's *Discours sur l'histoire universelle*. This work was constantly in Voltaire's mind. He pointed out that it had no claim to be universal ; it related only to four or five peoples, and especially the little Jewish nation which " was unknown to the rest of the world or justly despised," but which Bossuet made the centre of interest, as if the final cause of all the great empires of antiquity lay in their relations to the Jews. He had Bossuet in mind when he said "we will speak of the Jews as we would speak of Scythians or Greeks, weighing probabilities and discussing facts." In his new perspective the significance of Hebrew history is for the first time reduced to moderate limits.

But it was not only in this particular, though central, point that Voltaire challenged Bossuet's view. He eliminated final causes altogether, and Providence plays no part on his historical stage. Here his work reinforced the teaching of Montesquieu. Otherwise Montesquieu and Voltaire entirely differed in their methods. Voltaire concerned himself only with the causal enchainment of events and the immediate motives of men. His interpretation of history was confined to the discovery of particular causes; he did not consider the operation of those larger general causes which Montesquieu investigated. Montesquieu sought to show that the vicissitudes of societies were subject to law; Voltaire believed that events were determined by chance where they were not consciously guided by human reason. The element of chance is conspicuous even in legislation: "almost all laws have been instituted to meet passing needs, like remedies applied fortuitously, which have cured one patient and kill others."

On Voltaire's theory, the development of humanity might at any moment have been diverted into a different course; but whatever course it took the nature of human reason would have ensured a progress in civilisation. Yet the reader of the *Essay* and *Louis XIV*. might well have come away with a feeling that the security of Progress is frail and precarious. If fortune has governed events, if the rise and fall of empires, the succession of religions, the revolutions of states, and most of the great crises of history were decided by accidents, is there any cogent ground for believing that human reason, the principle to which Voltaire attributes the advance of civilisation, will prevail in the long run? Civilisation has been organised here and there, now and then, up to a certain point; there have been eras of rapid progress, but how can we be sure that these are not episodes, themselves also fortuitous? For growth has been followed by decay, progress by regress; can it be said that history authorises the conclusion that reason will ever gain such an ascendancy that the play of chance will no longer be able to thwart her will? Is such a conclusion more than a hope, unsanctioned by the data of past experience, merely one of the characteristics of the age of illumination?

Voltaire and Montesquieu thus raised fundamental questions of great moment for the doctrine of Progress, questions which belong to what was soon to be known as the Philosophy of History, a name invented by Voltaire, though hardly meant by him in the sense which it afterwards assumed.

3

Six years before Voltaire's *Essay* was published in its complete form a young man was planning a work on the same subject. Turgot is honourably remembered as an economist and administrator, but if he had ever written the *Discourses on Universal History* which he designed at the age of twenty-three his position in historical literature might have overshadowed his other claims to be remembered. We possess a partial sketch of its plan, which is supplemented by two lectures he delivered at the Sorbonne in 1750; so that we know his general conceptions.

He had assimilated the ideas of the *Esprit des lois*, and it is probable that he had read the parts of Voltaire's work which had appeared in a periodical. His work, like Voltaire's, was to be a challenge to Bossuet's view of history; his purpose was to trace the fortunes of the race in the light of the idea of Progress. He occasionally refers to Providence, but this is no more than a prudent lip-service. Providence has no functions in his scheme. The part which it played in Bossuet is usurped by those general causes which he had learned from Montesquieu. But his systematic mind would have organised and classified the ideas which Montesquieu left somewhat confused. He criticised the inductions drawn in the *Esprit des lois* concerning the influence of climate as hasty and exaggerated ; and he pointed out that the physical causes can only produce their effects by acting on "the hidden principles which contribute to form our mind and character." It follows that the psychical or moral causes are the first element to consider, and it is a fault of method to try to evaluate physical causes till we have exhausted the moral, and are certain that the phenomena cannot be explained by these alone. In other words, the study of the development of societies must be based on psychology ; and for Turgot, as for all his progressive contemporaries, psychology meant the philosophy of Locke.

General necessary causes, therefore, which we should rather call conditions, have determined the course of history—the nature of man, his passions, and his reason, in the first place ; and in the second, his environment,—geography and climate. But its course is a strict sequence of particular causes and effects, "which bind the state of the world (at a given moment) to all those which have preceded it." Turgot does not discuss the question of free-will, but his causal continuity does not exclude "the free action of great men."

He conceives universal history as the progress of the human race advancing as an immense whole steadily, though slowly, through alternating periods of calm and disturbance towards greater perfection. The various units of the entire mass do not move with equal steps, because nature is not impartial with her gifts. Some men have talents denied to others, and the gifts of nature are sometimes developed by circumstances, sometimes left buried in obscurity. The inequalities in the march of nations are due to the infinite variety of circumstances ; and these inequalities may be taken to prove that the world had a beginning, for in an eternal duration they would have disappeared.

But the development of human societies has not been guided by human reason. Men have not consciously made general happiness the end of their actions. They have been conducted by passion and ambition and have never known to what goal they were moving. For if reason had presided, progress would soon have been arrested. To avoid war peoples would have remained in isolation, and the race would have lived divided for ever into a multitude of isolated groups, speaking different tongues. All these groups would have been limited in the range of their ideas, stationary in science, art, and government, and would never have risen above mediocrity. The history of China is an example of the results of restricted intercourse among peoples. Thus the unexpected conclusion emerges, that without unreason and injustice there would have been no progress.

It is hardly necessary to observe that this argument is untenable. The hypothesis assumes that reason is in control among the primitive peoples, and at the same time supposes that its power would completely disappear if they attempted to engage in peaceful intercourse. But though Turgot has put his point in an unconvincing form, his purpose was to show that as a matter of fact "the tumultuous and dangerous passions" have been driving-forces which have moved the world in a desirable direction till the time should come for reason to take the helm.

Thus, while Turgot might have subscribed to Voltaire's assertion that history is largely "un ramas de crimes, de folies, et de malheurs," his view of the significance of man's sufferings is different and almost approaches the facile optimism of Pope— "whatever is, is right." He regards all the race's actual experiences as the indispensable mechanism of Progress, and does not regret its mistakes and calamities. Many changes and revolutions, he observes, may seem to have had most mischievous effects; yet every change has brought some advantage, for it has been a new experience and therefore has been instructive. Man advances by committing errors. The history of science shows (as Fontenelle had pointed out) that truth is reached over the ruins of false hypotheses.

The difficulty presented by periods of decadence and barbarism succeeding epochs of enlightenment is met by the assertion that in such dark times the world has not stood still; there has really been a progression which, though relatively inconspicuous, is not unimportant. In the Middle Ages, which are the prominent case, there were improvements in mechanical arts, in commerce, in some of the habits of civil life, all of which helped to prepare the way for happier times. Here Turgot's view of history is sharply opposed to Voltaire's. He considers Christianity to have been a powerful agent of civilisation, not a hinderer or an enemy. Had he executed his design, his work might well have furnished a notable makeweight to the view held by Voltaire, and afterwards more judicially developed by Gibbon, that "the triumph of barbarism and religion" was a calamity for the world.

Turgot also propounded two laws of development. He observed that when a people is progressing, every step it takes causes an acceleration in the rate of progress. And he anticipated Comte's famous "law" of the three stages of intellectual evolution, though without giving it the extensive and fundamental significance which Comte claimed for it. "Before man understood the causal connection of physical phenomena, nothing was so natural as to suppose they were produced by intelligent beings, invisible and resembling ourselves; for what else would they have resembled?" That is Comte's theological stage. "When philosophers recognised the absurdity of the fables about the gods, but had not yet gained an insight into natural history, they thought to explain the causes of phenomena by abstract expressions such as essences and faculties." That is the metaphysical stage. "It was only at a later period, that by observing the reciprocal mechanical action of bodies hypotheses were formed which could be developed by mathematics and verified by experience." There is the positive stage. The observation assuredly does not possess the far-reaching importance which Comte attached to it; but whatever value it has, Turgot deserves the credit of having been the first to state it.

The notes which Turgot made for his plan permit us to conjecture that his *Universal History* would have been a greater and more profound work than the *Essay* of Voltaire.   It would have embodied in a digested form the ideas of Montesquieu to which Voltaire paid little attention, and the author would have elaborated the intimate connection and mutual interaction among all social phenomena—government and morals, religion, science, and arts.   While his general thesis coincided with that of Voltaire—the gradual advance of humanity towards a state of enlightenment and reasonableness,—he made the idea of Progress more vital; for him it was an organising conception, just as the idea of Providence was for St. Augustine and Bossuet an organising conception, which gave history its unity and meaning. The view that man has throughout been blindly moving in the right direction is the counterpart of what Bossuet represented as a divine plan wrought out by the actions of men who are ignorant of it, and is sharply opposed to the views of Voltaire and the other philosophers of the day who ascribed Progress exclusively to human reason consciously striving against ignorance and passion.

CHAPTER VIII

THE ENCYCLOPAEDISTS AND ECONOMISTS

I

THE intellectual movement which prepared French opinion for the Revolution and supplied the principles for reconstituting society may be described as humanistic in the sense that man was the centre of speculative interest.

"One consideration especially that we ought never to lose from sight," says Diderot, " is that, if we ever banish a man, or the thinking and contemplative being, from above the surface of the earth, this pathetic and sublime spectacle of nature becomes no more than a scene of melancholy and silence . . . It is the presence of man that gives its interest to the existence of other beings. . . . Why should we not make him a common centre ? . . . Man is the single term from which we ought to set out." Hence psychology, morals, the structure of society, were the subjects which riveted attention instead of the larger supra-human problems which had occupied Descartes, Malebranche, and Leibnitz. It mattered little whether the universe was the best that could be constructed ; what mattered was the relation of man's own little world to his will and capacities.

Physical science was important only in so far as it could help social science and minister to the needs of man.   The closest analogy to this development of thought is not offered by the Renaissance, to which the description *humanistic* has been conventionally appropriated, but rather by the age of illumination in Greece in the latter half of the fifth century B.C., represented by Protagoras, Socrates, and others who turned from the ultimate problems of the cosmos, hitherto the main study of philosophers, to man, his nature and his works.

In this revised form of "anthropo-centrism" we see how the general movement of thought has instinctively adapted itself to the astronomical revolution. On the Ptolemaic system it was not incongruous or absurd that man, lord of the central domain in the universe, should regard himself as the most important cosmic creature.   This is the view, implicit in the Christian scheme, which had been constructed on the old erroneous cosmology.   When the true place of the earth was shown and man found himself in a tiny planet attached to one of innumerable solar worlds, his cosmic importance could no longer be maintained.   He was reduced to the condition of an insect creeping on a " tas de boue," which Voltaire so vividly illustrated in *Micromégas*.   But man is resourceful ; ἄπορος ἐπ' οὐδὲν ἔρχεται.   Displaced, along with his home, from the centre of things, he discovers a new means of restoring his self-importance ; he interprets his humiliation as a deliverance. Finding himself in an insignificant island floating in the immensity of space, he decides that he is at last master of his own destinies ; he can fling away the old equipment of final causes, original sin, and the

rest ; he can construct his own chart and, bound by
no cosmic scheme, he need take the universe into
account only in so far as he judges it to be to his
own profit.   Or, if he is a philosopher, he may say
that, after all, the universe for him is built out of his
own sensations, and that by virtue of this relativity
"anthropo-centrism" is restored in a new and more
effective form.

Built out of his own sensations : for the philosophy of Locke was now triumphant in France.
I have used the term Cartesianism to designate, not
the metaphysical doctrines of Descartes (innate
ideas, two substances, and the rest), but the great
principles which survived the passing of his
metaphysical system — the supremacy of reason,
and the immutability of natural laws, not subject
to providential interventions.   These principles still
controlled thought, but the particular views of
Descartes on mental phenomena were superseded
in France by the psychology of Locke, whose
influence was established by Voltaire and Condillac.
The doctrine that all our ideas are derived from the
senses lay at the root of the whole theory of man
and society, in the light of which the revolutionary
thinkers, Diderot, Helvétius, and their fellows, criticised the existing order and exposed the reigning
prejudices.   This sensationalism (which went beyond
what Locke himself had really meant) involved the
strict relativity of knowledge and led at once to the
old pragmatic doctrine of Protagoras, that man is
the measure of all things.   And the spirit of the
French philosophers of the eighteenth century was
distinctly pragmatic.   The advantage of man was
their principle, and the value of speculation was

judged by its definite service to humanity. " The value and rights of truth are founded on its utility," which is " the unique measure of man's judgements," one thinker asserts ; another declares that "the useful circumscribes everything," *l'utile circonscrit tout* ; another lays down that " to be virtuous is to be useful ; to be vicious is to be useless or harmful ; that is the sum of morality." Helvétius, anticipating Bentham, works out the theory that utility is the only possible basis of ethics. Bacon, the utilitarian, was extolled like Locke. As, a hundred years before, his influence had inspired the foundation of the Royal Society, so now his name was invoked by the founders of the Encyclopaedia.

Beneath all philosophical speculation there is an undercurrent of emotion, and in the French philosophers of the eighteenth century this emotional force was strong and even violent. They aimed at practical results. Their work was a calculated campaign to transform the principles and the spirit of governments and to destroy sacerdotalism. The problem for the human race being to reach a state of felicity by its own powers, these thinkers believed that it was soluble by the gradual triumph of reason over prejudice and knowledge over ignorance. Violent revolution was far from their thoughts ; by the diffusion of knowledge they hoped to create a public opinion which would compel governments to change the tenor of their laws and administration and make the happiness of the people their guiding principle. The optimistic confidence that man is *perfectible*, which means capable of indefinite improvement, inspired the movement as a whole, however greatly particular thinkers might differ in their views.

Belief in Progress was their sustaining faith, although, occupied by the immediate problems of amelioration, they left it rather vague and ill-defined. The word itself is seldom pronounced in their writings. The idea is treated as subordinate to the other ideas in the midst of which it had grown up : Reason, Nature, Humanity, Illumination (*lumières*). It has not yet entered upon an independent life of its own and received a distinct label, though it is already a vital force.

In reviewing the influences which were forming a new public opinion during the forty years before the Revolution, it is convenient for the present purpose to group together the thinkers (including Voltaire) associated with the Encyclopaedia, who represented a critical and consciously aggressive force against traditional theories and existing institutions. The constructive thinker Rousseau was not less aggressive, but he stands apart and opposed, by his hostility to modern civilisation. Thirdly, we must distinguish the school of Economists, also reformers and optimists, but of more conservative temper than the typical Encyclopaedists.

2

The *Encyclopaedia* (1751–1765) has rightly been pronounced the central work of the rationalistic movement which made the France of 1789 so different from the France of 1715. It was the organised section of a vast propaganda, speculative and practical, carried on by men of the most various views, most of whom were associated directly with it. As has well been observed, it did for the rationalism of the eighteenth century in

France much what the *Fortnightly Review*, under
the editorship of Mr. Morley (from 1868 to 1882)
did for that of the nineteenth in England, as an
organ for the penetrating criticism of traditional
beliefs.   If Diderot, who directed the Encyclopaedia
with the assistance of d'Alembert the mathematician,
had lived a hundred years later he would probably
have edited a journal.

We saw that the "solidarity" of the sciences was
one of the conceptions associated with the theory
of intellectual progress, and that the popularisation
of knowledge was another.   Both these conceptions
inspired the Encyclopaedia, which was to gather up
and concentrate the illumination of the modern age.
It was to establish the lines of communication among
all departments, "to enclose in the unity of a
system the infinitely various branches of knowledge."
And it was to be a library of popular instruction.
But it was also intended to be an organ of propaganda.   In the history of the intellectual revolution
it is in some ways the successor of the Dictionary
of Bayle, which, two generations before, collected
the material of war to demolish traditional doctrines.
The Encyclopaedia carried on the campaign against
authority and superstition by indirect methods, but
it was the work of men who were not sceptics like
Bayle, but had ideals, positive purposes, and social
hopes.   They were not only confident in reason
and in science, but most of them had also a more
or less definite belief in the possibility of an advance
of humanity towards perfection.

As one of their own band afterwards remarked,
they were less occupied in enlarging the bounds of
knowledge than in spreading the light and making

war on prejudice.[1] The views of the individual contributors differed greatly, and they cannot be called a school, but they agreed so far in common tendencies that they were able to form a co-operative alliance.

The propaganda of which the Encyclopaedia was the centre was reinforced by the independent publications of some of the leading men who collaborated or were closely connected with their circle, notably those of Diderot himself, Baron d'Holbach, and Helvétius.

3

The optimism of the Encyclopaedists was really based on an intense consciousness of the enlightenment of their own age. The progressiveness of knowledge was taken as axiomatic, but was there any guarantee that the light, now confined to small circles, could ever enlighten the world and regenerate mankind? They found the guarantee they required, not in an induction from the past experience of the race, but in an *a priori* theory: the indefinite malleability of human nature by education and institutions. This had been, as we saw, assumed by the Abbé de Saint-Pierre. It pervaded the speculation of the age, and was formally deduced from the sensational psychology of Locke and Condillac. It was developed, in an extreme form, in the work of Helvétius, *De l'esprit* (1758).

In this book, which was to exert a large influence in England, Helvétius sought, among other things, to show that the science of morals is equivalent to

---

[1] Condorcet, *Esquisse*, p. 206 (ed. 1822).

the science of legislation, and that in a well-organised
society all men are capable of rising to the highest
point of mental development. Intellectual and
moral inequalities between man and man arise
entirely from differences in education and social
circumstances. Genius itself is not a gift of
nature ; the man of genius is a product of circumstances—social, not physical, for Helvétius rejects
the influence of climate. It follows that if you
change education and social institutions you can
change the character of men.

The error of Helvétius in ignoring the irremovable physical differences between individuals,
the varieties of cerebral organisation, was at once
pointed out by Diderot. This error, however, was
not essential to the general theory of the immeasurable power of social institutions over human character,
and other thinkers did not fall into it. All alike,
indeed, were blind to the factor of heredity. But
the theory in its collective application contains a
truth which nineteenth century critics, biassed by
their studies in heredity, have been prone to over-
look. The social inheritance of ideas and emotions
to which the individual is submitted from infancy
is more important than the tendencies physically
transmitted from parent to child. The power of
education and government in moulding the members
of a society has recently been illustrated on a large
scale in the psychological transformation of the
German people in the life of a generation.

It followed from the theory expounded by
Helvétius that there is no impassable barrier
between the advanced and the stationary or retrograde races of the earth. "True morality," Baron

d'Holbach wrote, "should be the same for all the inhabitants of the globe. The savage man and the civilised; the white man, the red man, the black man; Indian and European, Chinaman and Frenchman, Negro and Lapp have the same nature. The differences between them are only modifications of the common nature produced by climate, government, education, opinions, and the various causes which operate on them. Men differ only in the ideas they form of happiness and the means which they have imagined to obtain it." Here again the eighteenth century theorists held a view which can no longer be dismissed as absurd. Some are coming round to the opinion that enormous differences in capacity which seem fundamental are a result of the differences in social inheritance, and that these again are due to a long sequence of historical circumstances; and consequently that there is no people in the world doomed by nature to perpetual inferiority or irrevocably disqualified by race from playing a useful part in the future of civilisation.

4

This doctrine of the possibility of indefinitely moulding the characters of men by laws and institutions—whether combined or not with a belief in the natural equality of men's faculties—laid a foundation on which the theory of the perfectibility of humanity could be raised. It marked, therefore, an important stage in the development of the doctrine of Progress.

It gave, moreover, a new and larger content to that doctrine by its applicability, not only to the peoples which are at present in the van of civilisation, but also to those which have lagged far behind and may appear irreclaimably barbarous — thus potentially including all humanity in the prospect of the future. Turgot had already conceived "the total mass of the human race moving always slowly forward"; he had declared that the human mind everywhere contains the germs of progress and that the inequality of peoples is due to the infinite variety of their circumstances. This enlarging conception was calculated to add strength to the idea of Progress, by raising it to a synthesis comprehending not merely the western civilised nations but the whole human world.

Interest in the remote peoples of the earth, in the unfamiliar civilisations of the East, in the untutored races of America and Africa, was vivid in France in the eighteenth century. Everyone knows how Voltaire and Montesquieu used Hurons or Persians to hold up the glass to Western manners and morals, as Tacitus used the Germans to criticise the society of Rome. But very few ever look into the seven volumes of the Abbé Raynal's *History of the Two Indies* which appeared in 1772. It is, however, one of the remarkable books of the century. Its immediate practical importance lay in the array of facts which it furnished to the friends of humanity in the movement against negro slavery. But it was also an effective attack on the Church and the sacerdotal system. The author's method was the same which his greater contemporary Gibbon employed on a larger scale. A history of facts was a more formidable indictment than any declamatory attack.

Raynal brought home to the conscience of Europeans the miseries which had befallen the natives of the New World through the Christian conquerors and their priests. He was not indeed an enthusiastic preacher of Progress. He is unable to decide between the comparative advantages of the savage state of nature and the most highly cultivated society. But he observes that "the human race is what we wish to make it," that the felicity of man depends entirely on the improvement of legislation; and in the survey of the history of Europe to which the last Book of his work is devoted, his view is generally optimistic.

5

Baron d'Holbach had a more powerful brain than Helvétius, but his writings had probably less influence, though he was the spiritual father of two prominent Revolutionaries, Hébert and Chaumette. His *System of Nature* (1770) develops a purely naturalistic theory of the universe, in which the prevalent Deism is rejected: there is no God; material Nature stands out alone, self-sufficing, *dominis privata superbis*. The book suggests how the Lucretian theory of development might have led to the idea of Progress. But it sent a chilly shock to the hearts of many and probably convinced few. The effective part was the outspoken and passionate indictment of governments and religions as causes of most of the miseries of mankind.

It is in other works, especially in his *Social System*, that his views of Progress are to be sought. Man is simply a part of nature; he has no privileged position, and he is born neither good nor bad.

Erras, as Seneca said, *si existumas vitia nobiscum esse: supervenerunt, ingesta sunt.*[1] We are made good or bad by education, public opinion, laws, government; and here the author points to the significance of the instinct of imitation as a social force, which a modern writer, M. Tarde, has worked into a system.

The evils, which are due to the errors of tyranny and superstition, the force of truth will gradually diminish if it cannot completely banish them; for our governments and laws may be perfected by the progress of useful knowledge. But the process will be a long one: centuries of continuous mental effort in unravelling the causes of social ill-being and repeated experiments to determine the remedies (*des expériences réitérées de la société*). In any case we cannot look forward to the attainment of an unchangeable or unqualified felicity. That is a mere chimera "incompatible with the nature of a being whose feeble machine is subject to derangement and whose ardent imagination will not always submit to the guidance of reason. Sometimes to enjoy, sometimes to suffer, is the lot of man; to enjoy more often than to suffer is what constitutes well-being."

D'Holbach was a strict determinist; he left no room for freewill in the rigorous succession of cause and effect, and the pages in which he drives home the theory of causal necessity are still worth reading. From his naturalistic principles he inferred that the distinction between nature and art is not fundamental; civilisation is as rational as the savage state. Here he was at one with Aristotle.

[1] Seneca, *Ep.* 124.

All the successive inventions of the human mind to change or perfect man's mode of existence and render it happier were only the necessary consequence of his essence and that of the existences which act upon him. All we do or think, all we are or shall be, is only an effect of what universal nature has made us. Art is only nature acting by the aid of the instruments which she has fashioned.

Progress, therefore, is natural and necessary, and to criticise or condemn it by appealing to nature is only to divide the house of nature against itself.

If d'Holbach had pressed his logic further, he would have taken a more indulgent and calmer view of the past history of mankind. He would have acknowledged that institutions and opinions to which modern reason may give short shrift were natural and useful in their day, and would have recognised that at any stage of history the heritage of the past is no less necessary to progress than the solvent power of new ideas. Most thinkers of his time were inclined to judge the past career of humanity anachronistically. All the things that had been done or thought which could not be justified in the new age of enlightenment, were regarded as gratuitous and inexcusable errors. The traditions, superstitions, and customs, the whole "code of fraud and woe" transmitted from the past, weighed then too heavily in France to allow the school of reform to do impartial justice to their origins. They felt a sort of resentment against history. D'Alembert said that it would be well if history could be destroyed; and the general tendency was to ignore the social memory and the common heritage of past experiences which mould a human society and make it something very different from a mere collection of individuals.

Belief in Progress, however, took no extravagant form. It did not beguile d'Holbach or any other of the leading thinkers of the Encyclopaedia epoch into optimistic dreams of the future which might await mankind. They had a much clearer conception of obstacles than the good Abbé de Saint-Pierre. Helvétius agrees with d'Holbach that progress will be slow, and Diderot is wavering and sceptical on the question of indefinite social improvement.

6

The reformers of the Encyclopaedia group were not alone in disseminating the idea of Progress. Another group of thinkers, who widely differed in their principles, though some of them had contributed articles to the Encyclopaedia,[1] also did much to make it a power. The rise of the special study of Economics was one of the most significant facts in the general trend of thought towards the analysis of civilisation. Economical students found that in seeking to discover a true theory of the production, distribution, and employment of wealth, they could not avoid the consideration of the constitution and purpose of society. The problems of production and distribution could not be divorced from political theory : production raises the question of the functions of government and the limits of its intervention in trade and industry ; distribution involves questions of property, justice, and equality. The employment of riches leads into the domain of morals.

The French Economists or " Physiocrats," as

---

[1] Quesnay and Turgot, who, though not professedly a Physiocrat, held the same views as the sect.

they were afterwards called, who formed a definite
school before 1760—Quesnay the master, Mirabeau,
Mercier de la Rivière, and the rest—envisaged their
special subject from a wide philosophical point of
view ; their general economic theory was equivalent
to a theory of human society.   They laid down
the doctrine of a Natural Order in political communities, and from it they deduced their economic
teaching.

They assumed, like the Encyclopaedists, that the
end of society is the attainment of terrestrial happiness by its members, and that this is the sole purpose
of government.   The object of a treatise by Mercier
de la Rivière [1] (a convenient exposition of the views
of the sect) is, in his own words, to discover the
natural order for the government of men living in
organised communities, which will assure to them
temporal felicity : an order in which everything is
well, necessarily well, and in which the interests of
all are so perfectly and intimately consolidated that
all are happy, from the ruler to the least of his
subjects.

But in what does this happiness consist ?   His
answer is that "humanly speaking, the greatest
happiness possible for us consists in the greatest
possible abundance of objects suitable to our enjoyment and in the greatest liberty to profit by them."
And liberty is necessary not only to enjoy them but
also to produce them in the greatest abundance,
since liberty stimulates human efforts.   Another
condition of abundance is the multiplication of the
race ; in fact, the happiness of men and their numbers
are closely bound up together in the system of

[1] *L'ordre naturel et essentiel des sociétés politiques*, 1767.

nature. From these axioms may be deduced the Natural Order of a human society, the reciprocal duties and rights whose enforcement is required for the greatest possible multiplication of products, in order to procure to the race the greatest sum of happiness with the maximum population.

Now, individual property is the indispensable condition for full enjoyment of the products of human labour; "property is the measure of liberty, and liberty is the measure of property." Hence, to realise general happiness it is only necessary to maintain property and consequently liberty in all their natural extent. The fatal error which has made history what it is has been the failure to recognise this simple fact; for aggression and conquest, the causes of human miseries, violate the law of property which is the foundation of happiness.

The practical inference was that the chief function of government was to protect property and that complete freedom should be left to private enterprise to exploit the resources of the earth. All would be well if trade and industry were allowed to follow their natural tendencies. This is what was meant by *Physiocracy*, the supremacy of the Natural Order. If rulers observed the limits of their true functions, Mercier thought that the moral effect would be immense. "The public system of government is the true education of moral man. *Regis ad exemplum totus componitur orbis.*" [1]

While they advocated a thorough reform of the

---

[1] The particulars of the Physiocratic doctrine as to the relative values of agriculture and commerce which Adam Smith was soon to criticise do not concern us; nor is it necessary to repeat the obvious criticisms on a theory which virtually reduced the science of society to a science of production and distribution.

principles which ruled the fiscal policy of governments, the Economists were not idealists, like the Encyclopaedic philosophers ; they sowed no seeds of revolution. Their starting-point was that which is, not that which ought to be. And, apart from their narrower point of view, they differed from the philosophers in two very important points. They did not believe that society was of human institution, and therefore they did not believe that there could be any deductive science of society based simply on man's nature. Moreover, they held that inequality of condition was one of its immutable features, immutable because it is a consequence of the inequality of physical powers.

But they believed in the future progress of society towards a state of happiness through the increase of opulence which would itself depend on the growth of justice and "liberty"; and they insisted on the importance of the increase and diffusion of knowledge. Their influence in promoting a belief in Progress is vouched for by Condorcet, the friend and biographer of Turgot. As Turgot stands apart from the Physiocrats (with whom indeed he did not identify himself) by his wider views on civilisation, it might be suspected that it is of him that Condorcet was chiefly thinking. Yet we need not limit the scope of his statement when we remember that as a sect the Economists assumed as their first principle the eudaemonic value of civilisation, declared that temporal happiness is attainable, and threw all their weight into the scales against the doctrine of Regress which had found a powerful advocate in Rousseau.

7

By liberty the Economists meant economic liberty. Neither they nor the philosophers nor Rousseau, the father of modern democracy, had any just conception of what political liberty means. They contributed much to its realisation, but their own ideas of it were narrow and imperfect. They never challenged the principle of a despotic government, they only contended that the despotism must be enlightened. The paternal rule of a Joseph or a Catherine, acting under the advice of philosophers, seemed to them the ideal solution of the problem of government; and when the progressive and disinterested Turgot, whom they might regard as one of themselves, was appointed financial minister on the accession of Louis XVI., it seemed that their ideal was about to be realised. His speedy fall dispelled their hopes, but did not teach them the secret of liberty. They had no quarrel with the principle of the censorship, though they writhed under its tyranny; they did not want to abolish it. They only complained that it was used against reason and light, that is against their own writings; and, if the Conseil d'État or the Parlement had suppressed the works of their obscurantist opponents, they would have congratulated themselves that the world was marching quickly towards perfection.

CHAPTER IX

I

THE optimistic theory of civilisation was not unchallenged by rationalists. In the same year (1750) in which Turgot traced an outline of historical Progress at the Sorbonne, Rousseau laid before the Academy of Dijon a theory of historical Regress. This Academy had offered a prize for the best essay on the question whether the revival of sciences and arts had contributed to the improvement of morals. The prize was awarded to Rousseau. Five years later the same learned body proposed another subject for investigation, the origin of Inequality among men. Rousseau again competed but failed to win the prize, though this second essay was a far more remarkable performance.

The view common to these two discourses, that social development has been a gigantic mistake, that the farther man has travelled from a primitive simple state the more unhappy has his lot become, that civilisation is radically vicious, was not original. Essentially the same issue had been raised in England, though in a different form, by Mandeville's

Fable of the Bees, the scandalous book which aimed at proving that it is not the virtues and amiable qualities of man that are the cement of civilised society, but the vices of its members which are the support of all trades and employments.[1]   In these vices, he said, "we must look for the true origin of all arts and sciences"; "the moment evil ceases, the society must be spoiled, if not totally dissolved."

The significance of Mandeville's book lay in the challenge it flung to the optimistic doctrines of Lord Shaftesbury, that human nature is good and all is for the best in this harmonious world. "The ideas he had formed," wrote Mandeville, "of the goodness and excellency of our nature were as romantic and chimerical as they are beautiful and amiable; he laboured hard to unite two contraries that can never be reconciled together, innocence of manners and worldly greatness."

Of these two views Rousseau accepted one and rejected the other. He agreed with Shaftesbury as to the natural goodness of man; he agreed with Mandeville that innocence of manners is incompatible with the conditions of a civilised society. He was an optimist in regard to human nature, a pessimist in regard to civilisation.

In his first *Discourse* he begins by appreciating the specious splendour of modern enlightenment, the voyages of man's intellect among the stars, and then goes on to assever that in the first place men have lost, through their civilisation, the original liberty for which they were born, and that arts and science, flinging garlands of flowers on the iron chains which bind them, make them love their

[1] The expanded edition was published in 1723.

slavery ; and secondly that there is a real depravity beneath the fair semblance and "our souls are corrupted as our sciences and arts advance to perfection." Nor is this only a modern phenomenon ; "the evils due to our vain curiosity are as old as the world." For it is a law of history that morals fall and rise in correspondence with the progress and decline of the arts and sciences as regularly as the tides answer to the phases of the moon. This "law" is exemplified by the fortunes of Greece, Rome, and China, to whose civilisations the author opposes the comparative happiness of the ignorant Persians, Scythians, and ancient Germans. "Luxury, dissoluteness, and slavery have been always the chastisement of the ambitious efforts we have made to emerge from the happy ignorance in which the Eternal Wisdom had placed us." There is the theological doctrine of the tree of Eden in a new shape.

Rousseau's attempt to show that the cultivation of science produces specific moral evils is feeble, and has little ingenuity ; it is a declamation rather than an argument ; and in the end he makes concessions which undo the effect of his impeachment. The essay did not establish even a plausible case, but it was paradoxical and suggestive, and attracted more attention than Turgot's thoughtful discourse in the Sorbonne. D'Alembert deemed it worthy of a courteous expression of dissent,[1] and Voltaire satirised it in his *Timon*.

2

In the *Discourse* on Inequality Rousseau dealt

[1] In the *Disc. Prél.* to the Encyclopaedia.

more directly with the effect of civilisation on happiness. He proposed to explain how it came about that right overcame the primitive reign of might, that the strong were induced to serve the weak, and the people to purchase a fancied tranquillity at the price of a real felicity. So he stated his problem ; and to solve it he had to consider the " state of nature " which Hobbes had conceived as a state of war and Locke as a state of peace. Rousseau imagines our first savage ancestors living in isolation, wandering in the forests, occasionally co-operating, and differing from the animals only by the possession of a faculty for improving themselves (*la faculté de se perfectionner*). After a stage in which families lived alone in a more or less settled condition, came the formation of groups of families, living together in a definite territory, united by a common mode of life and sustenance, and by the common influence of climate, but without laws or government or any social organisation.

It is this state, which was reached only after a long period, not the original state of nature, that Rousseau considers to have been the happiest period of the human race.

This period of the development of human faculties, holding a just mean between the indolence of the primitive state and the petulant activity of our self-love, must be the happiest and most durable epoch. The more we reflect on it, the more we find that this state was the least exposed to revolutions and the best for man ; and that he can have left it only through some fatal chance which, for the common advantage, should never have occurred. The example of the savages who have almost all been found in this state seems to bear out the conclusion that humanity was made to remain in it for ever,

that it was the true youth of the world, and that all further
progresses have been so many steps, apparently towards
the perfection of the individual, and really towards the
decrepitude of the species.

He ascribes to metallurgy and agriculture the
fatal resolution which brought this Arcadian existence to an end.   Agriculture entailed the origin of
property in land.   Moral and social inequality were
introduced by the man who first enclosed a piece of
land and said, This is mine, and found people simple
enough to believe him.   He was the founder of civil
society.

The general argument amounts to this : Man's
faculty of improving himself is the source of his
other faculties, including his sociability, and has been
fatal to his happiness.   The circumstances of his
primeval life favoured the growth of this faculty,
and in making man sociable they made him wicked ;
they developed the reason of the individual and
thereby caused the species to deteriorate.   If the
process had stopped at a certain point, all would
have been well ; but man's capacities, stimulated by
fortuitous circumstances, urged him onward, and
leaving behind him the peaceful Arcadia where he
should have remained safe and content, he set out
on the fatal road which led to the calamities of
civilisation.   We need not follow Rousseau in his
description of those calamities which he attributes
to wealth and the artificial conditions of society.
His indictment was too general and rhetorical to
make much impression.   In truth, a more powerful
and comprehensive case against civilised society
was drawn up about the same time, though with a
very different motive, by one whose thought repre-

sented all that was opposed to Rousseau's teaching. Burke's early work, *A Vindication of Natural Society*,[1] was written to show that all the objections which Deists like Bolingbroke urged against artificial religion could be brought with greater force against artificial society, and he worked out in detail a historical picture of the evils of civilisation which is far more telling than Rousseau's generalities.

3

If civilisation has been the curse of man, it might seem that the logical course for Rousseau to recommend was its destruction. This was the inference which Voltaire drew in *Timon*, to laugh the whole theory out of court. But Rousseau did not suggest a movement to destroy all the libraries and all the works of art in the world, to put to death or silence all the savants, to pull down the cities, and burn the ships. He was not a mere dreamer, and his Arcadia was no more than a Utopian ideal, by the light of which he conceived that the society of his own day might be corrected and transformed. He attached his hopes to equality, democracy, and a radical change in education.

Equality : this revolutionary idea was of course quite compatible with the theory of Progress, and was soon to be closely associated with it. But it is easy to understand that the two ideas should first have appeared in antagonism to each other. The advance of knowledge and the increase of man's power over nature had virtually profited only a minority. When Fontenelle or Voltaire vaunted the illumination of their age and glorified the modern

[1] A.D. 1756.

revolution in scientific thought, they took account
only of a small class of privileged people.   Higher
education, Voltaire observed, is not for cobblers or
kitchenmaids ; " on n'a jamais prétendu éclairer les
cordonniers et les servantes."   The theory of Progress had so far left the masses out of account.
Rousseau contrasted the splendour of the French
court, the luxury of the opulent, the enlightenment
of those who had the opportunity of education, with
the hard lot of the ignorant mass of peasants, whose
toil paid for the luxury of many of the idle enlightened people who amused themselves at Paris.
The horror of this contrast, which left Voltaire cold,
was the poignant motive which inspired Rousseau,
a man of the people, in constructing his new doctrine.
The existing inequality seemed an injustice which
rendered the self-complacency of the age revolting.
If this is the result of progressive civilisation, what
is progress worth?   The next step is to declare that
civilisation is the *causa malorum* and that what is
named progress is really regress.   But Rousseau
found a way of circumventing pessimism.   He asked
himself, cannot equality be realised in an organised
state, founded on natural right?   The *Social Contract* was his answer, and there we can see the living
idea of equality detaching itself from the dead theory
of degradation.

Arcadianism, which was thus only a side-issue
for Rousseau, was the extreme expression of tendencies which appear in the speculations of other
thinkers of the day.   Morelly and Mably argued in
favour of a reversion to simpler forms of life.   They
contemplated the foundation of socialistic communities by reviving institutions and practices which

belonged to a past period of social evolution. Mably, inspired by Plato, thought it possible by legislation to construct a state of antique pattern. They ascribed evils of civilisation to inequality arising from the existence of private property, but Morelly rejected the view of the "bold sophist" Rousseau that science and art were to blame. He thought that aided by science and learning man might reach a state based on communism, resembling the state of nature but more perfect, and he planned an ideal constitution in his romance of the *Floating Islands*.[1] Different as these views were, they represent the idea of regress; they imply a condemnation of the tendencies of actual social development and recommend a return to simpler and more primitive conditions.

Even Diderot, though he had little sympathy with Utopian speculations, was attracted by the idea of the simplification of society, and met Rousseau so far as to declare that the happiest state was a mean between savage and civilised life.

"I am convinced," he wrote, "that the industry of man has gone too far and that if it had stopped long ago and if it were possible to simplify the results, we should not be the worse. I believe there is a limit in civilisation, a limit more conformable to the felicity of man in general and far less distant from the savage state than is imagined; but how to return to it, having left it, or how to remain in it, if we were there? I know not."

His picture of the savages of Tahiti in the *Supplément au voyage de Bougainville* was not seriously

---

[1] *Naufrage des isles flottantes ou Basiliade du célèbre Pilpai* (1753). It begins: "je chante le règne aimable de la Vérité et de la Nature." Morelly's other work, *Code de la Nature*, appeared in 1755.

meant, but it illustrates the fact that in certain moods
he felt the fascination of Rousseau's Arcadia.

D'Holbach met all these theories by pointing out
that human development, from the "state of nature"
to social life and the ideas and commodities of
civilisation, is itself natural, given the innate tendency
of man to improve his lot. To return to the simpler
life of the forests—or to any bygone stage—would
be *dénaturer l'homme*, it would be contrary to nature;
and if he could do so, it would only be to re-
commence the career begun by his ancestors and
pass again through the same successive phases of
history.

There was, indeed, one question which caused
some embarrassment to believers in Progress. The
increase of wealth and luxury was evidently a salient
feature in modern progressive states; and it was
clear that there was an intimate connection between
the growth of knowledge and the growth of commerce and industrial arts, and that the natural
progress of these meant an ever-increasing accumulation of riches and the practice of more refined
luxury. The question, therefore, whether luxury is
injurious to the general happiness occupied the
attention of the philosophers. If it is injurious,
does it not follow that the forces on which admittedly
Progress depends are leading in an undesirable
direction? Should they be obstructed, or is it wiser
to let things follow their natural tendency (*laisser
aller les choses suivant leur pente naturelle*)?
Voltaire accepted wealth with all its consequences.
D'Holbach proved to his satisfaction that luxury
always led to the ruin of nations. Diderot and
Helvétius arrayed the arguments which could be

urged on both sides. Perhaps the most reasonable contribution to the subject was an essay of Hume.

4

It is obvious that Rousseau and all other theorists of Regress would be definitely refuted if it could be proved by an historical investigation that in no period in the past had man's lot been happier than in the present. Such an inquiry was undertaken by the Chevalier de Chastellux. His book *On Public Felicity, or Considerations on the lot of Men in the various Epochs of History*, appeared in 1772 and had a wide circulation.[1] It is a survey of the history of the western world and aims at proving the certainty of future Progress. It betrays the influence both of the Encyclopaedists and of the Economists. Chastellux is convinced that human nature can be indefinitely moulded by institutions; that enlightenment is a necessary condition of general happiness; that war and superstition, for which governments and priests are responsible, are the principal obstacles.

But he attempted to do what none of his masters had done, to test the question methodically from the data of history. Turgot, and Voltaire in his way, had traced the growth of civilisation; the originality of Chastellux lay in concentrating atten-tion on the eudaemonic issue, in examining each historical period for the purpose of discovering whether people on the whole were happy and enviable. Has there ever been a time, he inquired, in which public felicity was greater than in our own, in which it would have been desirable to remain for

---

[1] There was a new edition in 1776 with an important additional chapter.

ever, and to which it would now be desirable to return?

He begins by brushing away the hypothesis of an Arcadia. We know really nothing about primitive man, there is not sufficient evidence to authorise conjectures. We know man only as he has existed in organised societies, and if we are to condemn modern civilisation and its prospects, we must find our term of comparison not in an imaginary golden age but in a known historical epoch. And we must be careful not to fall into the mistakes of confusing public prosperity with general happiness, and of considering only the duration or aggrandisement of empires and ignoring the lot of the common people.

His survey of history is summary and superficial enough. He gives reasons for believing that no peoples from the ancient Egyptians and Assyrians to the Europeans of the Renaissance can be judged happy. Yet what about the Greeks? Theirs was an age of enlightenment. In a few pages he examines their laws and history, and concludes, "We are compelled to acknowledge that what is called the *bel âge* of Greece was a time of pain and torture for humanity." And in ancient history, generally, "slavery alone sufficed to make man's condition a hundred times worse than it is at present." The miseries of life in the Roman period are even more apparent than in the Greek. What Englishman or Frenchman would tolerate life as lived in ancient Rome? It is interesting to remember that four years later an Englishman who had an incomparably wider and deeper knowledge of history declared it to be probable that in the age of the Antonines civilised Europe enjoyed greater happiness than at any other period.

Rome declined and Christianity came. Its purpose was not to render men happy on earth, and we do not find that it made rulers less avaricious or less sanguinary, peoples more patient or quiet, crimes rarer, punishments less cruel, treaties more faithfully observed, or wars waged more humanely. The conclusion is that it is only those who are profoundly ignorant of the past who can regret " the good old times."

Throughout this survey Chastellux does not, like Turgot, make any attempt to show that the race was progressing, however slowly. On the contrary, he sets the beginning of, continuous Progress in the Renaissance—here agreeing with d'Alembert and Voltaire. The intellectual movement, which originated then and resulted in the enlightenment of his own day, was a condition of social progress. But alone it would not have been enough, as is proved by the fact that the intellectual brilliancy of the great age of Greece exerted no beneficent effects on the well-being of the people. Nor indeed was there any perceptible improvement in the prospect of happiness for the people at large during the sixteenth and seventeenth centuries, notwithstanding the progress of science and the arts. But the terrible wars of this period exhausted Europe, and this financial exhaustion has supplied the requisite conditions for attaining a measure of felicity never realised in the past.

Peace is an advantageous condition for the progress of reason, but especially when it is the result of the exhaustion of peoples and their satiety of fighting.

Frivolous ideas disappear; political bodies, like organisms, have the care of self-preservation impressed upon them by pain; the human mind, hitherto exercised on agreeable objects, falls back with more energy on useful objects; a more successful appeal can be made to the rights of humanity; and princes, who have become creditors and debtors of their subjects, permit them to be happy in order that they may be more solvent or more patient.

This is not very lucid or convincing; but the main point is that intellectual enlightenment would be ineffective without the co-operation of political events, and no political events would permanently help humanity without the progress of knowledge.

Public felicity consists—Chastellux follows the Economists—in external and domestic peace, abundance and liberty, the liberty of tranquil enjoyment of one's own; and ordinary signs of it are flourishing agriculture, large populations, and the growth of trade and industry. He is at pains to show the superiority of modern to ancient agriculture, and he avails himself of the researches of Hume to prove the comparatively greater populousness of modern European countries. As for the prospect of peace, he takes a curiously optimistic view. A system of alliances has made Europe a sort of confederated republic, and the balance of power has rendered the design of a universal monarchy, such as that which Louis XIV. essayed, a chimera. All the powerful nations are burdened with debt. War, too, is a much more difficult enterprise than it used to be; every campaign of the king of Prussia has been more arduous than all the conquests of Attila. It looks as if the Peace of 1762–3 possessed elements of finality. The chief danger he discerns in the overseas policy of the English—*auri sacra fames*. Divination of this kind has never been happy; a greater thinker, Auguste Comte, was to venture on more dogmatic predictions of the cessation of wars, which the event was no less utterly to belie.

As for equality among men, Chastellux admits its desirability, but observes that there is pretty much the same amount of happiness (*le bonheur se compense assez*) in the different classes of society. "Courtiers and ministers are not happier than husbandmen and artisans." Inequalities and disproportions in the lots of individuals are not incompatible with a positive measure of felicity. They are inconveniences incident to the perfectibility of the species, and they will be eliminated only when Progress reaches its final term. The best that can be done to remedy them is to accelerate the Progress of the race which will conduct it one day to the greatest possible happiness; not to restore a state of ignorance and simplicity, from which it would again escape.

The general argument of the book may be resumed briefly. Felicity has never been realised in any period of the past. No government, however esteemed, set before itself to achieve what ought to be the sole object of government, "the greatest happiness of the greatest number of individuals." Now, for the first time in human history, intellectual enlightenment, other circumstances fortunately concurring, has brought about a condition of things, in which this object can no longer be ignored, and there is a prospect that it

will gradually gain the ascendant. In the meantime, things have improved ; the diffusion of knowledge is daily ameliorating men's lot, and far from
envying any age in the past we ought to consider
ourselves much happier than the ancients.

We may wonder at this writer's easy confidence
in applying the criterion of happiness to different
societies. Yet the difficulty of such comparisons
was, I believe, first pointed out by Comte. It is
impossible, he says, to compare two states of
society and determine that in one more happiness
was enjoyed than in the other. The happiness of
an individual requires a certain degree of harmony
between his faculties and his environment. But
there is always a natural tendency towards the
establishment of such an equilibrium, and there is
no means of discovering by argument or by direct
experience the situation of a society in this respect.
Therefore, he concludes, the question of happiness
must be eliminated from any scientific treatment of
civilisation.

Chastellux won a remarkable success. His
work was highly praised by Voltaire, and was
translated into English, Italian, and German. It
condensed, on a single issue, the optimistic doctrines
of the philosophers, and appeared to give them a
more solid historical foundation than Voltaire's
Essay on Manners had supplied. It provided the
optimists with new arguments against Rousseau,
and must have done much to spread and confirm
faith in perfectibility.

CHAPTER X

THE YEAR 2440

I

THE leaders of thought in France did not look far forward into the future or attempt to trace the definite lines on which the human race might be expected to develop. They contented themselves with principles and vague generalities, and they had no illusions as to the slowness of the process of social amelioration; a rational morality, the condition of improvement, was only in its infancy. A passage in a work of the Abbé Morellet probably reflects faithfully enough the comfortable though not extravagant optimism which was current.

Let us hope for the amelioration of man's lot as a consequence of the progress of the enlightenment (*des lumières*) and labours of the educated (*des gens instruits*) ; let us trust that the errors and even the injustices of our age may not rob us of this consoling hope. The history of society presents a continuous alternation of light and darkness, reason and extravagance, humanity and barbarism ; but in the succession of ages we can observe good gradually increasing in ever greater proportion. What educated man, if he is not a misanthrope or misled by vain declamations, would really wish he had lived in the barbarous and poetical time which Homer paints in such fair and terrifying colours? Who regrets that he was not born at Sparta among those pretended heroes who made it a virtue to insult nature, practised theft, and gloried in the murder of a Helot ; or at Carthage, the scene of human sacrifices, or at Rome amid the proscriptions or under the rule of a Nero or a Caligula ? Let us agree that man advances, though slowly, towards light and happiness.

But though the most influential writers were sober in speculating about the future, it is significant of their effectiveness in diffusing the idea of Progress that now for the first time a prophetic Utopia was constructed. Hitherto, as I have before observed, ideal states were either projected into the remote past or set in some distant, vaguely-known region, where fancy could build freely. To project them into the future was a new thing, and when in 1770 Sébastien Mercier described what human civilisation would be in A.D. 2440, it was a telling sign of the power which the idea of Progress was beginning to exercise.

2

Mercier has been remembered, or rather forgotten, as an inferior dramatist. He was a good deal more, and the researches of M. Béclard into his life and works enable us to appreciate him. If it is an overstatement to say that his soul reflected in miniature the very soul of his age,[1] he was assuredly one of its characteristic products. He reminds us in some ways of the Abbé de Saint-Pierre, who was one of his heroes. All his activities were urged by the dream of a humanity regenerated

[1] L. Béclard, *Sébastien Mercier, sa vie, son œuvre, son temps* (1903), p. vii.

by reason, all his energy devoted to bringing about its accomplishment.   Saint-Pierre's idea of perpetual peace inspired an early essay on the scourge of war.

The theories of Rousseau exercised at first an irresistible attraction, but modern civilisation had too strong a hold on him ; he was too Parisian in temper to acquiesce for long in the doctrine of Arcadianism.   He composed a book on *The Savage* to illustrate the text that the true standard of morality is the heart of primitive man, and to prove that the best thing we could do is to return to the forest ; but in the process of writing it he seems to have come to the conclusion that the whole doctrine was fallacious.   The transformation of his opinions was the work of a few months.   He then came forward with the opposite thesis that all events have been ordered for man's felicity, and he began to work on an imaginary picture of the state to which man might find his way within seven hundred years.

L'an 2440 was published anonymously at Amsterdam in 1770.   Its circulation in France was rigorously forbidden, because it implied a merciless criticism of the administration.   It was reprinted in London and Neuchâtel, and translated into English and German.

3

As the motto of his prophetic vision Mercier takes the saying of Leibnitz that "the present is pregnant of the future."   Thus the phase of civilisation which he imagines is proposed as the outcome of the natural and inevitable march of history.

The world of A.D. 2440 in which a man born in the eighteenth century who has slept an enchanted sleep awakes to find himself, is composed of nations who live in a family concord rarely interrupted by war. But of the world at large we hear little; the imagination of Mercier is concentrated on France, and particularly Paris. He is satisfied with knowing that slavery has been abolished; that the rivalry of France and England has been replaced by an indestructible alliance; that the Pope, whose authority is still august, has renounced his errors and returned to the customs of the primitive Church; that French plays are performed in China. The changes in Paris are a sufficient index of the general transformation.

The constitution of France is still monarchical. Its population has increased by one half; that of the capital remains about the same. Paris has been rebuilt on a scientific plan; its sanitary arrangements have been brought to perfection; it is well lit; and every provision has been made for the public safety. Private hospitality is so large that inns have disappeared, but luxury at table is considered a revolting crime. Tea, coffee, and tobacco are no longer imported.[1] There is no system of credit; everything is paid for in ready money, and this practice has led to a remarkable simplicity in dress. Marriages are contracted only through mutual inclination; dowries have been abolished. Education is governed by the ideas of Rousseau, and is directed, in a narrow spirit, to the promotion of morality. Italian, German, English, and Spanish are taught in schools, but the study of the classical

---

[1] In the first edition of the book commerce was abolished.

languages has disappeared; Latin does not help a
man to virtue. History too is neglected and dis-
couraged, for it is "the disgrace of humanity, every
page being crowded with crimes and follies."
Theatres are government institutions, and have
become the public schools of civic duties and
morality.

The literary records of the past had been almost
all deliberately destroyed by fire. It was found
expedient to do away with useless and pernicious
books which only obscured truth or contained
perpetual repetitions of the same thing. A small
closet in the public library sufficed to hold the
ancient books which were permitted to escape the
conflagration, and the majority of these were
English. The writings of the Abbé de Saint-Pierre
were placed next those of Fénelon. "His pen was
weak, but his heart was sublime. Seven ages have
given to his great and beautiful ideas a just
maturity. His contemporaries regarded him as a
visionary; his dreams, however, have become
realities."

The importance of men of letters as a social
force was a favourite theme of Mercier, and in
A.D. 2440 this will be duly recognised. But the
State control which weighed upon them so heavily
in 1770 is not to be entirely abolished. There is
no preventive censorship to hinder publication, but
there are censors. There are no fines or imprison-
ment, but there are admonitions. And if any one
publishes a book defending principles which are
considered dangerous, he is obliged to go about in
a black mask.

There is a state religion, Deism. There is

probably no one who does not believe in God. But if any atheist were discovered, he would be put through a course of experimental physics. If he remained obdurate in his rejection of a "palpable and salutary truth," the nation would go into mourning and banish him from its borders.

Every one has to work, but labour no longer resembles slavery. As there are no monks, nor numerous domestics, nor useless valets, nor workmen employed on the production of childish luxuries, a few daily hours of labour are sufficient for the public wants. Censors inquire into men's capacities, assign tasks to the unemployed, and if a man be found fit for nothing but the consumption of food he is banished from the city.

These are some of the leading features of the ideal future to which Mercier's imagination reached. He did not put it forward as a final term. Later ages, he said, will go further, for "where can the perfectibility of man stop, armed with geometry and the mechanical arts and chemistry?" But in his scanty prophecies of what science might effect he showed curiously little resource. The truth is that this had not much interest for him, and he did not see that scientific discoveries might transmute social conditions. The world of 2440, its intolerably docile and virtuous society, reflects two capital weaknesses in the speculation of the Encyclopaedist period: a failure to allow for the strength of human passions and interests, and a deficient appreciation of the meaning of liberty. Much as the reformers acclaimed and fought for toleration, they did not generally comprehend the value of the principle. They did

not see that in a society organised and governed
by Reason and Justice themselves, the unreserved
toleration of false opinions would be the only
palladium of progress; or that a doctrinaire State,
composed of perfectly virtuous and deferential
people, would arrest development and stifle originality, by its ungenial if mild tyranny. Mercier's
is no exception to the rule that ideal societies
are always repellent; and there are probably few
who would not rather be set down in Athens in
the days of the "vile" Aristophanes, whose works
Mercier condemned to the flames, than in his Paris
of 2440.

4

That Bohemian man of letters, Restif de la
Bretonne, whose unedifying novels the Parisians
of 2440 would assuredly have rejected from their
libraries, published in 1790 a heroic comedy
representing how marriages would be arranged in
"the year 2000," by which epoch he conceived
that all social equalities would have disappeared
in a fraternal society and twenty nations be allied
to France under the wise supremacy of "our well-
beloved monarch Louis François XXII." It was
the Revolution that converted Restif to the conception of Progress, for hitherto his master had
been Rousseau; but it can hardly be doubted that
the *motif* and title of his play were suggested by the
romance of Mercier. *L'an 2440* and *L'an 2000*
are the first examples of the prophetic fiction which
Mr. Edward Bellamy's *Looking Backward* was to
popularise a hundred years later.

The Count de Volney's *Ruins* was another

popular presentation of the hopes which the theory
of Progress had awakened in France.   Although
the work was not published till after the outbreak of
the Revolution,[1] the plan had been conceived some
years before.   Volney was a traveller, deeply
interested in oriental and classical antiquities, and,
like Louis Le Roy, he approached the problem of
man's destinies from the point of view of a student
of the revolutions of empires.

The book opens with melancholy reflections
amid the ruins of Palmyra.   " Thus perish the
works of men, and thus do nations and empires
vanish away. . . . Who can assure us that deso-
lation like this will not one day be the lot of
our own country ? "   Some traveller like himself
will sit by the banks of the Seine, the Thames, or
the Zuyder Zee, amid silent ruins, and weep for a
people inurned and their greatness changed into
an empty name.   Has a mysterious Deity pronounced a secret malediction against the earth ?

In this disconsolate mood he is visited by an
apparition, who unveils the causes of men's misfortunes and shows that they are due to themselves.
Man is governed by natural invariable laws, and he
has only to study them to know the springs of
his destiny, the causes of his evils and their
remedies.   The laws of his nature are self-love,
desire of happiness, and aversion to pain ; these
are the simple and prolific principles of everything
that happens in the moral world.   Man is the
artificer of his own fate.   He may lament his
weakness and folly ; but " he has perhaps still more

---

[1] *Les Ruines des empires*, 1789.   An English translation ran to a second
edition (1795).

reason to be confident in his energies when he recollects from what point he has set out and to what heights he has been capable of elevating himself."

The supernatural visitant paints a rather rosy picture of the ancient Egyptian and Assyrian kingdoms.   But it would be a mistake to infer from their superficial splendour that the inhabitants generally were wise or happy.   The tendency of man to ascribe perfection to past epochs is merely "the discoloration of his chagrin."   The race is not degenerating ;   its misfortunes are due to ignorance and the mis-direction of self-love.   Two principal obstacles to improvement have been the difficulty of transmitting ideas from age to age, and that of communicating them rapidly from man to man.   These have been removed by the invention of printing.   The press is "a memorable gift of celestial genius."   In time all men will come to understand the principles of individual happiness and public felicity.   Then there will be established among the peoples of the earth an equilibrium of forces ;   there will be no more wars, disputes will be decided by arbitration, and "the whole species will become one great society, a single family governed by the same spirit and by common laws, enjoying all the felicity of which human nature is capable." The accomplishment of this will be a slow process, since the same leaven will have to assimilate an enormous mass of heterogeneous elements, but its operation will be effectual.

Here the genius interrupts his prophecy and exclaims, turning toward the west, "The cry of liberty uttered on the farther shores of the Atlantic has reached to the old continent." A prodigious movement is then visible to their eyes in a country at the extremity of the Mediterranean ; tyrants are overthrown, legislators elected, a code of laws is drafted on the principles of equality, liberty, and justice. The liberated nation is attacked by neighbouring tyrants, but her legislators propose to the other peoples to hold a general assembly, representing the whole world, and weigh every religious system in the balance. The proceedings of this congress follow, and the book breaks off incomplete.

It is not an arresting book ; to a reader of the present day it is positively tedious ; but it suited contemporary taste, and, appearing when France was confident that her Revolution would renovate the earth, it appealed to the hopes and sentiments of the movement. It made no contribution to the doctrine of Progress, but it undoubtedly helped to popularise it.

CHAPTER XI

I

THE authority which the advanced thinkers of France gained among the middle classes during the third quarter of the eighteenth century was promoted by the influence of fashion. The new ideas of philosophers, rationalists, and men of science had interested the nobles and higher classes of society for two generations, and were a common subject of discussion in the most distinguished salons. Voltaire's intimacy with Frederick the Great, the relations of d'Alembert and Diderot with the Empress Catherine, conferred on these men of letters, and on the ideas for which they stood, a prestige which carried great weight with the bourgeoisie. Humbler people, too, were as amenable as the great to the seduction of theories which supplied simple keys to the universe [1] and assumed that everybody was capable of judging for himself on the most difficult problems. As well as the Encyclopaedia, the works of nearly all the leading thinkers were written for the general public,

---

[1] Taine said of the *Contrat Social* that it reduces political science to the strict application of an elementary axiom which renders all study unnecessary (*La Révolution*, vol. i. c. iv. § iii.).

not merely for philosophers. The policy of the Government in suppressing these dangerous publications did not hinder their diffusion, and gave them the attraction of forbidden fruit. In 1770 the avocat général (Séguier) acknowledged the futility of the policy. "The philosophers," he said, "have with one hand sought to shake the throne, with the other to upset the altars. Their purpose was to change public opinion on civil and religious institutions, and the revolution has, so to speak, been effected. History and poetry, romances and even dictionaries, have been infected with the poison of incredulity. Their writings are hardly published in the capital before they inundate the provinces like a torrent. The contagion has spread into workshops and cottages."[1]

The contagion spread, but the official who wrote these words did not see that it was successful because it was opportune, and that the minds of men were prepared to receive the seed of revolutionary ideas by the unspeakable corruption of the Government and the Church. As Voltaire remarked about the same time, France was becoming Encyclopaedist, and Europe too.

2

The influence of the subversive and rationalistic thinkers in bringing about the events of 1789 has been variously estimated by historians. The truth probably lies in the succinct statement of Acton that "the confluence of French theory with American example caused the Revolution to break out" when it did. The theorists aimed at reform, not at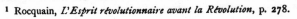

---

[1] Rocquain, *L'Esprit révolutionnaire avant la Révolution*, p. 278.

political revolution ; and it was the stimulus of the Declaration of Rights of 1774 and the subsequent victory of the Colonies that precipitated the convulsion, at a time when the country had a better prospect of improvement than it ever had before 1774, when Louis XVI. came to the throne.   But the theories had prepared France for radical changes, and they guided the phases of the Revolution.   The leaders had all the optimism of the Encyclopaedists ; yet the most powerful single force was Rousseau, who, though he denied Progress and blasphemed civilisation, had promulgated the doctrine of the sovereignty of the people, giving it an attractive appearance of mathematical precision ; and to this doctrine the revolutionaries attached their optimistic hopes.[1]   The theory of equality seemed no longer merely speculative ; for the American constitution was founded on democratic equality, whereas the English constitution, which before had seemed the nearest approximation to the ideal of freedom, was founded on inequality.   The philosophical polemic of the masters was waged with weapons of violence by the disciples.   Chaumette and Hébert, the followers of d'Holbach, were destroyed by the disciples of Rousseau.   In the name of the creed of the *Vicaire Savoyard* the Jacobin Club shattered the bust of Helvétius.   Mably and Morelly had their disciples in Babeuf and the socialists.

A naïve confidence that the political upheaval meant regeneration and inaugurated a reign of

---

[1] It is interesting to observe how Robespierre, to whom the doctrines of Rousseau were oracles, could break out into admiration of the progress of civilised man, as he did in the opening passage of his speech of 7th May 1794, proposing the decree for the worship of the Supreme Being (see the text in Stephen, *Orators of the French Revolution*, ii. 391-92).

justice and happiness pervaded France in the first
period of the Revolution, and found a striking
expression in the ceremonies of the universal
" Federation" in the Champ-de-Mars on 14th July
1790. The festival was theatrical enough, decreed
and arranged by the Constituent Assembly, but
the enthusiasm and optimism of the people who
gathered to swear loyalty to the new Constitution
were genuine and spontaneous. Consciously or
subconsciously they were under the influence of the
doctrine of Progress which leaders of opinion had
for several decades been insinuating into the public
mind. It did not occur to them that their oaths and
fraternal embraces did not change their minds or
hearts, and that, as Taine remarked, they remained
what ages of political subjection and one age of
political literature had made them. The assumption
that new social machinery could alter human nature
and create a heaven upon earth was to be swiftly
and terribly confuted.

Post uarios casus et tot discrimina rerum
uenimus in Latium,

but Latium was to be the scene of sanguinary
struggles.

Another allied and fundamental fallacy, into
which all the philosophers and Rousseau had more
or less fallen, was reflected and exposed by the
Revolution. They had considered man *in vacuo*.
They had not seen that the whole development of a
society is an enormous force which cannot be talked
or legislated away ; they had ignored the power of
social memory and historical traditions, and mis-
valued the strength of the links which bind genera-

tions together. So the Revolutionaries imagined that they could break abruptly with the past, and that a new method of government, constructed on mathematical lines, a constitution (to use words of Burke) "ready made and ready armed, mature in its birth, a perfect goddess of wisdom and of war, hammered by our blacksmith midwives out of the brain of Jupiter himself," would create a condition of idyllic felicity in France, and that the arrival of the millennium depended only on the adoption of the same principles by other nations. The illusions created by the Declaration of the Rights of Man on the 4th of August died slowly under the shadow of the Terror ; but though the hopes of those who believed in the speedy regeneration of the world were belied, some of the thoughtful did not lose heart. There was one at least who did not waver in his faith that the movement was a giant's step on the path of man towards ultimate felicity, however far he had still to travel. Condorcet, one of the younger Encyclopaedists, spent the last months of his life, under the menace of the guillotine, in projecting a history of human Progress.

3

Condorcet was the friend and biographer of Turgot, and it was not unfitting that he should resume the design of a history of civilisation, in the light of the idea of Progress, for which Turgot had only left luminous suggestions. He did not execute the plan, but he completed an elaborate sketch in which the controlling ideas of the scheme are fully set forth. His principles are to be found almost entirely in Turgot. But they have a new significance for Condorcet. He has given them wings. He has emphasised, and made deductions. Turgot wrote in the calm spirit of an inquirer. Condorcet spoke with the verve of a prophet. He was prophesying under the shadow of death. It is amazing that the optimistic *Sketch of a Historical Picture of the Progress of the Human Mind* should have been composed when he was hiding from Robespierre in 1793.[1]

Condorcet was penetrated with the spirit of the Encyclopaedists, of whom he had been one, and his attitude to Christianity was that of Voltaire and Diderot. Turgot had treated the received religion respectfully. He had acknowledged Providence, and, though the place which he assigned to Providence was that of a sort of honorary President of the development of civilisation who might disappear without affecting the proceedings, there was a real difference between his views and those of his friend as to the *rôle* of Christianity and the civilisation of the Middle Ages.

A more important difference between the two thinkers is connected with the different circumstances in which they wrote. Turgot did not believe in the necessity of violent changes ; he thought that steady reforms under the existing régime would do wonders for France. Before the Revolution Condorcet had agreed, but he was swept away by its enthusiasm. The victory of liberty in America and the increasing volume of the movement against slavery—one of the causes which most deeply stirred his heart—had heightened his natural optimism and confirmed his faith in the dogma of Progress. He felt the

[1] Published in 1795.

exhilaration of the belief that he was living through
"one of the greatest revolutions of the human
race," and he deliberately designed his book to be
opportune to a crisis of mankind, at which "a picture
of revolutions of the past will be the best guide."

Feeling that he is personally doomed, he consoles
himself with brooding on the time, however remote,
when the sun will shine "on an earth of none but
freemen, with no master save reason ; for tyrants and
slaves, priests and their stupid or hypocritical tools,
will all have disappeared." He is not satisfied with
affirming generally the certainty of an indefinite
progress in enlightenment and social welfare. He
sets himself to think out its nature, to forecast its
direction, and determine its goal, and insists, as his
predecessors had never done, on the prospects of
the distant future.

4

His ambitious design is, in his own words, to
show "the successive changes in human society, the
influence which each instant exerts on the succeeding
instant, and thus, in its successive modifications, the
advance of the human species towards truth or
happiness." Taken literally, this is an impossible
design, and to put it forward as a practical proposition is as if a man were to declare his intention of
writing a minute diary of the life of Julius Caesar
from his birth to his death. By stating his purpose
in such terms, Condorcet reveals that he had no
notion of the limitations which confine our knowledge
of the past, and that even if he had conceived a
more modest and practicable programme he would
have been incapable of executing it. His formula,

however, is worth remembering. For the unattainable ideal which it expresses reminds us how many periods and passages of human experience must always remain books with seven seals.

Condorcet distinguished ten periods of civilisation, of which the tenth lies in the future, but he has not justified his divisions and his epochs are not co-ordinate in importance. Yet his arrangement of the map of history is remarkable as an attempt to mark its sections not by great political changes but by important steps in knowledge. The first three periods—the formation of primitive societies, followed by the pastoral age, and the agricultural age—conclude with the invention of alphabetic writing in Greece. The fourth is the history of Greek thought, to the definite division of the sciences in the time of Aristotle. In the fifth knowledge progresses and suffers obscuration under Roman rule, and the sixth is the dark age which continues to the time of the Crusades. The significance of the seventh period is to prepare the human mind for the revolution which would be achieved by the invention of printing, with which the eighth period opens. Some of the best pages of the book develop the vast consequences of this invention. The scientific revolution effected by Descartes begins a new period, which is now closed by the creation of the French Republic.

The idea of the progress of knowledge had created the idea of social Progress and remained its foundation. It was therefore logical and inevitable that Condorcet should take advance in knowledge as the clew to the march of the human race. The history of civilisation is the history of enlightenment.

Turgot had justified this axiom by formulating the cohesion of all modes of social activity. Condorcet insists on "the indissoluble union" between intellectual progress and that of liberty, virtue, and the respect for natural rights, and on the effect of science in the destruction of prejudice. All errors in politics and ethics have sprung, he asserts, from false ideas which are closely connected with errors in physics and ignorance of the laws of nature. And in the new doctrine of Progress he sees an instrument of enlightenment which is to give "the last blow to the tottering edifice of prejudices."

It would not be useful to analyse Condorcet's sketch or dwell on his obsolete errors and the defects of his historical knowledge. His slight picture of the Middle Ages reflects the familiar view of all the eighteenth century philosophers. The only contribution to social amelioration which he can discover in a period of nearly a millennium is the abolition of domestic slavery. And so this period appears as an interruption of the onward march. His inability to appreciate the historical *rôle* of the Roman Empire exhibits more surprising ignorance and prejudice. But these particular defects are largely due to a fundamental error which runs through his whole book and was inherent in the social speculations of the Encyclopaedists. Condorcet, like all his circle, ignored the preponderant part which institutions have played in social development. So far as he considered them at all, he saw in them obstacles to the free play of human reason ; not the spontaneous expression of a society corresponding to its needs or embodying its ideals, but rather machinery deliberately contrived for oppressing the masses and keeping them in chains. He did not see that if the Progress in which he believed is a reality, its possibility depends on the institutions and traditions which give to societies their stability. In the following generation, it would be pointed out that he fell into a manifest contradiction when he praised the relative perfection reached in some European countries in the eighteenth century, and at the same time condemned as eminently retrograde all the doctrines and institutions which had been previously in control.[1] This error is closely connected with the other error, previously noticed, of conceiving man abstracted from his social environment and exercising his reason *in vacuo*.

5

The study of the history of civilisation has, in Condorcet's eyes, two uses. It enables us to establish the fact of Progress, and it should enable us to determine its direction in the future, and thereby to accelerate the rate of progression.

By the facts of history and the arguments they suggest, he undertakes to show that nature has set no term to the process of improving human faculties, and that the advance towards perfection is limited only by the duration of the globe. The movement may vary in velocity, but it will never be retrograde so long as the earth occupies its present place in the cosmic system and the general laws of this system do not produce some catastrophe or change which would deprive the human race of the faculties and resources which it has hitherto possessed. There will be no relapse into barbarism. The guarantees

[1] Comte, *Cours de philosophie positive*, iv. 258.

against this danger are the discovery of true methods in the physical sciences, their application to the needs of men, the lines of communication which have been established among them, the great number of those who study them, and finally the art of printing. And if we are sure of the continuous progress of enlightenment, we may be sure of the continuous improvement of social conditions.

It is possible to foresee events, if the general laws of social phenomena are known, and these laws can be inferred from the history of the past. By this statement Condorcet justifies his bold attempt to sketch his tenth period of human history which lies in the future ; and announces the idea which was in the next generation to be worked out by Comte. But he cannot be said to have deduced himself any law of social development. His forecast of the future is based on the ideas and tendencies of his own age.

Apart from scientific discoveries and the general diffusion of a knowledge of the laws of nature on which moral improvement depends, he includes in his prophetic vision the cessation of war and the realisation of the less familiar idea of the equality of the sexes. If he were alive to-day, he could point with triumph to the fact that of these far-reaching projects one is being accomplished in some of the most progressive countries and the other is looked upon as an attainable aim by statesmen who are not visionaries. The equality of the sexes was only a logical inference from the general doctrine of equality to which Condorcet's social theory is reducible. For him the goal of political progress is equality ; equality is to be the aim of social effort —the ideal of the Revolution.

For it is the multitude of men that must be considered—the mass of workers, not the minority who live on their labours. Hitherto they have been neglected by the historian as well as by the statesman. The true history of humanity is not the history of some men. The human race is formed by the mass of families who subsist almost entirely on the fruits of their own work, and this mass is the proper subject of history, not great men.

You may establish social equality by means of laws and institutions, yet the equality actually enjoyed may be very incomplete. Condorcet recognises this and attributes it to three principal causes : inequality in wealth ; inequality in position between the man whose means of subsistence are assured and can be transmitted to his family and the man whose means depend on his work and are limited by the term of his own life [1]; and inequality in education. He did not propose any radical methods for dealing with these difficulties, which he thought would diminish in time, without, however, entirely disappearing. He was too deeply imbued with the views of the Economists to be seduced by the theories of Rousseau, Mably, Babeuf, and others, into advocating communism or the abolition of private property.

Besides equality among the individuals composing a civilised society, Condorcet contemplated equality among all the peoples of the earth,—a uniform civilisation throughout the world, and the obliteration of the distinction between advanced and retrograde races. The backward peoples, he

---

[1] He looked forward to the mitigation of this inequality by the development of life insurance which was then coming to the front.

prophesied, will climb up to the condition of France and the United States of America, for no people is condemned never to exercise its reason. If the dogma of the perfectibility of human nature, unguarded by any restrictions, is granted, this is a logical inference, and we have already seen that it was one of the ideas current among the philosophers.

Condorcet does not hesitate to add to his picture adventurous conjectures on the improvement of man's physical organisation, and a considerable prolongation of his life. by the advance of medical science. We need only note this. More interest- ing is the prediction that, even if the compass of the human being's cerebral powers is inalterable, the range, precision, and rapidity of his mental operations will be augmented by the invention of new instruments and methods.

The design of writing a history of human civilisation was premature, and to have produced a survey of any durable value would have re- quired the equipment of a Gibbon. Condorcet was not even as well equipped as Voltaire.[1] The significance of his *Sketch* lies in this, that towards the close of an intellectual movement it con- centrated attention on the most important, though hitherto not the most prominent, idea which that movement had disseminated, and as it were officially announced human Progress as the leading problem that claimed the interest of mankind. With him Progress was associated intimately with particular eighteenth century doctrines, but these were not essential to it. It was a living idea ; it survived the compromising theories which began to fall into

---

[1] But as he wrote without books the *Sketch* was a marvellous *tour de force*.

discredit after the Revolution, and was explored
from new points of view. Condorcet, however,
wedded though his mind was to the untenable
views of human nature current in his epoch and
his circle, did not share the tendency of leading
philosophers to regard history as an unprofitable
record of folly and crime which it would be well to
obliterate or forget. He recognised the interpretation of history as the key to human development,
and this principle controlled subsequent speculations
on Progress in France.

6

Cabanis, the physician, was Condorcet's literary
executor, and a no less ardent believer in human
perfectibility. Looking at life and man from his
own special point of view, he saw in the study of
the physical organism the key to the intellectual
and moral improvement of the race. It is by
knowledge of the relations between his physical
states and moral states that man can attain happiness, through the enlargement of his faculties and
the multiplication of enjoyments, and that he will be
able to grasp, as it were, the infinite in his brief
existence by realising the certainty of indefinite
progress. His doctrine was a logical extension of
the theories of Locke and Condillac. If our knowledge is wholly derived from sensations, our sensations depend on our sensory organs, and mind becomes a function of the nervous system.

The events of the Revolution quenched in him
as little as in Condorcet the sanguine confidence
that it was the opening of a new era for science and
art, and thereby for the general Progress of man.

"The present is one of those great periods of history to which posterity will often look back" with gratitude.[1] He took an active part in the *coup d'État* of the 18th of Brumaire (1799) which was to lead to the despotism of Napoleon. He imagined that it would terminate oppression, and was as enthusiastic for it as he and Condorcet had been for the Revolution ten years before. "You philosophers," he wrote,[2] "whose studies are directed to the improvement and happiness of the race, you no longer embrace vain shadows. Having watched, in alternating moods of hope and sadness, the great spectacle of our Revolution, you now see with joy the termination of its last act; you will see with rapture this new era, so long promised to the French people, at last open, in which all the benefits of nature, all the creations of genius, all the fruits of time, labour, and experience will be utilised, an era of glory and prosperity in which the dreams of your philanthropic enthusiasm should end by being realised."

It was an over-sanguine and characteristic greeting of the eighteenth to the nineteenth century. Cabanis was one of the most important of those thinkers who, living into the new period, took care that the ideas of their own generation should not be overwhelmed in the rising flood of reaction.

[1] Picavet, *Les Idéologues*, p. 203. Cabanis was born in 1757 and died in 1808

[2] *Ib.* p. 224.

CHAPTER XII

THE THEORY OF PROGRESS IN ENGLAND

I

THE idea of Progress could not help crossing the Channel. France and England had been at war in the first year of the eighteenth century, they were at war in the last, and their conflict for supremacy was the leading feature of the international history of the whole century. But at no period was there more constant intellectual intimacy or more marked reciprocal influence between the two countries. It was a commonplace that Paris and London were the two great foci of civilisation, and they never lost touch of each other in the intellectual sphere. Many of the principal works of literature that appeared in either country were promptly translated, and some of the French books, which the censorship rendered it dangerous to publish in Paris, were printed in London.

It was not indeed to be expected that the theory should have the same kind of success, or exert the same kind of effect in England as in France. England had her revolution behind her, France had hers before her. England enjoyed what were then considered large political liberties, the envy of other lands ; France groaned under the tyranny of

worthless rulers. The English constitution satisfied
the nation, and the serious abuses which would now
appear to us intolerable were not sufficient to
awaken a passionate desire for reforms. The
general tendency of British thought was to see salvation in the stability of existing institutions, and to
regard change with suspicion. Now passionate
desire for reform was the animating force which
propagated the idea of Progress in France. And
when this idea is translated from the atmosphere of
combat, in which it was developed by French men
of letters, into the calm climate of England, it
appears like a cold reflection.

Again, English thinkers were generally inclined
to hold, with Locke, that the proper function of
government is principally negative, to preserve
order and defend life and property, not to aim
directly at the improvement of society, but to secure
the conditions in which men may pursue their own
legitimate aims. Most of the French theorists
believed in the possibility of moulding society
indefinitely by political action, and rested their

hopes for the future not only on the achievements
of science, but on the enlightened activity of
governments. This difference of view tended to
give to the doctrine of Progress in France more
practical significance than in England.

But otherwise British soil was ready to receive
the idea. There was the same optimistic temper
among the comfortable classes in both countries.
Shaftesbury, the Deist, had struck this note at the
beginning of the century by his sanguine theory,
which was expressed in Pope's banal phrase :
"Whatever is, is right," and was worked into a

system by Hutcheson. This optimism penetrated into orthodox circles. Progress, far from appearing as a rival of Providence, was discussed in the interests of Christianity by the Scotch theologian, Turnbull.[1]

2

The theory of the indefinite progress of civilisation left Hume cold. There is little ground, he argued, to suppose that "the world" is eternal or incorruptible. It is probably mortal, and must therefore, with all things in it, have its infancy, youth, manhood, and old age; and man will share in these changes of state. We must then expect that the human species should, when the world is in the age of manhood, possess greater bodily and mental vigour, longer life, and a stronger inclination and power of generation. But it is impossible to determine when this stage is reached. For the gradual revolutions are too slow to be discernible in the short period known to us by history and tradition. Physically and in mental powers men have been pretty much the same in all known ages. The sciences and arts have flourished now and have again decayed, but when they reached the highest perfection among one people, the neighbouring peoples were perhaps wholly unacquainted with them. We are therefore uncertain whether at present man is advancing to his point of perfection or declining from it.[2]

The argument is somewhat surprising in an eighteenth century thinker like Hume, but it did

[1] *The Principles of Modern Philosophy*, 1740.
[2] *Essay on the Populousness of Ancient Nations, ad init.*

not prevent him from recognising the superiority of modern to ancient civilisation. This superiority forms indeed the minor premiss in the general argument by which he confuted the commonly received opinion as to the populousness of ancient nations. He insisted on the improvements in art and industry, on the greater liberty and security enjoyed by modern men. "To one who considers coolly on the subject," he remarked, "it will appear that human nature in general really enjoys more liberty at present in the most arbitrary government of Europe than it ever did during the most flourishing period of ancient times." [1]

He discussed many of the problems of civilisation, especially the conditions in which the arts and sciences flourish,[2] and drew some general conclusions, but he was too sceptical to suppose that any general synthesis of history is possible, or that any considerable change for the better in the manners of mankind is likely to occur.[3]

The greatest work dealing with social problems, that Britain produced in the eighteenth century, was Adam Smith's *Wealth of Nations*, and his luminous exposition of the effects of the division of labour was the most considerable contribution made by British thinkers of the age to the study of human development. It is much more than a treatise on economic principles; it contains a history of the gradual economic progress of human society, and it suggests the expectation of an indefinite augmentation of wealth and well-being. Smith was entirely at one with the French Economists on the value

---

[1] The justification of this statement was the abolition of slavery in Europe.
[2] *Essay on the Rise of Arts and Sciences.*
[3] Cf. *Essay on the Idea of a Perfect Commonwealth, ad init.*

of opulence for the civilisation and happiness of mankind. But it was indirectly perhaps that his work contributed most effectively to the doctrine of the Progress of collective mankind. His teaching that the free commercial intercourse of all the peoples of the world, unfettered by government policies, was to the greatest advantage of each, presented an ideal of the economic "solidarity" of the race, which was one element in the ideal of Progress. And this principle soon began to affect practice. Pitt assimilated it when he was a young man, and it is one of the distinctions of his statesmanship that he endeavoured to apply the doctrines of his master so far as the prevailing prejudices would allow him.

3

A few writers of less weight and fame than Hume or Smith expressly studied history in the light of Progress. It would not help us, in following the growth of the idea, to analyse the works of Ferguson, Dunbar, or Priestley. But I will quote one passage from Priestley, the most eminent of the three, and the most enthusiastic for the Progress of man. As the division of labour—the chief principle of organised society—is carried further he anticipates that

. . . nature, including both its materials and its laws, will be more at our command ; men will make their situation in this world abundantly more easy and comfortable ; they will probably prolong their existence in it and will grow daily more happy. . . . Thus, whatever was the beginning of this world, the end will be glorious and paradisiacal beyond what our imaginations can now conceive.

Extravagant as some people may suppose these views to be, I think I could show them to be fairly suggested by the true theory of human nature and to arise from the natural course of human affairs.

The problem of dark ages, which an advocate of Progress must explain, was waved away by Priestley in his *Lectures on History* with the observation that they help the subsequent advance of knowledge by "breaking the progress of authority."[1] This is not much of a plea for such periods viewed as machinery in a Providential plan. The great history of the Middle Ages, which in the words of its author describes "the triumph of barbarism and religion," had been completed before Priestley's *Lectures* appeared, and it is remarkable that he takes no account of it, though it might seem to be a work with which a theory of Progress must come to terms.

Yet the sceptical historian of the *Decline and Fall of the Roman Empire*, who was more at home in French literature than any of his fellow-countrymen, was not opposed to the theory of Progress, and he even states it in a moderate form. Having given reasons for believing that civilised society will never again be threatened by such an irruption of barbarians as that which oppressed the arms and institutions of Rome, he allows us to "acquiesce in the pleasing conclusion that every age of the world has increased, and still increases, the real wealth, the happiness, the knowledge and perhaps the virtue of the human race."

"The discoveries of ancient and modern navi-

[1] This was doubtless suggested to him by some remarks of Hume in *The Rise of Arts and Sciences.*

gators, and the domestic history or tradition of the most enlightened nations, represent the *human savage*, naked both in mind and body, and destitute of laws, of arts, of ideas, and almost of language. From this abject condition, perhaps the primitive and universal state of man, he has gradually arisen to command the animals, to fertilise the earth, to traverse the ocean, and to measure the heavens. His progress in the improvement and exercise of his mental and corporeal faculties has been irregular and various, infinitely slow in the beginning, and increasing by degrees with redoubled velocity ; ages of laborious ascent have been followed by a moment of rapid downfall ; and the several climates of the globe have felt the vicissitudes of light and darkness. Yet the experience of four thousand years should enlarge our hopes and diminish our apprehensions ; we cannot determine to what height the human species may aspire in their advances towards perfection ; but it may safely be presumed that no people, unless the face of nature is changed, will relapse into their original barbarism." [1]

But Gibbon treats the whole subject as a speculation, and he treats it without reference to any of the general principles on which French thinkers had based their theory. He admits that his reasons for holding that civilisation is secure against a barbarous cataclysm may be considered fallacious ; and he also contemplates the eventuality that the fabric of sciences and arts, trade and manufacture, law and policy, might be "decayed by time." If so, the growth of civilisation would have to begin again, but not *ab initio*. For "the more

---

[1] *Decline and Fall of the Roman Empire*, ch. xxxviii. *ad fin.*

useful or at least more necessary arts," which do not require superior talents or national subordination for their exercise, and which war, commerce, and religious zeal have spread among the savages of the world, would certainly survive.

These remarks are no more than *obiter dicta*, but they show how the doctrine of Progress was influencing those who were temperamentally the least likely to subscribe to extravagant theories.

4

The outbreak of the French Revolution evoked a sympathetic movement among English progressive thinkers which occasioned the Government no little alarm. The dissenting minister Dr. Richard Price, whose *Observations on Civil Liberty* (1776), defending the action of the American colonies, had enjoyed an immense success, preached the sermon which provoked Burke to write his *Reflections*; and Priestley, no less enthusiastic in welcoming the Revolution, replied to Burke. The Government resorted to tyrannous measures; young men who sympathised with the French movement and agitated for reforms at home were sent to Botany Bay. Paine was prosecuted for his *Rights of Man*, which directly preached revolution. But the most important speculative work of the time, William Godwin's *Political Justice*, escaped the censorship because it was not published at a popular price.[1]

The *Enquiry concerning Political Justice*, begun

---

[1] Godwin had helped to get Paine's book published in 1791, and he was intimate with the group of revolutionary spirits who were persecuted by the Government. A good account of the episode will be found in Brailsford's *Shelley, Godwin, and their Circle*.

in 1791, appeared in 1793. The second edition, three years later, shows the influence of Condorcet's *Sketch*, which had appeared in the meantime. Godwin says that his original idea was to produce a work on political science to supersede Montesquieu. The note of Montesquieu's political philosophy was respect for social institutions. Godwin's principle was that social institutions are entirely pernicious, that they perpetuate harmful prejudices, and are an almost insuperable obstacle to improvement. If he particularly denounced monarchical government, he regarded all government as evil, and held that social progress would consist, not in the reformation of government, but in its abolition. While he recognised that man had progressed in the past, he considered history mainly a sequence of horrors, and he was incapable of a calm survey of the course of civilisation. In English institutions he saw nothing that did not outrage the principles of justice and benevolence. The present state of humanity is about as bad as it could be.

It is easy to see the deep influence which the teaching of Rousseau exercised on Godwin. Without accepting the theory of Arcadia Godwin followed him in unsparing condemnation of existing conditions. Rousseau and Godwin are the two great champions in the eighteenth century of the toiling and suffering masses. But Godwin drew the logical conclusion from Rousseau's premises which Rousseau hesitated to draw himself. The French thinker, while he extolled the anarchical state of uncivilised society, and denounced government as one of the sources of its corruption, nevertheless sought the remedy in new social and political institutions. Godwin said boldly, government is the evil; government must go. Humanity can never be happy until all political authority and social institutions disappear.

Now the peculiarity of Godwin's position as a doctrinaire of Progress lies in the fact that he entertained the same pessimistic view of some important sides of civilisation as Rousseau, and at the same time adopted the theories of Rousseau's opponents, especially Helvétius. His survey of human conditions seems to lead inevitably to pessimism; then he turns round and proclaims the doctrine of perfectibility.

The explanation of this argument was the psychological theory of Helvétius. He taught, as we saw, and Godwin developed the view in his own way, that the natures and characters of men are moulded entirely by their environment—not physical, but intellectual and moral environment, and therefore can be indefinitely modified. A man is born into the world without innate tendencies. His conduct depends on his opinions. Alter men's opinions and they will act differently. Make their opinions conformable to justice and benevolence, and you will have a just and benevolent society. Virtue, as Socrates taught, is simply a question of knowledge. The situation, therefore, is not hopeless. For it is not due to the radical nature of man; it is caused by ignorance and prejudice, by governments and institutions, by kings and priests. Transform the ideas of men, and society will be transformed The French philosopher considered that a reformed system of educating children would be one of the most powerful means for promoting progress and bringing about the reign of reason ; and Condorcet worked out a scheme of universal state education. This was entirely opposed to Godwin's principles. State schools would only be another instrument of power in the hands of a government, worse even than a state Church. They would strengthen the poisonous influence of kings and statesmen, and establish instead of abolishing prejudices. He seems to have relied entirely on the private efforts of enlightened thinkers to effect a gradual conversion of public opinion.

In his study of the perfectibility of man and the prospect of a future reign of general justice and benevolence, Godwin was even more visionary than Condorcet, as in his political views he was more radical than the Revolutionists. Condorcet had at least sought to connect his picture of the future with a reasoned survey of the past, and to find a chain of connection, but the perfectibility of Godwin hung in the air, supported only by an abstract theory of the nature of man.

It can hardly be said that he contributed anything to the theoretical problem of civilisation. His significance is that he proclaimed in England at an opportune moment, and in a more impressive and startling way than a sober apostle like Priestley, the creed of progress taught by French philosophers, though considerably modified by his own anarchical opinions.

5

Perfectibility, as expounded by Condorcet and Godwin, encountered a drastic criticism from

Malthus, whose *Essay on the Principle of Population* appeared in its first form anonymously in 1798. Condorcet had foreseen an objection which might be raised as fatal to the realisation of his future state. Will not the progress of industry and happiness cause a steady increase in population, and must not the time come when the number of the inhabitants of the globe will surpass their means of subsistence? Condorcet did not grapple with this question. He contented himself with saying that such a period must be very far away, and that by then "the human race will have achieved improvements of which we can now scarcely form an idea." Similarly Godwin, in his fancy picture of the future happiness of mankind, notices the difficulty and shirks it. "Three-fourths of the habitable globe are now uncultivated. The parts already cultivated are capable of immeasurable improvement. Myriads of centuries of still increasing population may pass away and the earth be still found sufficient for the subsistence of its inhabitants."

Malthus argued that these writers laboured under an illusion as to the actual relations between population and the means of subsistence. In present conditions the numbers of the race are only kept from increasing far beyond the means of subsistence by vice, misery, and the fear of misery.[1] In the conditions imagined by Condorcet and Godwin these checks are removed, and consequently the population would increase with great rapidity, doubling itself at least in twenty-five years.

[1] This observation had been made (as Hazlitt pointed out) before Malthus by Robert Wallace (see *A Dissertation on the Numbers of Mankind*, p. 13, 1753). It was another book of Wallace that suggested the difficulty to Godwin.

But the products of the earth increase only in an arithmetical progression, and in fifty years the food supply would be too small for the demand. Thus the oscillation between numbers and food supply would recur, and the happiness of the species would come to an end.

Godwin and his adherents could reply that one of the checks on over-population is prudential restraint, which Malthus himself recognised, and that this would come more extensively into operation with that progress of enlightenment which their theory assumed.[1] But the criticisms of Malthus dealt a trenchant blow to the doctrine that human reason, acting through legislation and government, has a virtually indefinite power of modifying the condition of society. The difficulty, which he stated so vividly and definitely, was well calculated to discredit the doctrine, and to suggest that the development of society could be modified by the conscious efforts of man only within restricted limits.[2]

6

The *Essay* of Malthus afterwards became one of the sacred books of the Utilitarian sect, and it is

[1] This is urged by Hazlitt in his criticism of Malthus in the *Spirit of the Age.*

[2] The recent conclusions of Mr. Knibbs, statistician to the Commonwealth of Australia, in vol. i. of his Appendix to the Census of the Commonwealth, have an interest in this connection. I quote from an article in the *Times* of August 5, 1918: "An eminent geographer, the late Mr. E. G. Ravenstein, some years ago, when the population of the earth was estimated at 1400 million, foretold that about the middle of this century population would have reached a limit beyond which increase would be disastrous. Mr. Knibbs is not so pessimistic and is much more precise; though he defers the disastrous culmination, he has no doubt as to its inevitability. The limits of human expansion, he assures us, are much nearer than popular opinion imagines; the difficulty of food supplies will soon be

interesting to notice what Bentham himself thought of perfectibility. Referring to the optimistic views of Chastellux and Priestley on progressive amelioration he observed that "these glorious expectations remind us of the golden age of poetry." For perfect happiness "belongs to the imaginary region of philosophy and must be classed with the universal elixir and the philosopher's stone." There will always be jealousies through the unequal gifts of nature and of fortune ; interests will never cease to clash and hatred to ensue; "painful labour, daily subjection, a condition nearly allied to indigence, will always be the lot of numbers"; in art and poetry the sources of novelty will probably be exhausted. But Bentham was far from being a pessimist. Though he believes that "we shall never make this world the abode of happiness," he asserts that it may be made a most delightful garden "compared with the savage forest in which men so long have wandered."[1]

7

The book of Malthus was welcomed at the moment by all those who had been thoroughly frightened by the French Revolution and saw in the "modern philosophy," as it was called, a serious danger to society.[2] Vice and misery and the in-

---

most grave ; the exhaustion of sources of energy necessary for any notable increase of population, or advance in the standards of living, or both combined, is perilously near. The present rate of increase in the world's population cannot continue for four centuries."

[1] *Works*, vol. i. p. 193 *seq.*

[2] Both Hazlitt and Shelley thought that Malthus was playing to the boxes, by sophisms "calculated to lull the oppressors of mankind into a security of everlasting triumph" (*Revolt of Islam*, Preface). Bentham refers in his *Book of Fallacies* (*Works*, ii. p. 462) to the unpopularity of the views of Priestley, Godwin, and Condorcet : "to aim at perfection has been pronounced to be utter folly or wickedness."

exorable laws of population were a godsend to rescue the state from " the precipice of perfectibility." We can understand the alarm occasioned to believers in the established constitution of things, for Godwin's work—now virtually forgotten, while Malthus is still appealed to as a discoverer in social science — produced an immense effect on impressionable minds at the time. All who prized liberty, sympathised with the downtrodden, and were capable of falling in love with social ideals, hailed Godwin as an evangelist. " No one," said a contemporary, " was more talked of, more looked up to, more sought after ; and wherever liberty, truth, justice was the theme, his name was not far off." Young graduates left the Universities to throw themselves at the feet of the new Gamaliel ; students of law and medicine neglected their professional studies to dream of " the renovation of society and the march of mind." Godwin carried with him " all the most sanguine and fearless understandings of the time." [1]

The most famous of his disciples were the poets Wordsworth, Coleridge, Southey, and after-wards Shelley. Wordsworth had been an ardent sympathiser with the French Revolution. In its early days he had visited Paris :

> An emporium then
> Of golden expectations and receiving
> Freights every day from a new world of hope.

He became a Godwinian in 1795, when the Terror had destroyed his faith in Revolutionary France. Southey, who had come under the influence of Rousseau, was initiated by Coleridge into Godwin's theories, and in their utopian enthusiasm they formed

---

[1] Hazlitt, *Spirit of the Age* : article on Godwin (written in 1814).

the design of founding a "pantisocratic" settlement in America, to show how happiness could be realised in a social environment in which duty and interest coincide and consequently all are virtuous. The plan anticipated the experiments of Owen and Cabet; but the pantisocrats did not experience the disappointments of the socialists, for it was never carried out. Coleridge and Southey as well as Wordsworth soon abandoned their Godwinian doctrines.[1] They had, to use a phrase of Hazlitt, lost their way in Utopia, and they gave up the abstract and mechanical view of society which the French philosophy of the eighteenth century taught, for an organic conception in which historic sentiment and the wisdom of our ancestors had their due place. Wordsworth could presently look back and criticise his Godwinian phase as that of

> A proud and most presumptuous confidence
> In the transcendent wisdom of the age
> And its discernment.[2]

He and Southey became conservative pillars of the state. Yet Southey, reactionary as he was in politics, never ceased to believe in social Progress,[3] Amelioration was indeed to be effected by slow and cautious reforms, with the aid of the Church, but the intellectual aberrations of his youth had left an abiding impression.

While these poets were sitting at Godwin's feet,

---

[1] In letters of 1797 and 1798 Coleridge repudiated the French doctrines and Godwin's philosophy. See Cestre, *La Révolution française et les poètes anglais* (1789–1809), pp. 389, 414.

[2] *Excursion*, Book ii.

[3] See his *Colloquies*; and Shelley, writing in 1811, says that Southey "looks forward to a state when all shall be perfected and matter become subjected to the omnipotence of mind" (Dowden, *Life of Shelley*, i. p. 212). Compare below, p. 325.

Shelley was still a child. But he came across *Political Justice* at Eton ; in his later life he re-read it almost every year ; and when he married Godwin's daughter he was more Godwinian than Godwin himself.   Hazlitt, writing in 1814, says that Godwin's reputation had "sunk below the horizon," but Shelley never ceased to believe in his theory, though he came to see that the regeneration of man would be a much slower process than he had at first imagined.   In the immature poem *Queen Mab* the philosophy of Godwin was behind his description of the future, and it was behind the longer and more ambitious poems of his maturer years.   The city of gold, of the *Revolt of Islam*, is Godwin's future society, and he describes that poem as "an experiment on the temper of the public mind as to how far a thirst for a happier condition of moral and political society survives, among the enlightened and refined, the tempests which have shaken the age in which we live."   As to *Prometheus Unbound* his biographer observes :[1]

All the glittering fallacies of " Political Justice "—now sufficiently tarnished—together with all its encouraging and stimulating truths, may be found in the *caput mortuum* left when the critic has reduced the poetry of the " Prometheus " to a series of doctrinaire statements.

The same dream inspired the final chorus of *Hellas*. Shelley was the poet of perfectibility.

8

The attraction of perfectibility reached beyond

[1] Dowden, *ib.* ii. p. 264.   Elsewhere Dowden remarks on the singular insensibility of Shelley's mind "to the wisdom or sentiment of history" (i. p. 55).

the ranks of men of letters, and in Robert Owen, the benevolent millowner of Lanark, it had an apostle who based upon it a very different theory from that of *Political Justice* and became one of the founders of modern socialism.

The success of the idea of Progress has been promoted by its association with socialism.[1] The first phase of socialism, what has been called its sentimental phase, was originated by Saint-Simon in France and Owen in England at about the same time; Marx was to bring it down from the clouds and make it a force in practical politics. But both in its earlier and in its later forms the economical doctrines rest upon a theory of society depending on the assumption, however disguised, that social institutions have been solely responsible for the vice and misery which exist, and that institutions and laws can be so changed as to abolish misery and vice. That is pure eighteenth century doctrine; and it passed from the revolutionary doctrinaires of that period to the constructive socialists of the nineteenth century.

Owen learned it probably from Godwin, and he did not disguise it. His numerous works enforce it *ad nauseam*. He began the propagation of his gospel by his "New View of Society, or Essays on the formation of the human character, preparatory to the development of a plan for gradually ameliorating the condition of mankind," which he

---

[1] The word was independently invented in England and France. An article in the *Poor Man's Guardian* (a periodical edited by H. Hetherington, afterwards by Bronterre O'Brien), Aug. 24, 1833, is signed "A Socialist"; and in 1834 *socialisme* is opposed to individualism by P. Leroux in an article in the *Revue Encyclopédique*. The word is used in the *New Moral World*, and from 1836 was applied to the Owenites. See Dolléans, *Robert Owen* (1907), p. 305.

dedicated to the Prince Regent.[1] Here he lays down that "any general character, from the best to the worst, may be given to any community, even to the world at large, by the application of proper means; which means are to a great extent at the command and under the control of those who have influence in the affairs of men."[2] The string on which he continually harps is that it is the cardinal error in government to suppose that men are responsible for their vices and virtues, and therefore for their actions and characters. These result from education and institutions, and can be transformed automatically by transforming those agencies. Owen founded several short-lived journals to diffuse his theories. The first number of the *New Moral World* (1834–36)[3] proclaimed the approach of an ideal society in which there will be no ignorance, no poverty, and no charity—a system "which will ensure the happiness of the human race throughout all future ages," to replace one "which, so long as it shall be maintained, must produce misery to all." His own experimental attempt to found such a society on a miniature scale in America proved a ludicrous failure.

It is to be observed that in these socialist theories the conception of Progress as indefinite

---

[1] 3rd ed. 1817. The Essays had appeared separately in 1813–14.

[2] P. 19.

[3] This was not a journal, but a series of pamphlets which appeared in 1836–1844. Other publications of Owen were: *Outline of the Rational System of Society* (6th ed., Leeds, 1840); *The Revolution in the Mind and Practice of the Human Race, or the coming change from Irrationality to Rationality* (1849); *The Future of the Human Race, or a great, glorious and peaceful Revolution, near at hand, to be effected through the agency of departed spirits of good and superior men and women* (1853); *The New Existence of Man upon Earth*, Parts i.-viii., 1854–55.

tends to vanish or to lose its significance. If the millennium can be brought about at a stroke by a certain arrangement of society, the goal of development is achieved; we shall have reached the term, and shall have only to live in and enjoy the ideal state—a menagerie of happy men. There will be room for further, perhaps indefinite, advance in knowledge, but civilisation in its social character becomes stable and rigid. Once man's needs are perfectly satisfied in a harmonious environment there is no stimulus to cause further changes, and the dynamic character of history disappears.

Theories of Progress are thus differentiating into two distinct types, corresponding to two radically opposed political theories and appealing to two antagonistic temperaments. The one type is that of constructive idealists and socialists, who can name all the streets and towers of "the city of gold," which they imagine as situated just round a promontory. The development of man is a closed system; its term is known and is within reach. The other type is that of those who, surveying the gradual ascent of man, believe that by the same interplay of forces which have conducted him so far and by a further development of the liberty which he has fought to win, he will move slowly towards conditions of increasing harmony and happiness. Here the development is indefinite; its term is unknown, and lies in the remote future. Individual liberty is the motive force, and the corresponding political theory is liberalism; whereas the first doctrine naturally leads to a symmetrical system in which the authority of the state is preponderant, and the individual has little

more value than a cog in a well-oiled wheel : his
place is assigned ; it is not his right to go his own
way.   Of this type the principal example that is
not socialistic is, as we shall see, the philosophy of
Comte.

CHAPTER XIII

GERMAN SPECULATIONS ON PROGRESS

I

THE philosophical views current in Germany during the period in which the psychology of Locke was in fashion in France and before the genius of Kant opened a new path, were based on the system of Leibnitz. We might therefore expect to find a theory of Progress developed there, parallel to the development in France though resting on different principles. For Leibnitz, as we saw, provided in his cosmic optimism a basis for the doctrine of human Progress, and he had himself incidentally pointed to it. This development, however, was delayed. It was only towards the close of the period—which is commonly known as the age of "Illumination"—that Progress came to the front, and it is interesting to observe the reason.

Wolf was the leading successor and interpreter of Leibnitz. He constrained that thinker's ideas into a compact logical system which swayed Germany till Kant swept it away. In such cases it usually happens that some striking doctrines and tendencies of the master are accentuated and enforced, while others are suffered to drop out of sight.

So it was here. In the Wolfian system, Leibnitz's conception of development was suffered to drop out of sight, and the dynamic element which animated his speculation disappeared. In particular, he had laid down that the sum of motive forces in the physical world is constant. His disciples proceeded to the inference that the sum of morality in the ethical world is constant. This dogma obviously eliminates the possibility of ethical improvement for collective humanity. And so we find Mendelssohn, who was the popular exponent of Wolf's philosophy, declaring that "progress is only for the individual; but that the whole of humanity here below in the course of time shall always progress and perfect itself seems to me not to have been the purpose of Providence."

The publication of the *Nouveaur Essais* in 1765 induced some thinkers to turn from the dry bones of Wolf to the spirit of Leibnitz himself. And at the same time French thought was penetrating. In consequence of these influences the final phase of the German "Illumination" is marked by the appearance of two or three works in which Progress is a predominating idea.

We see this reaction against Wolf and his static school in a little work published by Herder in 1774 —"a philosophy of history for the cultivation of mankind." There is continuous development, he declares, and one people builds upon the work of another. We must judge past ages, not by the present, but relatively to their own particular conditions. What exists now was never possible before, for everything that man accomplishes is conditioned by time, climate, and circumstances.

Six years later Lessing's pamphlet on the *Education of the Human Race* appeared, couched in the form of aphoristic statements, and to a modern reader, one may venture to say, singularly wanting in argumentative force. The thesis is that the drama of history is to be explained as the education of man by a progressive series of religions, a series not yet complete, for the future will produce another revelation to lift him to a higher plane than that to which Christ has drawn him up. This interpretation of history proclaimed Progress, but assumed an ideal and applied a measure very different from those of the French philosophers. The goal is not social happiness, but a full comprehension of God. Philosophy of religion is made the key to the philosophy of history. The work does not amount to more than a suggestion for a new synthesis, but it was opportune and arresting.

Herder meanwhile had been thinking, and in 1784 he gave the German world his survey of man's career—*Ideas of the Philosophy of the History of Humanity*. In this famous work, in which we can mark the influence of French thinkers, especially Montesquieu, as well as of Leibnitz, he attempted, though on very different lines, the same task which Turgot and Condorcet planned, a universal history of civilisation.

The Deity designed the world but never interferes in its process, either in the physical cosmos or in human history. Human history itself, civilisation, is a purely natural phenomenon. Events are strictly enchained; continuity is unbroken; what happened at any given time could have happened only then, and nothing else could have happened. Herder's rigid determinism not only excludes Voltaire's chance but also suppresses the free play of man's intelligent will. Man cannot guide his own destinies; his actions and fortunes are determined by the nature of things, his physical organisation and physical environment. The fact that God exists in inactive ease hardly affects the fatalistic complexion of this philosophy ; but it is perhaps a mitigation that the world was made for man ; humanity is its final cause.

The variety of the phases of civilisation that have appeared on earth is due to the fact that the possible manifestations of human nature are very numerous and that they must all be realised. The lower forms are those in which the best, which means the most human, faculties of our nature are undeveloped. The highest has not yet been realised. "The flower of humanity, captive still in its germ, will blossom out one day into the true form of man like unto God, in a state of which no terrestrial man can imagine the greatness and the majesty."

Herder is not a systematic thinker—indeed his work abounds in contradictions—and he has not made it clear how far this full epiphany results from the experiences of mankind in preceding phases. He believes that life is an education for humanity (he has taken the phrase of Lessing), that good progressively develops, that reason and justice become more powerful. This is a doctrine of Progress, but he distinctly opposes the hypothesis of a final and unique state of perfection as the goal of history, which would imply that earlier generations exist for the sake of the later and suffer in order to ensure the felicity of remote posterity — a theory which offends his sense of justice and fitness. On the

contrary, man can realise happiness equally in every
stage of civilisation. All forms of society are equally
legitimate, the imperfect as well as the perfect; all
are ends in themselves, not mere stages on the way
to something better. And a people which is happy
in one of these inferior states has a perfect right to
remain in it.

Thus the Progress which Herder sees is, to
use his own geometrical illustration, a sequence
of unequal and broken curves, corresponding to
different maxima and minima. Each curve has
its own equation, the history of each people is
subject to the laws of its own environment; but
there is no general law controlling the whole career
of humanity.

Herder brought down his historical survey only
as far as the sixteenth century. It has been suggested [1] that if he had come down further he might
have comprehended the possibility of a deliberate
transformation of societies by the intelligent action
of the human will—an historical force to which he
does not do justice, apparently because he fancied it
incompatible with strict causal sequence. The value
of his work does not lie in the philosophical principles
which he applied. Nor was it a useful contribution
to history; of him it has been said, as of Bossuet,
that facts bent like grass under his feet.[2] But it
was a notable attempt to do for human phenomena
what Leibnitz in his *Theodicy* sought to do for the
cosmos, and it pointed the way to the rationalistic
philosophies of history which were to be a feature
of the speculations of the following century.

[1] Javary, *De l'idée de progrès*, p. 69.
[2] Jouffroy, *Mélanges*, p. 81.

2

The short essay of Kant, which he clumsily called the *Idea of a Universal History on a Cosmopolitical Plan*,[1] approaches the problems raised by the history of civilisation from a new point of view.

He starts with the principle of invariable law. On any theory of free will, he says, human actions are as completely under the control of universal laws of nature as any other physical phenomena. This is illustrated by statistics. Registers of births, deaths, and marriages show that these events occur with as much conformity to laws of nature as the oscillations of the weather.

It is the same with the great sequence of historical events. Taken alone and individually, they seem incoherent and lawless; but viewed in their connection, as due to the action not of individuals but of the human species, they do not fail to reveal "a regular stream of tendency." Pursuing their own often contradictory purposes, individual nations and individual men are unconsciously promoting a process to which if they perceived it they would pay little regard.

Individual men do not obey a law. They do not obey the laws of instinct like animals, nor do they obey, as rational citizens of the world would do, the laws of a preconcerted plan. If we look at the stage of history we see scattered and occasional indications of wisdom, but the general sum of men's actions is "a web of folly, childish vanity, and often even of the idlest wickedness and spirit of destruction."

[1] 1784.

The problem for the philosopher is to discover a meaning in this senseless current of human actions, so that the history of creatures who pursue no plan of their own may yet admit of a systematic form. The clew to this form is supplied by the predispositions of human nature.

I have stated this problem almost in Kant's words, and as he might have stated it if he had not introduced the conception of final causes. His use of the postulate of final causes without justifying it is a defect in his essay. He identifies what he well calls a stream of tendency with "a natural purpose." He makes no attempt to show that the succession of events is such that it cannot be explained without the postulate of a purpose. His solution of the problem is governed by this conception of finality, and by the unwarranted assumption that nature does nothing in vain.

He lays down that all the tendencies to which any creature is predisposed by its nature must in the end be developed perfectly and agreeably to their final purpose. Those predispositions in man which serve the use of his reason are therefore destined to be fully developed. This destiny, however, cannot be realised in the individual; it can only be realised in the species. For reason works tentatively, by progress and regress. Each man would require an inordinate length of time to make a perfect use of his natural tendencies. Therefore, as life is short, an incalculable series of generations is needed.

The means which nature employs to develop these tendencies is the antagonism which in man's social state exists between his gregarious and his antigregarious tendencies. His antigregarious nature expresses itself in the desire to force all things to comply to his own humour.   Hence ambition, love of honour, avarice.   These were necessary to raise mankind from the savage to the civilised state.   But for these antisocial propensities men would be gentle as sheep, and "an Arcadian life would arise, of perfect harmony and mutual love, such as must suffocate and stifle all talents in their very germs." Nature, knowing better than man what is good for the species, ordains discord.   She is to be thanked for competition and enmity, and for the thirst of power and wealth.   For without these the final purpose of realising man's rational nature would remain unfulfilled.   This is Kant's answer to Rousseau.

The full realisation of man's rational nature is possible only in a "universal civil society" founded on political justice.   The establishment of such a society is the highest problem for the human species. Kant contemplates, as the political goal, a confederation of states in which the utmost possible freedom shall be united with the most rigorous determination of the boundaries of freedom.

Is it reasonable to suppose that a universal or cosmopolitical society of this kind will come into being; and if so, how will it be brought about? Political changes in the relations of states are generally produced by war. Wars are tentative endeavours to bring about new relations and to form new political bodies.   Are combinations and re-combinations to continue until by pure chance some rational self-supporting system emerges?   Or is it possible that no such condition of society may ever arrive, and that ultimately all progress may be overwhelmed by a hell of evils?   Or, finally, is Nature pursuing her regulai course of raising the species by its own spontaneous efforts and developing, in the apparently wild succession of events, man's originally implanted tendencies?

Kant accepts the last alternative on the ground that it is not reasonable to assume a final purpose in particular natural processes and at the same time to assume that there is no final purpose in the whole. Thus his theory of Progress depends on the hypothesis of final causes.

It follows that to trace the history of mankind is equivalent to unravelling a hidden plan of Nature for accomplishing a perfect civil constitution for a universal society ; since a universal society is the sole state in which the tendencies of human nature can be fully developed. We cannot determine the orbit of the development, because the whole period is so vast and only a small fraction is known to us, but this is enough to show that there is a definite course.

Kant thinks that such a "cosmopolitical" history, as he calls it, is possible, and that if it were written it would give us a clew opening up "a consolatory prospect into futurity, in which at a remote distance we shall discover the human species seated upon an eminence won by infinite toil, where all the germs are unfolded which nature has implanted and its own destination upon this earth accomplished."

3

But to see the full bearing of Kant's discussion we must understand its connection with his ethics. For his ethical theory is the foundation and the motive of his speculation on Progress. The pro-

gress on which he lays stress is moral amelioration ;
he refers little to scientific or material progress.
For him morality was an absolute obligation
founded in the nature of reason. Such an obligation presupposes an end to be attained, and this
end is a reign of reason under which all men
obeying the moral law mutually treat each other
as ends in themselves. Such an ideal state must
be regarded as possible, because it is a necessary
postulate of reason. From this point of view it
may be seen that Kant's speculation on universal
history is really a discussion whether the ideal state,
which is required as a subjective postulate in the
interest of ethics, is likely to be realised objectively.

Now, Kant does not assert that because our
moral reason must assume the possibility of this
hypothetical goal civilisation is therefore moving
towards it. That would be a fallacy into which
he was incapable of falling. Civilisation is a
phenomenon, and anything we know about it can
only be inferred from experience. His argument
is that there are actual indications of progress in
this desirable direction. He pointed to the contemporary growth of civil liberty and religious
liberty, and these are conditions of moral improvement. So far his argument coincides in principle
with that of French theorists of Progress. But
Kant goes on to apply to these data the debatable
conception of final causes, and to infer a purpose
in the development of humanity. Only this
inference is put forward as a hypothesis, not as a
dogma.

It is probable that what hindered Kant from
broaching his theory of Progress with as much

confidence as Condorcet was his perception that nothing could be decisively affirmed about the course of civilisation until the laws of its movement had been discovered. He saw that this was a matter for scientific investigation. He says expressly that the laws are not yet known, and suggests that some future genius may do for social phenomena what Kepler and Newton did for the heavenly bodies. As we shall see, this is precisely what some of the leading French thinkers of the next generation will attempt to do.

But cautiously though he framed the hypothesis Kant evidently considered Progress probable. He recognised that the most difficult obstacle to the moral advance of man lies in war and the burdens which the possibility of war imposes. And he spent much thought on the means by which war might be abolished. He published a philosophical essay on *Perpetual Peace*, in which he formulated the articles of an international treaty to secure the disappearance of war. He considered that, while a universal republic would be the *positive* ideal, we shall probably have to be contented with what he calls a *negative* substitute, consisting in a federation of peoples bound by a peace-alliance guaranteeing the independence of each member. But to assure the permanence of this system it is essential that each state should have a democratic constitution. For such a constitution is based on individual liberty and civil equality. All these changes should be brought about by legal reforms; revolutions—he was writing in 1795—cannot be justified.

We see the influence of Rousseau's *Social Contract* and that of the Abbé de Saint-Pierre, with whose works Kant was acquainted. There can be little doubt that it was the influence of French thought, so powerful in Germany at this period, that turned Kant's mind towards these speculations, which belong to the latest period of his life and form a sort of appendix to his philosophical system. The theory of Progress, the idea of universal reform, the doctrine of political equality — Kant examined all these conceptions and appropriated them to the service of his own highly metaphysical theory of ethics. In this new association their spirit was changed.

In France, as we saw, the theory of Progress was generally associated with ethical views which could find a metaphysical basis in the sensationalism of Locke. A moral system which might be built on sensation, as the primary mental fact, was worked out by Helvétius. But the principle that the supreme law of conduct is to obey nature had come down as a practical philosophy from Rabelais and Montaigne through Molière to the eighteenth century. It was reinforced by the theory of the natural goodness of man. Jansenism had struggled against it and was defeated. After theology it was the turn of metaphysics. Kant's moral imperative marked the next stage in the conflict of the two opposite tendencies which seek natural and ultra-natural sanctions for morality.

Hence the idea of progress had a different significance for Kant and for its French exponents, though his particular view of the future possibly in store for the human species coincided in some essential points with theirs. But his theory of life gives a different atmosphere to the idea. In

France the atmosphere is emphatically eudaemonic ; happiness is the goal. Kant is an uncompromising opponent of eudaemonism. " If we take enjoyment or happiness as the measure, it is easy," he says, " to evaluate life. Its value is less than nothing. For who would begin one's life again in the same conditions, or even in new natural conditions, if one could choose them oneself, but of which enjoyment would be the sole end ? "

There was, in fact, a strongly-marked vein of pessimism in Kant. One of the ablest men of the younger generation who were brought up on his system founded the philosophical pessimism—very different in range and depth from the sentimental pessimism of Rousseau — which was to play a remarkable part in German thought in the nine-teenth century. Schopenhauer's unpleasant con-clusion that of all conceivable worlds this is the worst, is one of the speculations for which Kant may be held ultimately responsible.

4

Kant's considerations on historical development are an appendix to his philosophy; they are not a necessary part, wrought into the woof of his system. It was otherwise with his successors the Idealists, for whom his system was the point of departure, though they rejected its essential feature, the limitation of human thought. With Fichte and Hegel progressive development was directly deduced from their principles. If their particular interpreta-tions of history have no permanent value, it is significant that, in their ambitious attempts to explain the universe *a priori*, history was conceived as progressive, and their philosophies did much to reinforce a conception which on very different principles was making its way in the world. But the progress which their systems involved was not bound up with the interest of human happiness, but stood out as a fact which, whether agreeable or not, is a consequence of the nature of thought.

The process of the universe, as it appeared to Fichte,[1] tends to a full realisation of "freedom"; that is its end and goal, but a goal that always recedes. It can never be reached; for its full attainment would mean the complete suppression of Nature. The process of the world, therefore, consists in an indefinite approximation to an unattainable ideal: freedom is being perpetually realised more and more; and the world, as it ascends in this direction, becomes more and more a realm of reason.

What Fichte means by freedom may be best explained by its opposition to instinct. A man acting instinctively may be acting quite reasonably, in a way which any one fully conscious of all the implications and consequences of the action would judge to be reasonable. But in order that his actions should be free he must himself be fully conscious of all those implications and consequences.

It follows that the end of mankind upon earth is to reach a state in which all the relations of life shall be ordered according to reason, not instinctively but with full consciousness and deliberate purpose. This end should govern the ethical rules

---

[1] Fichte's philosophy of history will be found in *Die Grundzüge des gegenwärtigen Zeitalters* (1806), lectures which he delivered at Berlin in 1804-5.

of conduct, and it determines the necessary stages of history.

It gives us at once two main periods, the earliest and the latest : the earliest, in which men act reasonably by instinct, and the latest, in which they are conscious of reason and try to realise it fully. But before reaching this final stage they must pass through an epoch in which reason is conscious of itself, but not regnant. And to reach this they must have emancipated themselves from instinct, and this process of emancipation means a fourth epoch. But they could not have wanted to emancipate themselves unless they had felt instinct as a servitude imposed by an external authority, and therefore we have to distinguish yet another epoch wherein reason is expressed in authoritarian institutions to which men blindly submit. In this way Fichte deduces five historical epochs : two in which progress is blind, two in which it is free, and an intermediate in which it is struggling to consciousness.[1] But there are no locked gates between these periods ; they overlap and mingle ; each may have some of the characteristics of another ; and in each there is a vanguard leading the way and a rearguard lagging behind.

At present (1804) we are in the third age ; we have broken with authority, but do not yet possess a clear and disciplined knowledge of reason.[2]

---

[1] *First* Epoch : that of instinctive reason ; the age of innocence. *Second* : that of authoritarian reason. *Third* : that of enfranchisement ; the age of scepticism and unregulated liberty. *Fourth* : that of conscious reason, as science. *Fifth* : that of regnant reason, as art.

[2] Three years later, however, Fichte maintained in his patriotic *Discourses to the German Nation* (1807) that in 1804 man had crossed the threshold of the fourth epoch. He asserted that the progress of " culture " and science will depend henceforward chiefly on Germany.

Fichte has deduced this scheme purely *a priori* without any reference to actual experience. " The philosopher," he says, " follows the *a priori* thread of the world-plan which is clear to him without any history ; and if he makes use of history, it is not to prove anything, since his theses are already proved independently of all history."

Historical development is thus presented as a necessary progress towards a goal which is known but cannot be reached. And this fact as to the destiny of the race constitutes the basis of morality, of which the fundamental law is to act in such a way as to promote the free realisation of reason upon earth. It has been claimed by a recent critic that Fichte was the first modern philosopher to humanise morals. He completely rejected the individualistic conception which underlay Kantian as well as Christian ethics. He asserted that the true motive of morality is not the salvation of the individual man but the Progress of humanity. In fact, with Fichte Progress is the principle of ethics. That the Christian ideal of ascetic saintliness detached from society has no moral value is a plain corollary from the idea of earthly Progress.

One other point in Fichte's survey of history deserves notice—the social *rôle* of the savant. It is the function of the savant to discover the truths which are a condition of moral progress ; he may be said to incarnate reason in the world. We shall see how this idea played a prominent part in the social schemes of Saint-Simon and Comte.

5

Hegel's philosophy of history is better known

than Fichte's.   Like Fichte, he deduced the phases
a priori from his metaphysical principles, but he
condescended to review in some detail the actual
phenomena.   He conceived the final cause of the
world as Spirit's consciousness of its own freedom.
The ambiguous term "freedom" is virtually equivalent to self-consciousness, and Hegel defines
Universal History as the description of the process
by which Spirit or God comes to the consciousness of its own meaning.   This freedom does not
mean that Spirit could choose at any moment to
develop in a different way; its actual development
is necessary and is the embodiment of reason.
Freedom consists in fully recognising the fact.

Of the particular features which distinguish
Hegel's treatment, the first is that he identifies
"history" with political history, the development of
the state.   Art, religion, philosophy, the creations
of social man, belong to a different and higher stage
of Spirit's self-revelation.[1]   In the second place,
Hegel ignores the primitive prehistoric ages of man,
and sets the beginning of his development in the
fully-grown civilisation of China.   He conceives
the Spirit as continually moving from one nation to
another in order to realise the successive stages of
its self-consciousness : from China to India, from
India to the kingdoms of Western Asia ; then from
the Orient to Greece, then to Rome, and finally to
the Germanic world.   In the East men knew only
that *one* is free, the political characteristic was
despotism ; in Greece and Rome they knew that
some are free, and the political forms were aristocracy

---

[1] The three phases of Spirit are (1) subjective ; (2) objective ; (3) absolute.
Psychology, *e.g.*, is included in (1), law and history in (2), religion in (3).

and democracy; in the modern world they know that *all* are free, and the political form is monarchy. The first period. he compared to childhood, the second to youth (Greece) and manhood (Rome), the third to old age, old but not feeble. The third, which includes the medieval and modern history of Europe, designated by Hegel as the Germanic world—for "the German spirit is the spirit of the modern world"—is also the final period. In it God realises his freedom completely in history, just as in Hegel's own absolute philosophy, which is final, God has completely understood his own nature.

And here is the most striking difference between the theories of Fichte and Hegel. Both saw the goal of human development in the realisation of "freedom," but, while with Fichte the development never ends as the goal is unattainable, with Hegel the development is already complete, the goal is not only attainable but has now been attained. Thus Hegel's is what we may call a closed system. History has been progressive, but no path is left open for further advance. Hegel views this con-clusion of development with perfect complacency. To most minds that are not intoxicated with the Absolute it will seem that, if the present is the final state to which the evolution of Spirit has conducted, the result is singularly inadequate to the gigantic process. But his system is eminently inhuman. The happiness or misery of individuals is a matter of supreme indifference to the Absolute, which, in order to realise itself in time, ruthlessly sacrifices sentient beings.

The spirit of Hegel's philosophy, in its bearing

on social life, was thus antagonistic to Progress as a practical doctrine. Progress there had been, but Progress had done its work; the Prussian monarchical state was the last word in history. Kant's cosmopolitical plan, the liberalism and individualism which were implicit in his thought, the democracies which he contemplated in the future, are all cast aside as a misconception. Once the needs of the Absolute Spirit have been satisfied, when it has seen its full power and splendour revealed in the Hegelian philosophy, the world is as good as it can be. Social amelioration does not matter, nor the moral improvement of men, nor the increase of their control over physical forces.

6

The other great representative of German idealism, who took his departure from Kant, also saw in history a progressive revelation of divine reason. But it was the processes of nature, not the career of humanity, that absorbed the best energies of Schelling, and the elaboration of a philosophical idea of organic evolution was the prominent feature of his speculation. His influence—and it was wide, reaching even scientific biologists—lay chiefly in diffusing this idea, and he thus contributed to the formation of a theory which was afterwards to place the idea of Progress on a more imposing base.

Schelling influenced, among others, his contemporary Krause, a less familiar name, who worked out a philosophy of history in which this idea is fundamental. Krause conceived history, which is the expression of the Absolute, as the development of life; society as an organism; and social growth as a process which can be deduced from abstract biological principles.

All these transcendent speculations had this in common that they pretended to discover the necessary course of human history on metaphysical principles, independent of experience. But it has been rightly doubted whether this alleged independence was genuine. We may question whether any of them would have produced the same sequence of periods of history, if the actual facts of history had been to them a sealed book. Indeed we may be sure that they were surreptitiously and subconsciously using experience as a guide, while they imagined that abstract principles were entirely responsible for their conclusions. And this is equivalent to saying that their ideas of progressive movement were really derived from that idea of Progress which the French thinkers of the eighteenth century had attempted to base on experience.

The influence, direct and indirect, of these German philosophers reached far beyond the narrow circle of the bacchants or even the wandbearers of idealism. They did much to establish the notion of progressive development as a category of thought, almost as familiar and indispensable as that of cause and effect. They helped to diffuse the idea of "an increasing purpose" in history. Augustine or Bossuet might indeed have spoken of an increasing purpose, but the "purpose" of their speculations was subsidiary to a future life. The purpose of the German idealists could be fulfilled in earthly conditions and required no theory of personal immortality.

This atmosphere of thought affected even in-

telligent reactionaries who wrote in the interest
of orthodox Christianity and the Catholic Church.
Progressive development is admitted in the lectures
on the *Philosophy of History* of Friedrich von
Schlegel.[1] He denounced Condorcet, and opposed
to perfectibility the corruptible nature of man.   But
he asserted that the philosophy of history is to
be found in "the principles of social progress."[2]
These principles are three : the hidden ways of
Providence emancipating the human race ; the
freewill of man ; and the power which God permits
to the agents of evil,—principles which Bossuet
could endorse, but the novelty is that here they are
arrayed as forces of Progress.   In fact, the point
of von Schlegel's pretentious, unilluminating book
is to rehabilitate Christianity by making it the key
to that new conception of life which had taken
shape among the enemies of the Church.

7

As biological development was one of the
constant preoccupations of Goethe, whose doctrine
of metamorphosis and "types" helped to prepare
the way for the evolutionary hypothesis, we might
have expected to find him interested in theories
of social progress, in which theories of biological
development find a logical extension.   But the
French speculations on Progress did not touch
his imagination ; they left him cool and sceptical.
Towards the end of his life, in conversation with
Eckermann, he made some remarks which indicate
his attitude.[3]

---

[1] Translated into English in 2 vols., 1835.
[2] *Op. cit* ii. p. 194, *sqq.*
[3] *Gespräche mit Goethe*, 23 Oktober 1828.

" 'The world will not reach its goal so quickly as we think and wish. The retarding demons are always there, intervening and resisting at every point, so that, though there is an advance on the whole, it is very slow. Live longer and you will find that I am right.'

" 'The development of humanity,' said Eckermann, 'appears to be a matter of thousands of years.'

" 'Who knows?' Goethe replied, 'perhaps of millions. But let humanity last as long as it will, there will always be hindrances in its way, and all kinds of distress, to make it develop its powers. Men will become more clever and discerning, but not better nor happier nor more energetic, at least except for limited periods. I see the time coming when God will take no more pleasure in the race, and must again proceed to a rejuvenated creation. I am sure that this will happen and that the time and hour in the distant future are already fixed for the beginning of this epoch of rejuvenation. But that time is certainly a long way off, and we can still for thousands and thousands of years enjoy ourselves on this dear old playing-ground, just as it is.' "

That is at once a plain rejection of perfectibility, and an opinion that intellectual development is no highroad to the gates of a golden city.

CHAPTER XIV

CURRENTS OF THOUGHT IN FRANCE AFTER
THE REVOLUTION

I

THE failure of the Revolution to fulfil the visionary hopes which had dazzled France for a brief
period—a failure intensified by the horrors that
had attended the experiment — was followed by
a reaction against the philosophical doctrines and
tendencies which had inspired its leaders. Forces,
which the eighteenth century had underrated or
endeavoured to suppress, emerged in a new shape,
and it seemed for a while as if the new century
might definitely turn its back on its predecessor.
There was an intellectual rehabilitation of Catholicism,
which will always be associated with the names of
four thinkers of exceptional talent, Chateaubriand,
De Maistre, Bonald, and Lamennais.

But the outstanding fame of these great reactionaries must not mislead us into exaggerating
the reach of this reaction. The spirit and tendencies
of the past century still persisted in the circles
which were most permanently influential. Many
eminent savants who had been imbued with the
ideas of Condillac and Helvétius, and had taken

part in the Revolution and survived it, were active under the Empire and the restored Monarchy, still true to the spirit of their masters, and commanding influence by the value of their scientific work. M. Picavet's laborious researches into the activities of this school of thinkers has helped us to understand the transition from the age of Condorcet to the age of Comte. The two central figures are Cabanis, the friend of Condorcet,[1] and Destutt de Tracy. M. Picavet has grouped around them, along with many obscurer names, the great scientific men of the time, like Laplace, Bichat, Lamarck, as all in the direct line of eighteenth century thought. " Ideologists " he calls them.[2]   Ideology, the science of ideas, was the word invented by de Tracy to distinguish the investigation of thought in accordance with the methods of Locke and Condillac from old-fashioned metaphysics. The guiding principle of the ideologists was to apply reason to observed facts and eschew *a priori* deductions.   Thinkers of this school had an influential organ, the *Décade philosophique*, of which J. B. Say the economist was one of the founders in 1794. The Institut, which had been established by the Convention, was crowded with " ideologists," and may be said to have continued the work of the Encyclopaedia.[3] These men had a firm faith in the indefinite progress of knowledge, general enlightenment, and " social reason."

[1] He has already claimed our notice, above, p. 215.

[2] Ideology is now sometimes used to convey a criticism ; for instance, to contrast the methods of Lamarck with those of Darwin.

[3] Picavet, *op. cit.* p. 69.   The members of the 2nd Class of the Institut, that of moral and political science, were so predominantly Ideological that the distrust of Napoleon was excited, and he abolished it in 1803, distributing its members among the other Classes.

2

Thus the ideas of the "sophists" of the age of Voltaire were alive in the speculative world, notwithstanding political, religious, and philosophical reaction. But their limitations were to be transcended, and account taken of facts and aspects which their philosophy had ignored or minimised. The value of the reactionary movement lay in pressing these facts and aspects on the attention, in reopening chambers of the human spirit which the age of Voltaire had locked and sealed.

The idea of Progress was particularly concerned in the general change of attitude, intellectual and emotional, towards the Middle Ages. A fresh interest in the great age of the Church was a natural part of the religious revival, but extended far beyond the circle of ardent Catholics. It was a characteristic feature, as every one knows, of the Romantic movement. It did not affect only creative literature, it occupied speculative thinkers and stimulated historians. For Guizot, Michelet, and Auguste Comte, as well as for Chateaubriand and Victor Hugo, the Middle Ages have a significance which Frenchmen of the previous generation could hardly have comprehended.

We saw how that period had embarrassed the first pioneers who attempted to trace the course of civilisation as a progressive movement, how lightly they passed over it, how unconvincingly they explained it away. At the beginning of the nineteenth century the medieval question was posed in such a way that any one who undertook to develop the doctrine of Progress would have to explore it more seriously. Madame de Staël saw this when she wrote her book on *Literature considered in its Relation to Social Institutions* (1801). She was then under the influence of Condorcet and an ardent believer in perfectibility, and the work is an attempt to extend this theory, which she testifies was falling into discredit, to the realm of literature. She saw that, if man regressed instead of progressing for ten centuries, the case for Progress was gravely compromised, and she sought to show that the Middle Ages contributed to the development of the intellectual faculties and to the expansion of civilisation, and that the Christian religion was an indispensable agent. This contention that Progress was uninterrupted is an advance on Condorcet and an anticipation of Saint-Simon and Comte.

A more eloquent and persuasive voice was raised in the following year from the ranks of reaction. Chateaubriand's *Génie du Christianisme* appeared in 1802, "amidst the ruins of our temples," as the author afterwards said, when France was issuing from the chaos of her revolution. It was a declaration of war against the spirit of the eighteenth century which had treated Christianity as a barbarous system whose fall was demanded in the name of Progress. But it was much more than polemic. Chateaubriand arrayed arguments in support of orthodox dogmas, original sin, primitive degeneration, and the rest ; but the appeal of the book did not lie in its logic, it lay in the appreciation of Christianity from a new point of view. He approached it in the spirit of an artist, as an aesthete, not as a philosopher, and so far as he proved anything he proved that Christianity is valuable because

it is beautiful, not because it is true.   He aimed at
showing that it can "enchanter l'âme aussi divine-
ment que les dieux de Virgile et d'Homère."   He
might call to his help the Fathers of the Church,
but it was on Dante, Milton, Racine that his case
was really based.   The book is an apologia, from
the aesthetic standpoint of the Romantic school.
"Dieu ne défend pas les routes fleuries quand elles
servent à revenir à lui."

It was a matter of course that the defender of
original sin should reject the doctrine of perfectibility.   "When man attains the highest point of
civilisation," wrote Chateaubriand in the vein of
Rousseau, "he is on the lowest stair of morality ; if
he is free, he is rude ; by civilising his manners, he
forges himself chains.   His heart profits at the
expense of his head, his head at the expense of his
heart."   And, apart from considerations of Christian
doctrine, the question of Progress had little interest
for the Romantic school.   Victor Hugo, in the
famous Preface to his *Cromwell* (1827), where he
went more deeply than Chateaubriand into the
contrasts between ancient and modern art, revived
the old likeness of mankind to an individual man,
and declared that classical antiquity was the time of
its virility and that we are now spectators of its
imposing old age.

From other points of view powerful intellects
were reverting to the Middle Ages and eager to
blot out the whole development of modern society
since the Reformation, as the Encyclopaedic philosophers had wished to blot out the Middle Ages.
The ideal of Bonald, De Maistre, and Lamennais
 was a sacerdotal government of the world, and the

English constitution was hardly less offensive to
their minds than the Revolution which De Maistre
denounced as "satanic."   Advocates as they were
of the dead system of theocracy, they contributed,
however, to the advance of thought, not only by
forcing medieval institutions on the notice of the
world but also by their perception that society had
been treated in the eighteenth century in too
mechanical a way, that institutions grow, that the
conception of individual men divested of their life in
society is a misleading abstraction.   They put this
in extravagant and untenable forms, but there was a
large measure of truth in their criticism, which did
its part in helping the nineteenth century to revise
and transcend the results of eighteenth century
speculation.

In this reactionary literature we can see the
struggle of the doctrine of Providence, declining
before the doctrine of Progress, to gain the upper-
hand again.   Chateaubriand, Bonald, De Maistre,
Lamennais firmly held the dogma of an original
golden age and the degradation of man, and denounced the whole trend of progressive thought
from Bacon to Condorcet.   These writers were unconsciously helping Condorcet's doctrine to assume
a new and less questionable shape.

3

Along with the discovery of the Middle Ages
came the discovery of German literature.   In the
intellectual commerce between the two countries in
the age of Frederick the Great, France had been
exclusively the giver, Germany the recipient.   It
was due, above all, to Madame de Staël that the

tide began to flow the other way. Among the
writers of the Napoleonic epoch, Madame de Staël
is easily first in critical talent and intellectual breadth.
Her study of the Revolution showed a more dis-
passionate appreciation of that convulsion than any
of her contemporaries were capable of forming.
But her *chef-d'œuvre* is her study of Germany, *De
l'Allemagne*,[1] which revealed the existence of a
world of art and thought, unsuspected by the French
public.   Within the next twenty years Herder and
Lessing, Kant and Hegel were exerting their influence at Paris.   She did in France what Coleridge
was doing in England for the knowledge of German
thought.

Madame de Staël had raised anew the question
which had been raised in the seventeenth century
and answered in the negative by Voltaire: is there
progress in aesthetic literature?   Her early book
on *Literature* had clearly defined the issue.   She
did not propose the thesis that there is any progress
or improvement (as some of the Moderns had contended in the famous Quarrel) in artistic form.
Within the limits of their own thought and emotional
experience the ancients achieved perfection of expression, and perfection cannot be surpassed.   But
as thought progresses, as the sum of ideas increases
and society changes, fresh material is supplied to
art, there is "a new development of sensibility"
which enables literary artists to compass new kinds
of charm.   The *Génie du Christianisme* embodied a
commentary on her contention, more arresting than
any she could herself have furnished.   Here the
reactionary joined hands with the disciple of

---

[1] A.D. 1813.

Condorcet, to prove that there is progress in the domain of art. Madame de Staël's masterpiece, *Germany*, was a further impressive illustration of the thesis that the literature of the modern European nations represents an advance on classical literature, in the sense that it sounds notes which the Greek and Roman masters had not heard, reaches depths which they had not conjectured, unlocks chambers which to them were closed,— as a result of the progressive experiences of the human soul.[1]

This view is based on the general propositions that all social phenomena closely cohere and that literature is a social phenomenon ; from which it follows that if there is a progressive movement in society generally, there is a progressive movement in literature. Her books were true to the theory ; they inaugurated the methods of modern criticism, which studies literary works in relation to the social background of their period.

4

France, then, under the Bourbon Restoration began to seek new light from the obscure profundities of German speculation which Madame de Staël proclaimed. Herder's *Ideas* were translated by Edgar Quinet, Lessing's *Education* by Eugène Rodrigues. Cousin sat at the feet of Hegel. At the same time a new master, full of suggestiveness for those who were interested in the philosophy of

---

[1] We can see the effect of her doctrine in Guizot's remarks (*Histoire de la civilisation en Europe*, 2ᵉ leçon) where he says of modern literatures that " sous le point de vue du fond des sentiments et des idées elles sont plus fortes et plus riches [than the ancient]. On voit que l'âme humaine a été remuée sur un plus grand nombre de points à une plus grande profondeur " —and to this very fact he ascribes their comparative imperfection in form.

history, was discovered in Italy.   The *Scienza nuova* of Vico was translated by Michelet.

The book of Vico was now a hundred years old. I did not mention him in his chronological place, because he exercised no immediate influence on the world.   His thought was an anachronism in the eighteenth century, it appealed to the nineteenth. He did not announce or conceive any theory of Progress, but his speculation, bewildering enough and confused in its exposition, contained principles which seemed predestined to form the basis of such a doctrine.   His aim was that of Cabanis and the ideologists, to set the study of society on the same basis of certitude which had been secured for the study of nature through the work of Descartes and Newton.

His fundamental idea was that the explanation of the history of societies is to be found in the human mind.   The world at first is felt rather than thought ; this is the condition of savages in the state of nature, who have no political organisation. The second mental state is imaginative knowledge, "poetical wisdom" ; to this corresponds the higher barbarism of the heroic age.   Finally, comes conceptual knowledge, and with it the age of civilisation.   These are the three stages through which every society passes, and each of these types determines law, institutions, language, literature, and the characters of men.

Vico's strenuous researches in the study of Homer and early Roman history were undertaken in order to get at the point of view of the heroic age.   He insisted that it could not be understood unless we transcended our own abstract ways of thinking and looked at the world with primitive eyes, by a forced effort of imagination. He was convinced that history had been vitiated by the habit of ignoring psychological differences, by the failure to recapture the ancient point of view. Here he was far in advance of his own times.

Concentrating his attention above all on Roman antiquity, he adopted—not altogether advantageously for his system—the revolutions of Roman history as the typical rule of social development. The succession of aristocracy (for the early kingship of Rome and Homeric royalty are merely forms of aristocracy in Vico's view), democracy, and monarchy is the necessary sequence of political governments. Monarchy (the Roman Empire) corresponds to the highest form of civilisation. What happens when this is reached? Society declines into an anarchical state of nature, from which it again passes into a higher barbarism or heroic age, to be followed once more by civilisation. The dissolution of the Roman Empire and the barbarian invasions are followed by the Middle Ages, in which Dante plays the part of Homer; and the modern period with its strong monarchies corresponds to the Roman Empire. This is Vico's principle of reflux. If the theory were sound, it would mean that the civilisation of his day must again relapse into barbarism and the cycle begin again. He did not himself state this conclusion directly or venture on any prediction.

It is obvious how readily his doctrine could be adapted to the conception of Progress as a spiral movement. Evidently the corresponding periods in his cycles are not identical or really homogeneous. Whatever points of likeness may be discovered between early Greek or Roman and medieval societies, the points of unlikeness are still more numerous and manifest. Modern civilisation differs in fundamental and far-reaching ways from Greek and Roman. It is absurd to pretend that the general movement brings man back again and again to the point from which he started, and therefore, if there is any value in Vico's reflux, it can only mean that the movement of society may be regarded as a spiral ascent, so that each stage of an upward progress corresponds, in certain general aspects, to a stage which has already been traversed, this correspondence being due to the psychical nature of man.

A conception of this kind could not be appreciated in Vico's day or by the next generation. The *Scienza nuova* lay in Montesquieu's library, and he made no use of it. But it was natural that it should arouse interest in France at a time when the new idealistic philosophies of Germany were attracting attention, and when Frenchmen, of the ideological school, were seeking, like Vico himself, a synthetic principle to explain social phenomena. Different though Vico was in his point of departure as in his methods from the German idealists, his speculations nevertheless had something in common with theirs. Both alike explained history by the nature of mind which necessarily determined the stages of the process ; Vico as little as Fichte or Hegel took eudaemonic considerations into account. The difference was that the German thinkers sought their principle in logic and applied it *a priori*, while Vico sought his in concrete psychology and engaged in laborious research to establish it *a posteriori* by the actual data of history.

But both speculations suggested that the course of human development corresponds to the fundamental character of mental processes and is not diverted either by Providential intervention or by free acts of human will.

5

These foreign influences co-operated in determining the tendencies of French speculation in the period of the restored monarchy, whereby the idea of Progress was placed on new basements and became the headstone of new "religions." Before we consider the founders of sects, we may glance briefly at the views of some eminent savants who had gained the ear of the public before the July Revolution—Jouffroy, Cousin, and Guizot.

Cousin, the chief luminary in the sphere of pure philosophy in France in the first half of the nineteenth century, drew his inspiration from Germany. He was professedly an eclectic, but in the main his philosophy was Hegelian. He might endow God with consciousness and speak of Providence, but he regarded the world-process as a necessary evolution of thought, and he saw, not in religion but in philosophy, the highest expression of civilisation. In 1828 he delivered a course of lectures on the philosophy of history. He divided history into three periods, each governed by a master idea: the first by the idea of the infinite (the Orient); the second by that of the finite (classical antiquity); the third by that of the relation of finite to infinite (the modern age). As with Hegel, the future is ignored, progress is confined within a closed system, the highest circle has already been reached.

As an opponent of the ideologists and the sensational philosophy on which they founded their speculations, Cousin appealed to the orthodox and all those to whom Voltairianism was an accursed thing, and for a generation he exercised a considerable influence. But his work—and this is the important point for us—helped to diffuse the idea, which the ideologists were diffusing on very different lines — that human history has been a progressive development.

Progressive development was also the theme of Jouffroy in his slight but suggestive introduction to the philosophy of history (1825),[1] in which he posed the same problem which, as we shall see, Saint-Simon and Comte were simultaneously attempting to solve. He had not fallen under the glamour of German idealism, and his results have more affinity with Vico's than with Hegel's.

He begins with some simple considerations which conduct to the doubtful conclusion that all the historical changes in man's condition are due to the operation of his intelligence. The historian's business is to trace the succession of the actual changes. The business of the philosopher of history is to trace the succession of ideas and study the correspondence between the two developments. This is the true philosophy of history : "the glory of our age is to understand it."

Now it is admitted to-day, he says, that the human intelligence obeys invariable laws, so that a further problem remains. The actual succession of ideas has to be deduced from these necessary laws.

---

[1] " Réflexions sur la philosophie de l'histoire," in *Mélanges philosophiques*, 2nd edition, 1838.

When that deduction is effected—a long time hence—history will disappear; it will be merged in science.

Jouffroy then presented the world with what he calls the *fatality of intellectual development*, to take the place of Providence or Destiny. It is a fatality, he is careful to explain, which, so far from compromising, presupposes individual liberty. For it is not like the fatality of sensual impulse which guides the brute creation. What it implies is this: if a thousand men have the same idea of what is good, this idea will govern their conduct in spite of their passions, because, being reasonable and free, they are not blindly submissive to passion, but can deliberate and choose.

This explanation of history as a necessary development of society corresponding to a necessary succession of ideas differs in two important points from the explanations of Hegel and Cousin. The succession of ideas is not conceived as a transcendent logic, but is determined by the laws of the *human* mind and belongs to the domain of psychology. Here Jouffroy is on the same ground as Vico. In the second place, it is not a closed system; room remains for an indefinite development in the future.

6

While Cousin was discoursing on philosophy at Paris in the days of the last Bourbon king, Guizot was drawing crowded audiences to his lectures on the history of European civilisation,[1] and the keynote of these lectures was Progress. He

[1] *Histoire de la civilisation en Europe.*

approached it with a fresh mind, unencumbered with any of the philosophical theories which had attended and helped its growth.

Civilisation, he said, is the supreme fact so far as man is concerned, "the fact *par excellence*, the general and definite fact in which all other facts merge." And "civilisation" means progress or development. The word "awakens, when it is pronounced, the idea of a people which is in motion, not to change its place but to change its state, a people whose condition is expanding and improving. The idea of progress, development, seems to me to be the fundamental idea contained in the word *civilisation*."

There we have the most important positive idea of eighteenth century speculation, standing forth detached and independent, no longer bound to a system. Fifty years before, no one would have dreamed of defining civilisation like that and counting on the immediate acquiescence of his audience.

But progress has to be defined. It does not merely imply the improvement of social relations and public well-being. France in the seventeenth and eighteenth centuries was behind Holland and England in the sum and distribution of well-being among individuals, and yet she can claim that she was the most "civilised" country in those ages. The reason is that civilisation also implies the development of the individual life, of men's private faculties, sentiments, and ideas. The progress of man therefore includes both these developments. But they are intimately connected. We may observe how moral reformers generally recommend their proposals by promising social amelioration as a result, and that progressive politicians maintain that the progress of society necessarily induces moral improvement. The connection may not always be apparent, and at different times one or other kind of progress predominates. But one is followed by the other ultimately, though it may be after a long interval, for " la Providence a ses aises dans le temps." The rise of Christianity was one of the crises of civilisation, yet it did not in its early stages aim at any improvement of social conditions; it did not attack the great injustices which were wrought in the world. It meant a great crisis because it changed the beliefs and sentiments of individuals; social effects came afterwards.

The civilisation of modern Europe has grown through a period of fifteen centuries and is still progressing. The rate of progress has been slower than that of Greek civilisation, but on the other hand it has been continuous, uninterrupted, and we can see "the vista of an immense career."

The effects of Guizot's doctrine in propagating the idea of Progress were all the greater for its divorce from philosophical theory. He did not touch perplexing questions like fatality, or discuss the general plan of the world ; he did not attempt to rise above common-sense; and he did not essay any premature scheme of the universal history of man. His masterly survey of the social history of Europe exhibited progressive movement as a fact, in a period in which to the thinkers of the eighteenth century it had been almost invisible. This of course was far from proving that Progress is the key to the history of the world and human destinies. The equation of civilisation with progress remains an assumption. For the question at once arises : Can civilisation reach a state of equilibrium from which no further advance is possible ; and if it can, does it cease to be civilisation ? Is Chinese civilisation mis-called, or has there been here too a progressive movement all the time, however slow? Such questions were not raised by Guizot. But his view of history was effective in helping to establish the association of the two ideas of civilisation and progress, which to-day is taken for granted as evidently true.

7

The views of these eminent thinkers Cousin, Jouffroy, and Guizot show that—quite apart from the doctrines of ideologists and of the " positivists," Saint-Simon and Comte, of whom I have still to speak — there was a common trend in French thought in the Restoration period towards the conception of history as a progressive movement. Perhaps there is no better illustration of the infectiousness of this conception than in the *Historical Studies* which Chateaubriand gave to the world in 1831. He had learned much, from books as well as from politics, since he wrote the *Genius of Christianity*. He had gained some acquaintance with German philosophy and with Vico. And in this work of his advanced age he accepts the idea of Progress, so far as it could be accepted by an orthodox son of the Church. He believes that the advance of knowledge will lead to social progress, and that society, if it seems sometimes to move backward, is always really moving forward. Bossuet, for whom he had no word of criticism thirty years before, he now convicts of "an imposing error." That great man, he writes, "has confined historical events in a circle as rigorous as his genius. He has imprisoned them in an inflexible Christianity—a terrible hoop in which the human race would turn in a sort of eternity, without progress or improvement." The admission from such a quarter shows eloquently how the wind was setting.

The notions of development and continuity which were to control all departments of historical study in the later nineteenth century were at the same time being independently promoted by the young historical school in Germany which is associated with the names of Eichhorn, Savigny, and Niebuhr. Their view that laws and institutions are a natural growth or the expression of a people's mind, represents another departure from the ideas of the eighteenth century. It was a repudiation of that "universal reason" which desired to reform the world and its peoples indiscriminately without taking any account of their national histories.

CHAPTER XV

AMID the intellectual movements in France described in the last chapter the idea of Progress passed into a new phase of its growth. Hitherto it had been a vague optimistic doctrine which encouraged the idealism of reformers and revolutionaries, but could not guide them. It had waited like a handmaid on the abstractions of Nature and Reason ; it had hardly realised an independent life. The time had come for systematic attempts to probe its meaning and definitely to ascertain the direction in which humanity is moving. Kant had said that a Kepler or a Newton was needed to find the law of the movement of civilisation. Several Frenchmen now undertook to solve the problem. They did not solve it ; but the new science of sociology was founded ; and the idea of Progress, which presided at its birth, has been its principal problem ever since.

I

The three thinkers who claimed to have discovered the secret of social development had also in view the practical object of remoulding society on

general scientific principles, and they became the
founders of sects, Fourier, Saint-Simon, and Comte.
They all announced a new era of development as
a necessary sequel of the past, an inevitable and
desirable stage in the march of humanity, and
delineated its features.

Comte was the successor of Saint-Simon, as
Saint-Simon himself was the successor of Condorcet.
Fourier stands quite apart. He claimed that he
broke entirely new ground, and acknowledged no
masters. He regarded himself as a Newton for
whom no Kepler or Galileo had prepared the way.
The most important and sanest part of his work was
the scheme for organising society on a new principle
of industrial co-operation. His general theory of
the universe and man's destinies which lay behind
his practical plans is so fantastic that it sounds like
the dream of a lunatic. Yet many accepted it as the
apocalypse of an evangelist.

Fourier was moved by the far-reaching effects of
Newton's discovery to seek a law which would co-
ordinate facts in the moral world as the principle of
gravitation had co-ordinated facts in the physical
world, and in 1808 he claimed to have found the
secret in what he called the law of Passional
Attraction.[1] The human passions have hitherto
been sources of misery; the problem for man is to
make them sources of happiness. If we know the
law which governs them, we can make such changes
in our environment that none of the passions will
need to be curbed, and the free indulgence of one

---

[1] *Théorie des quatre mouvements et des destinées générales.* General
accounts of his theories will be found in *Charles Fourier, sa vie et sa théorie*,
by his disciple Dr. Ch. Pellarin (2nd ed., 1843), and in Flint, *Hist. of
Philosophy of History in France*, etc., pp. 408 *sqq.*

will not hinder or compromise the satisfaction of the others.

His worthless law for harmonising the passions without restraining them need not detain us. The structure of society, by which he proposed to realise the benefits of his discovery, was based on co-opera-tion, but was not socialistic. The family as a social unit was to be replaced by a larger unit (*phalange*), economically self-sufficing, and consisting of about 1800 persons, who were to live together in a vast building (*phalansère*), surrounded by a domain sufficient to produce all they required. Private property is not abolished; the community will include both rich and poor; all the products of their work are distributed in shares according to the labour, talents, and capital of each member, but a fixed minimum is assured to every one. The scheme was actually tried on a small scale near the forest of Rambouillet in 1832.

This transformation of society, which is to have the effect of introducing harmony among the passions, will mark the beginning of a new epoch. The duration of man's earthly career is 81,000 years, of which 5000 have elapsed. He will now enter upon a long period of increasing harmony, which will be followed by an equal period of decline—like the way up and the way down of Heraclitus. His brief past, the age of his infancy, has been marked by a decline of happiness leading to the present age of "civilisation" which is thoroughly bad—here we see the influence of Rousseau—and from it Fourier's discovery is the clue to lead humanity forth into the epoch in which harmony begins to emerge. But men who have lived in the bad ages need not be

pitied, and those who live to-day need not be
pessimistic.   For Fourier believed in metem-
psychosis, and could tell you, as if he were the
private secretary of the Deity calculating the
arithmetical details of the cosmic plan, how many
very happy, tolerably happy, and unhappy lives fall
to the lot of each soul during the whole 81,000
years.   Nor does the prospect end with the life of
the earth.   The soul of the earth and the human
souls attached to it will live again in comets, planets,
and suns, on a system of which Fourier knew all
the particulars.[1]

These silly speculations would not deserve even
this slight indication of their purport were it not
that Fourier founded a sect and had a considerable
body of devoted followers.   His "discovery" was
acclaimed by Béranger :

> Fourier nous dit : Sors de la fange,
>   Peuple en proie aux déceptions,
> Travaille, groupé par phalange,
>   Dans un cercle d'attractions ;
> La terre, après tant de désastres,
>   Forme avec le ciel un hymen,
> Et la loi qui régit les astres,
>   Donne la paix au genre humain.

Ten years after his death (1837) an English writer
tells us that "the social theory of Fourier is at the
present moment engrossing the attention and exciting
the apprehensions of thinking men, not only in
France but in almost every country in Europe."
Grotesque as was the theoretical background of his
doctrines, he helped to familiarise the world with
the idea of indefinite Progress.

[1] Details will be found in the *Théorie de l'unité universelle*, originally
published under the title *Association domestique-agricole* in 1822.

2

" The imagination of poets has placed the golden age in the cradle of the human race. It was the age of iron they should have banished there. The golden age is not behind us, but in front of us. It is the perfection of social order. Our fathers have not seen it; our children will arrive there one day, and it is for us to clear the way for them."

The Comte de Saint-Simon, who wrote these words in 1814, was one of the liberal nobles who had imbibed the ideas of the Voltairian age and sympathised with the spirit of the Revolution. In his literary career from 1803 to his death in 1825 he passed through several phases of thought,[1] but his chief masters were always Condorcet and the physiologists, from whom he derived his two guiding ideas that ethics and politics depend ultimately on physics and that history is progress.

Condorcet had interpreted history by the progressive movement of knowledge. That, Saint-Simon said, is the true principle, but Condorcet applied it narrowly, and committed two errors. He did not understand the social import of religion, and he represented the Middle Ages as a useless interruption of the forward movement. Here Saint-Simon learned from the religious reaction. He saw that religion has a natural and legitimate social *rôle* and cannot be eliminated as a mere perversity. He expounded the doctrine that all social phenomena cohere. A religious system, he said, always corresponds to the stage of science which the society

---

[1] They are traced in G. Weill's valuable monograph, *Saint-Simon et son œuvre*, 1894.

wherein it appears has reached; in fact, religion is merely science clothed in a form suitable to the emotional needs which it satisfies. And as a religious system is based on the contemporary phase of scientific development, so the political system of an epoch corresponds to the religious system. They all hang together. Medieval Europe does not represent a temporary triumph of obscurantism, useless and deplorable, but a valuable and necessary stage in human progress. It was a period in which an important principle of social organisation was realised, the right relation of the spiritual and temporal powers.

It is evident that these views transformed the theory of Condorcet into a more acceptable shape. So long as the medieval tract of time appeared to be an awkward episode, contributing nothing to the forward movement but rather thwarting and retarding it, Progress was exposed to the criticism that it was an arbitrary synthesis, only partly borne out by historical facts and supplying no guarantees for the future. And so long as rationalists of the Encyclopaedic school regarded religion as a tiresome product of ignorance and deceit, the social philosophy which lay behind the theory of Progress was condemned as unscientific; because, in defiance of the close cohesion of social phenomena, it refused to admit that religion, as one of the chief of those phenomena, must itself participate and co-operate in Progress.

Condorcet had suggested that the value of history lies in affording data for foreseeing the future. Saint-Simon raised this suggestion to a dogma. But prevision was impossible on Condorcet's unscientific method. In order to foretell, the law of the movement must be discovered, and Condorcet had not found or even sought a law. The eighteenth century thinkers had left Progress a mere hypothesis based on a very insufficient induction; their successors sought to lift it to the rank of a scientific hypothesis, by discovering a social law as valid as the physical law of gravitation. This was the object both of Saint-Simon and of Comte.

The "law" which Saint-Simon educed from history was that epochs of organisation or construction, and epochs of criticism or revolution, succeed each other alternately. The medieval period was a time of organisation, and was followed by a critical, revolutionary period, which has now come to an end and must be succeeded by another epoch of organisation. Having discovered the clew to the process, Saint-Simon is able to predict. As our knowlege of the universe has reached or is reaching a stage which is no longer conjectural but *positive* in all departments, society will be transformed accordingly; a new *physicist* religion will supersede Christianity and Deism; men of science will play the *rôle* of organisers which the clergy played in the Middle Ages.

As the goal of the development is social happiness, and as the working classes form the majority, the first step towards the goal will be the amelioration of the lot of the working classes. This will be the principal problem of government in reorganising society, and Saint-Simon's solution of the problem was socialism. He rejected the watchwords of liberalism—democracy, liberty, and equality—with as much disdain as De Maistre and the reactionaries.

The announcement of a future age of gold, which I quoted above, is taken from a pamphlet which he issued, in conjunction with his secretary, Augustin Thierry the historian, after the fall of Napoleon.[1] In it he revived the idea of the Abbé de Saint-Pierre for the abolition of war, and proposed a new organisation of Europe more ambitious and utopian than the Abbé's league of states. At this moment he saw in parliamentary government, which the restored Bourbons were establishing in France, a sovran remedy for political disorder, and he imagined that if this political system were introduced in all the states of Europe a long step would have been taken to the perpetuation of peace. If the old enemies France and England formed a close alliance there would be little difficulty in creating ultimately a European state like the American Commonwealth, with a parliamentary government supreme over the state governments. Here is the germ of the idea of a "parliament of man."

3

Saint-Simon, however, did not construct a definite system for the attainment of social perfection. He left it to disciples to develop the doctrine which he sketched. In the year of his death (1825) Olinde Rodrigues and Enfantin founded a journal, the *Producteur*, to present to humanity the one thing which humanity, in the opinion of their master then most needed, a new general doctrine.

History shows that peoples have been moving

---

[1] *De la réorganisation de la société européenne*, p. 111 (1814).

from isolation to union, from war to peace, from antagonism to association. The programme for the future is association scientifically organised. The Catholic Church in the Middle Ages offered the example of a great social organisation resting on a general doctrine. The modern world must also be a social organisation, but the general doctrine will be scientific, not religious. The spiritual power must reside, not in priests but in savants, who will direct the progress of science and public education. Each member of the community will have his place and duties assigned to him. Society consists of three classes of workers—industrial workers, savants, and artists. A commission of eminent workers of each class will determine the place of every individual according to his capacities. Complete equality is absurd; inequality, based on merit, is reasonable and necessary. It is a modern error to distrust state authority. A power directing national forces is requisite, to propose great ideas and to make the innovations necessary for Progress. Such an organisation will promote progress in all domains : in science by co-operation, in industry by credit, and in art too, for artists will learn to express the ideas and sentiments of their own age There are signs already of a tendency towards something of this kind ; its realisation must be procured, not by revolution but by gradual change.

In the authoritarian character of the organisation to which these apostles of Progress wished to entrust the destinies of man we may see the influence of the great theocrat and antagonist of Progress, Joseph de Maistre. He taught them the necessity of a strong central power and the danger of liberty.

But the fullest exposition of the Saint-Simonian doctrine of development was given by Bazard, one of the chief disciples, a few years later.[1] The human race is conceived as a collective being which unfolds its nature in the course of generations, according to a law—the law of Progress—which may be called the physiological law of the human species, and was discovered by Saint-Simon. It consists in the alternation of *organic* and *critical* epochs.

In an organic epoch men discern a destination and harmonise all their energies to reach it. In a critical epoch they are not conscious of a goal, and their efforts are dispersed and discordant. There was an organic period in Greece before the age of Socrates. It was succeeded by a critical epoch lasting to the barbarian invasions. Then came an organic period in the homogeneous societies of Europe from Charlemagne to the end of the fifteenth century, and a new critical period opened with Luther and has lasted till to-day. Now it is time to prepare the advent of the organic age which must necessarily follow.

The most salient fact observable in history is the continual extension of the principle of association, in the series of family, city, nation, supernational Church. The next term must be a still vaster association comprehending the whole race.

In consequence of the incompleteness of association, the exploitation of the weak by the strong has been a capital feature in human societies, but

---

[1] *Exposition de la doctrine saint-simonienne*, 2 vols., 1830–1.

its successive forms exhibit a gradual mitigation. Cannibalism is followed by slavery, slavery by serfdom, and finally comes industrial exploitation by the capitalist. This latest form of the oppression of the weak depends on the right of property, and the remedy is to transfer the right of inheriting the property of the individual from the family to the state. The society of the future must be socialistic.

The new social doctrine must not only be diffused by education and legislation, it must be sanctioned by a new religion. Christianity will not serve, for Christianity is founded on a dualism between matter and spirit, and has laid a curse on matter. The new religion must be monistic, and its principles are, briefly : God is one, God is all that is, all is God. He is universal love, revealing itself as mind and matter. And to this triad correspond the three domains of religion, science, and industry.

In combining their theory with a philosophical religion the Saint-Simonian school was not only true to its master's teaching but obeying an astute instinct. As a purely secular movement for the transformation of society, their doctrine would not have reaped the same success or inspired the same enthusiasm. They were probably influenced too by the pamphlet of Lessing to which Madame de Staël had invited attention, and which one of Saint-Simon's disciples translated.

The fortunes of the school, the life of the community at Ménilmontant under the direction of Enfantin, the persecution, the heresies, the dispersion, the attempt to propagate the movement in Egypt, the philosophical activity of Enfantin and

Lemonnier under the Second Empire, do not claim our attention ; the curious story is told in M. Weill's admirable monograph.[1] The sect is now extinct, but its influence was wide in its day, and it propagated faith in Progress as the key to history and the law of collective life.[2]

[1] Weill, *L'Ecole saint-simonienne, son histoire, son influence jusqu'à nos jours* (1896).

[2] Two able converts to the ideas of Saint-Simon seceded from the school at an early stage in consequence of Enfantin's aberrations: Pierre Leroux, whom we shall meet again, and P. J. B. Buchez, who in 1833 published a thoughtful *Introduction à la science de l'histoire*, where history is defined as "a science whose end is to foresee the social future of the human species in the order of its free activity" (vol. i. p. 60, ed. 2, 1842).

CHAPTER XVI

THE SEARCH FOR A LAW OF PROGRESS:
II. COMTE

I

AUGUSTE COMTE did more than any preceding thinker to establish the idea of Progress as a luminary which could not escape men's vision. The brilliant suggestions of Saint-Simon, the writings of Bazard and Enfantin, the vagaries of Fourier, might be dismissed as curious rather than serious propositions, but the massive system wrought out by Comte's speculative genius—his organic scheme of human knowledge, his elaborate analysis of history, his new science of sociology— was a great fact with which European thought was forced to reckon. The soul of this system was Progress, and the most important problem he set out to solve was the determination of its laws.

His originality is not dimmed by the fact that he owed to Saint-Simon more than he afterwards admitted or than his disciples have been willing to allow. He collaborated with him for several years, and at this time enthusiastically acknowledged the intellectual stimulus he received from the elder savant. But he derived from Saint-Simon much more than the stimulation of his thoughts in a

certain direction. He was indebted to him for
some of the characteristic ideas of his own system.
He was indebted to him for the principle which lay
at the very basis of his system, that the social
phenomena of a given period and the intellectual
state of the society cohere and correspond. The
conception that the coming age was to be a period
of organisation like the Middle Ages, and the idea
of the government of savants, are pure Saint-
Simonian doctrine. And the fundamental idea of
a *positive* philosophy had been apprehended by
Saint-Simon long before he was acquainted with his
youthful associate.

But Comte had a more methodical and scientific
mind, and he thought that Saint-Simon was premature in drawing conclusions as to the reformation
of societies and industries before the positive
philosophy had been constructed. He published—
he was then only twenty-two—in 1822 a *Plan of
the scientific operations necessary for the re-organ-
isation of society*, which was published under another
title two years later by Saint-Simon, and it was
over this that the friends quarrelled. This work
contains the principles of the positive philosophy
which he was soon to begin to work out; it
announces already the "law of the Three Stages."

The first volume of the *Cours de philosophie
positive* appeared in 1830; it took him twelve years
more to complete the exposition of his system.[1]

2

The "law of Three Stages" is familiar to many
who have never read a line of his writings. That

---

[1] With vol. vi., 1842.

men first attempted to explain natural phenomena by the operation of imaginary deities, then sought to interpret them by abstractions, and finally came to see that they could only be understood by scientific methods, observation, and experiment—this was a generalisation which had already been thrown out by Turgot. Comte adopted it as a fundamental psychological law, which has governed every domain of mental activity and explains the whole story of human development. Each of our principal conceptions, every branch of knowledge, passes successively through these three states which he names the theological, the metaphysical, and the positive or scientific. In the first, the mind invents; in the second, it abstracts; in the third, it submits itself to positive facts; and the proof that any branch of knowledge has reached the third stage is the recognition of invariable natural laws.

But, granting that this may be the key to the history of the sciences, of physics, say, or botany, how can it explain the history of man, the sequence of actual historical events? Comte replies that history has been governed by ideas; "the whole social mechanism is ultimately based on opinions." Thus man's history is essentially a history of his opinions; and these are subject to the fundamental psychological law.

It must, however, be observed that all branches of knowledge are not in the same stage simultaneously. Some may have reached the metaphysical, while others are still lagging behind in the theological; some may have become scientific, while others have not passed from the metaphysical. Thus the study of physical phenomena has already reached the positive stage; but the study of social phenomena has not. The central aim of Comte, and his great achievement in his own opinion, was to raise the study of social phenomena from the second to the third stage.

When we proceed to apply the law of the three stages to the general course of historical development, we are met at the outset by the difficulty that the advance in all the domains of activity is not simultaneous. If at a given period thought and opinions are partly in the theological, partly in the metaphysical, and partly in the scientific state, how is the law to be applied to general development? One class of ideas, Comte says, must be selected as the criterion, and this class must be that of social and moral ideas, for two reasons. In the first place, social science occupies the highest rank in the hierarchy of sciences, on which he laid great stress. In the second, those ideas play the principal part for the majority of men, and the most ordinary phenomena are the most important to consider. When, in other classes of ideas, the advance is at any time more rapid, this only means an indispensable preparation for the ensuing period.

The movement of history is due to the deeply rooted though complex instinct which pushes man to ameliorate his condition incessantly, to develop in all ways the sum of his physical, moral, and intellectual life. And all the phenomena of his social life are closely cohesive, as Saint-Simon had pointed out. By virtue of this cohesion, political, moral, and intellectual progress are inseparable from material progress, and so we find that the phases of his material development correspond to intellectual changes.

The principle of consensus or "solidarity," which secures harmony and order in the development, is as important as the principle of the three stages which governs the onward movement. This movement, however, is not in a right line, but displays a series of oscillations, unequal and variable, round a mean motion which tends to prevail. The three general causes of variation, according to Comte, are race, climate, and deliberate political action (such as the retrograde policies of Julian the Apostate or Napoleon). But while they cause deflections and oscillation, their power is strictly limited; they may accelerate or retard the movement, but they cannot invert its order; they may affect the intensity of the tendencies in a given situation, but cannot change their nature.

3

In the demonstration of his laws by the actual course of civilisation, Comte adopts what he calls "the happy artifice of Condorcet," and treats the successive peoples who pass on the torch as if they were a single people running the race. This is "a rational fiction," for a people's true successors are those who pursue its efforts. And, like Bossuet and Condorcet, he confined his review to European civilisation; he considered only the *élite* or advance guard of humanity. He deprecated the introduction of China or India, for instance, as a confusing complication. He ignored the *rôles* of Brahmanism, Buddhism, Mohammedanism. His synthesis, therefore, cannot claim to be a synthesis of universal history; it is only a synthesis of the movement of European history.

In accordance with the law of the three stages, the development falls into three great periods. The first or Theological came to an end about A.D. 1400, and the second or Metaphysical is now nearing its close, to make way for the third or Positive, for which Comte was preparing the way.

The Theological period has itself three stages, in which Fetishism, Polytheism, and Monotheism successively prevail. The chief social characteristics of the Polytheistic period are the institution of slavery and the coincidence or " confusion " of the spiritual and temporal powers. It has two stages : the theocratic, represented by Egypt, and the military, represented by Rome, between which Greece stands in a rather embarrassing and uneasy position.

The initiative for the passage to the Monotheistic period came from Judaea, and Comte attempts to show that this could not have been otherwise. His analysis of this period is the most interesting part of his survey. The chief feature of the political system corresponding to monotheism is the separation of the spiritual and temporal powers ; the function of the spiritual power being concerned with education, and that of the temporal with action, in the wide senses of those terms. The defects of this dual system were due to the irrational theology. But the theory of papal infallibility was a great step in intellectual and social progress, by providing a final jurisdiction, without which society would have been troubled incessantly by contests arising from the vague formulae of dogmas. Here Comte had learned from Joseph de Maistre. But that thinker would not have been edified when Comte went on to declare that in the passage from polytheism to monotheism the religious spirit had really declined, and that one of the merits of Catholicism was that it augmented the domain of human wisdom at the expense of divine inspiration.[1] If it be said that the Catholic system promoted the empire of the clergy rather than the interests of religion, this was all to the good; for it placed the practical use of religion in "the provisional elevation of a noble speculative corporation eminently able to direct opinions and morals."

But Catholic monotheism could not escape dissolution. The metaphysical spirit began to operate powerfully on the notions of moral philosophy, as soon as the Catholic organisation was complete; and Catholicism, because it could not assimilate this intellectual movement, lost its progressive character and stagnated.

The decay began in the fourteenth century, where Comte dates the beginning of the Metaphysical period—a period of revolution and disorder. In the fourteenth and fifteenth centuries the movement is spontaneous and unconscious; from the sixteenth till to-day it has proceeded under the direction of a philosophical spirit which is negative and not constructive. This critical philosophy has only accelerated a decomposition which began spontaneously. For as theology progresses it becomes less consistent and less durable, and as its conceptions become less irrational, the intensity of the emotions which they excite decreases. Fetishism had deeper roots than polytheism and lasted longer; and polytheism surpassed monotheism in vigour and vitality.

Yet the critical philosophy was necessary to

---

[1] *Cours de philosophie positive*, vi. 354.

exhibit the growing need of solid reorganisation
and to prove that the decaying system was incapable
of directing the world any longer.   Logically it was
very imperfect, but it was justified by its success.
The destructive work was mainly done in the
seventeenth century by Hobbes, Spinoza, and
Bayle, of whom Hobbes was the most effective.   In
the eighteenth all prominent thinkers participated
in developing this negative movement, and Rousseau
gave it the practical stimulus which saved it from
degenerating into an unfruitful agitation.   Of particular importance was the great fallacy, which
Helvétius propagated, that human intellects are
equal.   This error was required for the full development of the critical doctrine.   For it supported the
dogmas of popular sovranty and social equality,
and justified the principle of the right of private
judgement.

These three principles—popular sovranty, equality,
and what he calls the right of free examination—are
in Comte's eyes vicious and anarchical.[1]   But it was
necessary that they should be promulgated, because
the transition from one organised social system to
another cannot be direct ; it requires an anarchical
interregnum.   Popular sovranty is opposed to
orderly institutions and condemns all superior
persons to dependence on the multitude of their
inferiors.   Equality, obviously anarchical in its
tendency, and obviously untrue (for, as men are not
equal or even equivalent to one another, their rights
cannot be identical), was similarly necessary to break
down the old institutions.   The universal claim to
the right of free judgement merely consecrates the

[1] *Op. cit.* iv. 36-38.

transitional state of unlimited liberty in the interim between the decline of theology and the arrival of positive philosophy.   Comte further remarks that the fall of the spiritual power had led to anarchy in international relations, and if the spirit of nationality were to prevail too far, the result would be a state of things inferior to that of the Middle Ages.

But Comte says for the metaphysical spirit in France that with all its vices it was more disengaged from the prejudices of the old theological régime, and nearer to a true rational positivism than either the German mysticism or the English empiricism of the same period.

The Revolution was a necessity, to disclose the chronic decomposition of society from which it resulted, and to liberate the modern social elements from the grip of the ancient powers.   Comte has praise for the Convention, which he contrasts with the Constituent Assembly with its political fictions and inconsistencies.   He pointed out that the great vice in the " metaphysics " of the crisis—that is, in the principles of the revolutionaries—lay in conceiving society out of relation to the past, in ignoring the Middle Ages, and borrowing from Greek and Roman society retrograde and contradictory ideals.

Napoleon restored order, but he was more injurious to humanity than any other historical person.   His moral and intellectual nature was incompatible with the true direction of Progress, which involves the extinction of the theological and military régime of the past.   Thus his work, like Julian the Apostate's, exhibits an instance of deflection from the line of Progress.   Then came the parliamentary system of the restored Bourbons which Comte designates as a political Utopia, destitute of social principles, a foolish attempt to combine political retrogression with a state of permanent peace.

4

The critical doctrine has performed its historical function, and the time has come for man to enter upon the Positive stage of his career. To enable him to take this step forward, it is necessary that the study of social phenomena should become a positive science. As social science is the highest in the hierarchy of sciences, it could not develop until the two branches of knowledge which come next in the scale, biology and chemistry, assumed a scientific form. This has recently been achieved, and it is now possible to found a scientific sociology.

This science, like mechanics and biology, has its statics and its dynamics. The first studies the laws of co-existence, the second those of succession ; the first contains the theory of order, the second that of progress. The law of consensus or cohesion is the fundamental principle of social statics ; the law of the three stages is that of social dynamics. Comte's survey of history, of which I have briefly indicated the general character, exhibits the application of these sociological laws.

The capital feature of the third period, which we are now approaching, will be the organisation of society by means of scientific sociology. The world will be guided by a general theory, and this means that it must be controlled by those who understand the theory and will know how to apply it. Therefore society will revive the principle which was realised in the great period of Monotheism, the distinction of a spiritual and a temporal order. But the spiritual order will consist of savants who will direct social life not by theological fictions but by the positive truths of science. They will administer a system of universal education and will draw up the final code of ethics. They will be able, more effectively than the Church, to protect the interests of the lower classes.

Comte's conviction that the world is prepared for a transformation of this kind is based principally on signs of the decline of the theological spirit and of the military spirit, which he regarded as the two main obstacles to the reign of reason. Catholicism, he says, is now no more than "an imposing historical ruin." As for militarism, the epoch has arrived in which serious and lasting warfare among the *élite* nations will totally cease. The last general cause of warfare has been the competition for colonies. But the colonial policy is now in its decadence (with the temporary exception of England), so that we need not look for future trouble from this source. The very sophism, sometimes put forward to justify war, that it is an instrument of civilisation, is a homage to the pacific nature of modern society.

We need not follow further the details of Comte's forecast of the Positive period, except to mention that he did not contemplate a political federation. The great European nations will develop each in its own way, with their separate "temporal" organisations. But he contemplated the intervention of a common "spiritual" power, so that all nationalities "under the direction of a homogeneous speculative class will contribute to an identical work, in a spirit of active European patriotism, not of sterile cosmopolitanism."

Comte claimed, like Saint-Simon, that the data of history, scientifically interpreted, afford the means of prevision. It is interesting to observe how he failed himself as a diviner; how utterly he misapprehended the vitality of Catholicism, how completely his prophecy as to the cessation of wars was belied by the event. He lived to see the Crimean war.[1] As a diviner he failed as completely as Saint-Simon and Fourier, whose dream that the nineteenth century would see the beginning of an epoch of harmony and happiness was to be fulfilled by a deadly struggle between capitalism and labour, the civil war in America, the war of 1870, the Commune, Russian pogroms, Armenian massacres, and finally the universal catastrophe of 1914.

5

For the comprehension of history we have perhaps gained as little from Comte's positive laws as from Hegel's metaphysical categories. Both thinkers had studied the facts of history only slightly and partially, a rather serious drawback which enabled them to impose their own constructions with the greater ease. Hegel's method of *a priori* synthesis was enjoined by his philosophical theory; but in Comte we also find a tendency to *a priori* treatment. He expressly remarks that the chief social features of the Monotheistic period might almost be constructed *a priori*.

The law of the Three Stages is discredited. It

[1] He died in 1857.

may be contended that general Progress depends on intellectual progress, and that theology, metaphysics, and science have common roots, and are ultimately identical, being merely phases in the movement of the intelligence. But the law of this movement, if it is to rank as a scientific hypothesis, must be properly deduced from known causes, and must then be verified by a comparison with historical facts. Comte thought that he fulfilled these requirements, but in both respects his demonstration was defective.

The gravest weakness perhaps in his historical sketch is the gratuitous assumption that man in the earliest stage of his existence had animiṣtic beliefs and that the first phase of his progress was controlled by fetishism. There is no valid evidence that fetishism is not a relatively late development, or that in the myriads of years stretching back beyond our earliest records, during which men decided the future of the human species by their technical inventions and the discovery of fire, they had any views which could be called religious or theological. The psychology of modern savages is no clew to the minds of the people who wrought tools of stone in the world of the mammoth and the *Rhinoceros tichorhinus*. If the first stage of man's development, which was of such critical importance for his destinies, was pre-animistic, Comte's law of progress fails, for it does not cover the ground.

In another way, Comte's system may be criticised for failing to cover the ground, if it is regarded as a philosophy of history. In accordance with "the happy artifice of Condorcet," he assumes that the growth of European civilisation is the only history that matters, and discards entirely the civilisations, for instance, of India and China. This assumption is much more than an artifice, and he has not scientifically justified it.

The reader of the *Philosophie positive* will also observe that Comte has not grappled with a fundamental question which has to be faced in unravelling the woof of history or seeking a law of events. I mean the question of contingency. It must be remembered that contingency does not in the least affect the doctrine of determinism; it is compatible with the strictest interpretation of the principle of causation. A particular example may be taken to show what it implies.

It may plausibly be argued that a military dictatorship was an inevitable sequence of the French Revolution. This may not be true, but let us assume it. Let us further assume that, given Napoleon, it was inevitable that he should be the dictator. But Napoleon's existence was due to an independent causal chain which had nothing whatever to do with the course of political events. He might have died in his boyhood by disease or by an accident, and the fact that he survived was due to causes which were similarly independent of the causal chain which, as we are assuming, led necessarily to an epoch of monarchical government. The existence of a man of his genius and character at the given moment was a contingency which profoundly affected the course of history. If he had not been there another dictator would have grasped the helm, but obviously would not have done what Napoleon did.

It is clear that the whole history of man has

been modified at every stage by such contingencies, which may be defined as the collisions of two independent causal chains.   Voltaire was perfectly right when he emphasised the *rôle* of chance in history, though he did not realise what it meant.   This factor would explain the oscillations and deflections which Comte admits in the movement of historical progression.   But the question arises whether it may not also have once and again definitely altered the direction of the movement.   Can the factor be regarded as virtually negligible by those who, like Comte, are concerned with the large perspective of human development and not with the details of an episode ?   Or was Renouvier right in principle when he maintained " the real possibility that the sequence of events from the Emperor Nerva to the Emperor Charlemagne might have been radically different from what it actually was " ?.[1]

6

It does not concern us here to examine the defects of Comte's view of the course of European history.   But it interests us to observe that his synthesis of human Progress is, like Hegel's, what I have called a closed system.   Just as his own absolute philosophy marked for Hegel the highest and ultimate term of human development, so for Comte the coming society whose organisation he adumbrated was the final state of humanity beyond which there would be no further movement.   It would take time to perfect the organisation, and

---

[1] He illustrated this proposition by a fanciful reconstruction of European history from 100 to 800 A.D. in his *Uchronie*, 1876.   He contended that there is no definite law of progress : " The true law lies in the equal possibility of progress or regress for societies as for individuals."

the period would witness a continuous increase
of knowledge, but the main characteristics were
definitely fixed. Comte did not conceive that the
distant future, could he survive to experience it,
could contain any surprises for him. His theory
of Progress thus differed from the eighteenth
century views which vaguely contemplate an indefinite development and only profess to indicate
some general tendencies. He expressly repudiated
this notion of *indefinite* progress; the data, he said,
justify only the inference of *continuous* progress,
which is a different thing.

A second point in which Comte in his view of
Progress differed from the French philosophers of
the preceding age is this. Condorcet and his predecessors regarded it exclusively from the eudaemonic point of view. The goal of Progress for
them was the attainment of human felicity. With
felicity Comte is hardly more concerned than
Hegel. The establishment of a fuller harmony
between men and their environment in the third
stage will no doubt mean happiness. But this consideration lies outside the theory, and to introduce
it would only intrude an unscientific element into the
analysis. The course of development is determined
by intellectual ideas, and he treats these as independent of, and indifferent to, eudaemonic motives.

A third point to be noted is the authoritarian
character of the régime of the future. Comte's
ideal state would be as ill to live in for any
unfortunate being who values personal liberty as
a theocracy or any socialistic utopia. He had as
little sympathy with liberty as Plato or as Bossuet,
and less than the eighteenth century philosophers.

This feature, common to Comte and the Saint-Simonians, was partly due to the reaction against the Revolution, but it also resulted from the logic of the man of science. If sociological laws are positively established as certainly as the law of gravitation, no room is left for opinion ; right social conduct is definitely fixed ; the proper functions of every member of society admit of no question ; therefore the claim to liberty is perverse and irrational. It is the same argument which some modern exponents of Eugenics use to advocate a state tyranny in the matter of human breeding.

When Comte was writing, the progressive movement in Europe was towards increase of liberty in all its forms, national, civic, political, and economical. On one hand there was the agitation for the release of oppressed nationalities, on the other the growth of liberalism in England and France. The aim of the liberalism of that period was to restrict the functions of government ; its spirit was distrust of the state. As a political theory it was defective, as modern Liberals acknowledge, but it was an important expression of the feeling that the interests of society are best furthered by the free interplay of individual actions and aims. It thus implicitly contained or pointed to a theory of Progress sharply opposed to Comte's : that the realisation of the fullest possible measure of individual liberty is the condition of ensuring the maximum of energy and effectiveness in improving our environment, and therefore the condition of attaining public felicity. Right or wrong, this theory reckons with fundamental facts of human nature which Comte ignored.

7

Comte spent the later years of his life in composing another huge work, on social reorganisation. It included a new religion, in which Humanity was the object of worship, but made no other important addition to the speculations of his earlier manhood, though he developed them further.

The *Course of Positive Philosophy* was not a book that took the public by storm. We are told by a competent student of social theories in France that the author's name was little known in his own country till about 1855, when his greatness began to win recognition, and his influence to operate.[1] Even then his work can hardly have been widely read. But through men like Littré and Taine, whose conceptions of history were moulded by his teaching, and men like Mill, whom he stimulated, as well as through the disciples who adopted Positivism as a religion, his leading principles, detached from his system, became current in the world of speculation.

He laid the foundations of sociology, convincing many minds that the history of civilisation is subject to general laws, or, in other words, that a science of society is possible. In England this idea was still a novelty when Mill's *System of Logic* appeared in 1843.

The publication of this work, which attempted to define the rules for the investigation of truth in all fields of inquiry and to provide tests for the hypotheses of science, was a considerable event, whether we regard its value and range or its prolonged influence on education. Mill, who had

---

[1] Weill, *Hist. du mouvement social*, p. 21.

followed recent French thought attentively and was particularly impressed by the system of Comte, recognised that a new method of investigating social phenomena had been inaugurated by the thinkers who set out to discover the "law" of human progression. He proclaimed and welcomed it as superior to previous methods, and at the same time pointed out its limitations.

Till about fifty years ago, he said, generalisations on man and society have erred by implicitly assuming that human nature and society will for ever revolve in the same orbit and exhibit virtually the same phenomena. This is still the view of the ostentatiously practical votaries of common sense in Great Britain ; whereas the more reflective minds of the present age, analysing historical records more minutely, have adopted the opinion that the human race is in a state of necessary progression. The reciprocal action between circumstances and human nature, from which social phenomena result, must produce either a cycle or a trajectory. While Vico maintained the conception of periodic cycles, his successors have universally adopted the idea of a trajectory or progress, and are endeavouring to discover its law.

But they have fallen into a misconception in imagining that if they can find a law of uniformity in the succession of events they can infer the future from the past terms of the series. For such a law would only be an "empirical law" ; it would not be a causal law or an ultimate law. However rigidly uniform, there is no guarantee that it would apply to phenomena outside those from which it was derived. It must itself depend on laws of mind and character (psychology and ethology). When those laws are known and the nature of the dependence is explained, when the determining causes of all the changes constituting the progress are understood, then the empirical law will be elevated to a scientific law, then only will it be possible to predict.

Thus Mill asserted that if the advanced thinkers who are engaged on the subject succeed in discovering an empirical law from the data of history, it may be converted into a scientific law by deducing it *a priori* from the principles of human nature. In the meantime, he argued that what is already known of those principles justifies the important conclusion that the order of general human progression will mainly depend on the order of progression in the intellectual convictions of mankind.

Throughout his exposition Mill uses "progress" in a neutral sense, without implying that the progression necessarily means improvement. Social science has still to demonstrate that the changes determined by human nature do mean improvement. But in warning the reader of this he declares himself to be personally an optimist, believing that the general tendency, saving temporary exceptions, is in the direction of a better and happier state.

8

Twenty years later[1] Mill was able to say that the conception of history as subject to general laws had "passed into the domain of newspaper and ordinary political discussion." Buckle's *History of Civilisation in England*,[2] which enjoyed an

---

[1] In later editions of the *Logic*.
[2] Vol. i. appeared in 1857, vol. ii. in 1861.

immediate success, did a great deal to popularise
the idea.   In this stimulating work Buckle took the
fact of Progress for granted ; his purpose was to in-
vestigate its causes.   Considering the two general
conditions on which all events depend, human nature
and external nature, he arrived at two conclusions :
(1) In the early stage of history the influence of
man's external environment is the more decisive
factor ; but as time goes on the *rôles* are gradually
inverted, and now it is his own nature that is principally responsible for his development.   (2) Progress
is determined, not by the emotional and moral
faculties, but by the intellect ;[1] the emotional and
moral faculties are stationary, and therefore religion
is not a decisive influence in the onward movement
of humanity.   "I pledge myself to show that the
progress Europe has made from barbarism to civilisation is entirely due to its intellectual activity. . . .
In what may be called the innate and original
morals of mankind there is, so far as we are aware,
no progress."

Buckle was convinced that social phenomena
exhibit the same undeviating regularity as natural
phenomena.   In this belief he was chiefly influenced
by the investigations of the Belgian statistician
Quetelet (1835).   "Statistics," he said, "has already
thrown more light on the study of human nature
than all the sciences put together."   From the
regularity with which the same crimes recur in the
same state of society, and many other constant
averages, he inferred that all actions of individuals
result directly from the state of society in which
they live, and that laws are operating which, if we

[1] This was the view of Jouffroy, Comte, and Mill ; Buckle popularised it.

take large enough numbers into account, scarcely undergo any sensible perturbation.[1]   Thus the evidence of statistics points to the conclusion that progress is not determined by the acts of individual men, but depends on general laws of the intellect which govern the successive stages of public opinion. The totality of human actions at any given time depends on the totality of knowledge and the extent of its diffusion.

There we have the theory that history is subject to general laws in its most unqualified form, based on a fallacious view of the significance of statistical facts.   Buckle's attempt to show the operation of general laws in the actual history of man was disappointing.   When he went on to review the concrete facts of the historical process, his own political principles came into play, and he was more concerned with denouncing the tendencies of which he did not approve than with extricating general laws from the sequence of events.   His comments on religious persecution and the obscurantism of governments and churches were instructive and timely, but they did not do much to exhibit a set of rigid laws governing and explaining the course of human development.

The doctrine that history is under the irresistible control of law was also popularised by an American physiologist, J. W. Draper, whose *History of the Intellectual Development of Europe* appeared in 1864 and was widely read.   His starting-point was a superficial analogy between a society and an individual.   " Social advancement is as completely

---

[1] Kant had already appealed to statistics in a similar sense ; see above, p. 243.

under the control of natural law as a bodily growth. The life of an individual is a miniature of the life of a nation," and "particles" in the individual organism answer to persons in the political organism. Both have the same epochs — infancy, childhood, youth, manhood, old age—and therefore European progress exhibits five phases, designated as Credulity, Inquiry, Faith, Reason, Decrepitude. Draper's conclusion was that Europe, now in the fourth period, is hastening to a long period of decrepitude. The prospect did not dismay him; decrepitude is the culmination of Progress, and means the organisation of national intellect. That has already been achieved in China, and she owes to it her well-being and longevity. "Europe is inevitably hastening to become what China is. In her we may see what we shall be like when we are old."

Judged by any standard, Draper's work is much inferior to Buckle's, but both these books, utterly different though they were in both conception and treatment, performed a similar function. Each in its own way diffused the view which had originated in France, that civilisation is progression and, like nature, subject to general laws.

CHAPTER XVII

"PROGRESS" IN THE FRENCH REVOLUTIONARY MOVEMENT (1830–1851)

I

IN 1850 there appeared at Paris a small book by M. A. Javary, with the title *De l'idée du progrès*. Its interest lies in the express recognition that Progress was the characteristic idea of the age, ardently received by some, hotly denounced by others.

"If there is any idea," he says, "that belongs properly to one century, at least by the importance accorded to it, and that, whether accepted or not, is familiar to all minds, it is the idea of Progress conceived as the general law of history and the future of humanity."

He observes that some, intoxicated by the spectacle of the material improvements of modern civilisation and the results of science, set no limits to man's power or his hopes; while others, unable to deny the facts, say that this progress serves only the lower part of human nature, and refuse to look with complacency on a movement which means, they assert, a continuous decadence of the nobler part. To which it is replied that, if moral decadence is a fact, it is only transient; it is a necessary phase of a development which means moral progress in the end, for it is due to the process by which the beliefs, ideas, and institutions of the past disappear and make way for new and better principles.

And Javary notes a prevailing tendency in France to interpret every contemporary movement as progressive, while all the social doctrinaires justify their particular reforms by invoking the law of Progress. It was quite true that during the July monarchy nearly all serious speculations on society and history were related to that idea. It was common to Michelet and Quinet, who saw in the march of civilisation the gradual triumph of liberty; to Leroux and Cabet, who preached humanitarian communism; to Louis Blanc and to Proudhon; to the bourgeois, who were satisfied with the régime of Louis Philippe and grew rich, following the precept of Guizot, as well as to the workers who overthrew it. It is significant that the journal of Louis Blanc, in which he published his book on the *Organisation of Work* (1839), was entitled *Revue des progrès.* The political question as to the due limits between government and individual freedom was discussed in terms of Progress: is personal liberty or state authority the efficient means of progressing? The metaphysical question of necessity and freewill acquired a new interest: is Progress a fatality, independent of human purposes, determined by general, ineluctable, historical laws? Quinet and Michelet argued vigorously against the optimism of Cousin, who with Hegel held that history is just what it ought to be and could not be improved.

2

Among the competing theories of the time, and sharply opposed to the views of Comte, was the idea, derived from the Revolution, that the world is moving towards universal equality and the obliteration of class distinctions, that this is the true direction of Progress. This view, represented by leaders of the popular movement against the bourgeois ascendency, derived powerful reinforcement from one of the most enlightened political thinkers of the day. The appearance of de Tocqueville's renowned study of American democracy was the event of 1834. He was convinced that he had discovered on the other side of the Atlantic the answer to the question whither the world is tending. In American society he found that equality of conditions is the generating fact on which every other fact depends. He concluded that equality is the goal of humanity, providentially designed.

" The gradual development of equality of conditions has the principal characteristics of a providential fact. It is universal, it is permanent, it eludes human power; all events and all men serve this development. . . . This whole book has been written under the impression of a sort of religious terror produced in the author's soul by the view of this irresistible revolution which for so many centuries has been marching across all obstacles, and which is to-day seen still advancing in the midst of the ruins it has made. . . . If the men of our time were brought to see that the gradual and progressive development of equality is at once the

past and the future of their history, this single
discovery would give that development the sacred
character of the will of the sovran master."

Here we have a view of the direction of Progress
and the meaning of history, pretending to be
based upon the study of facts and announced with
the most intense conviction. And behind it is
the fatalistic doctrine that the movement cannot
be arrested or diverted; that it is useless to
struggle against it; that men, whatever they may
do, cannot deflect the clock-like motion regulated
by a power which de Tocqueville calls Providence
but to which his readers might give some other
name.

3

It has been conjectured,[1] and seems probable
enough, that de Tocqueville's book was one of
the influences which wrought upon the mind of
Proudhon. The speculations of this remarkable
man, who, like Saint-Simon and Comte, sought to
found a new science of society, attracted general
attention in the middle of the century. His hostility
to religion, his notorious dictum that "property is
theft," his gospel of "anarchy," and the defiant,
precipitous phrases in which he clothed his ideas,
created an impression that he was a dangerous
anti-social revolutionary. But when his ideas are
studied in their context and translated into sober
language, they are not so unreasonable. Notwithstanding his communistic theory of property and
his ideal of equality, he was a strong individualist.
He held that the future of civilisation depends on

---

[1] Georges Sorel, *Les Illusions du progrès*, pp. 247-8 (1908).

the energy of individuals, that liberty is a condition
of its advance, and that the end to be kept in
view is the establishment of justice, which means
equality. He saw the difficulty of reconciling
liberty with complete equality, but hoped that the
incompatibility would be overcome by a gradual
reduction of the natural differences in men's
capacities. He said, "I am an anarchist," but his
anarchy only meant that the time would come when
government would be superfluous, when every
human being could be trusted to act wisely and
morally without a restraining authority or external
sanctions. Nor was he a Utopian. He comprehended that such a transformation of society would
be a long, slow process, and he condemned the
schools of Saint-Simon and Fourier for imagining
that a millennium might be realised immediately
by a change of organisation.

He tells us that all his speculations and contro-
versial activities are penetrated with the idea of
Progress, which he described as "the railway of
liberty"; and his radical criticism on current social
theories, whether conservative or democratic, was
that they did not take Progress seriously though
they invoked it.

"What dominates in all my studies, what forms
their beginning and end, their summit and their
base, their reason, what makes my originality as a
thinker (if I have any), is that I affirm Progress
resolutely, irrevocably, and everywhere, and deny
the Absolute. All that I have ever written, all I
have denied or affirmed, I have written, denied or
affirmed in the name of one unique idea, Progress.
My adversaries, on the other hand, are all partisans

of the Absolute, *in omni genere, casu, et numero,* to
use the phrase of Sganarelle."

4

A vague confidence in Progress had lain behind
and encouraged the revolution of 1789, but in the
revolution of 1848 the idea was definitely enthroned
 as the regnant principle.   It presided over the
session of the Committee which drew up the Constitution of the second Republic.   Armand Marrast,
the most important of the men who framed
that document, based the measure of universal
suffrage upon "the invisible law which rules
societies," the law of progress which has been so
long denied but which is rooted in the nature of
man.   His argument was this : Revolutions are due
to the repression of progress, and are the expression
and triumph of a progress which has been achieved.
But such convulsions are an undesirable method
of progressing ; how can they be avoided?   Only
by organising elastic institutions in which new ideas
of amelioration can easily be incorporated, and laws
which can be accommodated without struggle or
friction to the rise of new opinions.   What is
needed is a flexible government open to the pene-
tration of ideas, and the key to such a government
is universal suffrage.

Universal suffrage was practical politics, but the
success of the revolution fluttered agreeably all the
mansions of Utopia, and social reformers of every
type sought to improve the occasion.   In the history
of the political struggles of 1848 the names are
written of Proudhon, of Victor Considérant the
disciple of Fourier, of Pierre Leroux the humani-

tarian communist, and his devoted pupil George Sand.   The chief title of Leroux to be remembered is just his influence over the soul of the great novelist. Her later romances are pervaded by ideas derived from his teaching.   His communism was vague and ineffectual, but he was one of the minor forces in the thought of the period, and there are some features in his theory which deserve to be pointed out.

Leroux had begun as a member of the Saint-Simonian school, but he diverged into a path of his own.   He reinstated the ideal of equality which Saint-Simon rejected, and made the approach to that ideal the measure of Progress.   The most significant process in history, he held, is the gradual breaking down of caste and class : the process is now approaching its completion; "to-day *man* is synonymous with *equal.*"

In order to advance to the city of the future we must have a force and a lever.   Man is the force, and the lever is the idea of Progress.   It is supplied by the study of history which displays the improvement of our faculties, the increase of our power over nature, the possibility of organising society more efficaciously.   But the force and the lever are not enough.   A fulcrum is also required, and this is to be found in the "solidarity" of the human race.   But this conception meant for Leroux something different from what is ordinarily meant by the phrase, a deeper and even mystical bond.   Human "solidarity" was a corollary from the pantheistic religion of the Saint-Simonians, but with Leroux, as with Fourier, it was derived from the more difficult doctrine of palingenesis.   We of this generation, he believed, are not merely the sons and descendants of past generations, we are the past generations themselves, which have come to birth again in us.

Through many pages of the two volumes[1] in which he set forth his thesis, Leroux expended much useless learning in endeavouring to establish this doctrine, which, were it true, might be the central principle in a new religion of humanity, a transformed Pythagoreanism. It is easy to understand the attractiveness of palingenesis to a believer in Progress : for it would provide a solution of the anomaly that generations after generations are sacrificed for the sake of posterity, and so appear to have no value in themselves. Believers in Progress, who are sensitive to the sufferings of mankind, past and present, need a stoical resolution to face this fact. We saw how Herder refused to accept it. A pantheistic faith, like that of the Saint-Simonian Church, may help some, it cannot do more, to a stoical acquiescence. The palingenesis of Leroux or Fourier removes the radical injustice. The men of each generation are sacrificed and suffer for the sake of their descendants, but as their descendants are themselves come to life again, they are really suffering in their own interests. They will themselves reach the desirable state to which the slow, painful process of history is tending.

But palingenesis, notwithstanding all the ancient opinions and traditions that the researches of Leroux might muster, could carry little conviction to those who were ceasing to believe in the familiar doctrine of a future life detached from earth, and Madame Dudevant was his only distinguished convert.

---

[1] *De l'humanité*, 1840 (dedicated to Béranger).

5

The ascendency of the idea of Progress among thoughtful people in France in the middle of the last century is illustrated by the work which Ernest Renan composed under the immediate impression of the events of 1848. He desired to understand the significance of the current revolutionary doctrines, and was at once involved in speculation on the future of humanity. This is the purport of *L'Avenir de la science*.[1]

The author was then convinced that history has a goal, and that mankind tends perpetually, though in an oscillating line, towards a more perfect state, through the growing dominion of reason over instinct and caprice. He takes the French Revolution as the critical moment in which humanity first came to know itself. That revolution was the first attempt of man to take the reins into his own hands. All that went before we may call, with Owen, the irrational period of human existence.

We have now come to a point at which we must choose between two faiths. If we despair of reason, we may find a refuge from utter scepticism in a belief in the external authority of the Roman Church. If we trust reason, we must accept the march of the human mind and justify the modern spirit. And it can be justified only by proving that it is a necessary step towards perfection. Renan affirmed his belief in the second alternative, and felt confident that science — including philology, on the human bearings of which he enlarged, —

---

[1] *L'Avenir de la science—Pensées de* (1848). Published in 1890.

philosophy, and art would ultimately enable men to realise an ideal civilisation, in which all would be equal. The state, he said, is the machine of Progress, and the Socialists are right in formulating the problem which man has to solve, though their solution is a bad one. For individual liberty, which socialism would seriously limit, is a definite conquest, and ought to be preserved inviolate.

Renan wrote this work in 1848 and 1849, but did not publish it at the time. He gave it to the world forty years later. Those forty years had robbed him of his early optimism. He continues to believe that the unfortunate conditions of our race might be ameliorated by science, but he denounces the view that men can ever be equal. Inequality is written in nature; it is not only a necessary consequence of liberty, but a necessary postulate of Progress. There will always be a superior minority. He criticises himself too for having fallen into the error of Hegel, and assigned to man an unduly important place in the universe.

In 1890 there was nothing left of the sentimental socialism which he had studied in 1848; it had been blown away by the cold wind of scientific socialism which Marx and Engels created. And Renan had come to think that in this new form socialism would triumph.[1] He had criticised Comte for believing that "man lives exclusively by science, or rather little verbal tags, like geometrical theorems, dry formulae." Was he satisfied by the concrete doctrine of Marx that all the phenomena of civilisation at a given period are

---

[1] He reckoned without the new forces, opposed to socialism as well as to parliamentary democracy, represented by Bakunin and men like Georges Sorel.

determined by the methods of production and distribution which then prevail? But the future of socialism is a minor issue, and the ultimate goal of humanity is quite uncertain. " Ce qu'il y a de consolant, c'est qu'on arrive nécessairement quelque part." We may console ourselves with the certainty that we must get somewhere.

6

Proudhon described the idea of Progress as the railway of liberty. It certainly supplied motive power to social ideals which were repugnant and alarming to the authorities of the Catholic Church. At the Vatican it was clearly seen that the idea was a powerful engine driven by an enemy ; and in the famous *Syllabus* of errors which Pope Pius IX. flung in the face of the modern world at the end of 1864, Progress had the honour of being censured. The eightieth error, which closes the list, runs thus :

Romanus Pontifex potest ac debet cum progressu, cum liberalismo et cum recenti civilitate sese reconciliare et componere.

" The Roman Pontiff can, and ought to, be reconciled and come to terms with progress, with liberalism, and with modern civilisation."

No wonder, seeing that Progress was invoked to justify every movement that offended the nostrils of the Vatican—liberalism, toleration, democracy, and socialism. And the Roman Church well understood the intimate connection of the idea with the advance of rationalism.

CHAPTER XVIII

I

IT is not easy for a new idea of the speculative
order to penetrate and inform the general consciousness of a community until it has assumed some
external and concrete embodiment or is recom-
mended by some striking material evidence.   In the
case of Progress both these conditions were fulfilled
in the period 1820 to 1850.   In the Saint Simonian
Church, and in the attempts of Owen and Cabet to
found ideal societies, people saw practical enterprises
inspired by the idea.   They might have no sympathy with these enterprises, but their attention was
attracted.   And at the same time they were witness-
ing a rapid transformation of the external conditions
of life, a movement to the continuation of which
there seemed no reason for setting any limit in the
future.   The spectacular results of the advance of
science and mechanical technique brought home to
the mind of the average man the conception of an
indefinite increase of man's power over nature as
his brain penetrated her secrets.   This evident
material progress which has continued incessantly

ever since has been a mainstay of the general belief
in Progress which is prevalent to-day.

England was the leader in this material progress,
of which the particulars are familiar and need not be
enumerated here.   The discovery of the power of
steam and the potentialities of coal revolutionised
the conditions of life.   Men who were born at the
beginning of the century had seen, before they had
passed the age of thirty, the rapid development of
steam navigation, the illumination of towns and
houses by gas, the opening of the first railway.

It was just before this event, the opening of the
Liverpool and Manchester railway, which showed
how machinery would abbreviate space as it had
revolutionised industry, that Southey published his
*Sir Thomas More, or Colloquies on the Progress of
Society* (1829).   There we see the effect of the new
force on his imagination.   " Steam," he says, " will
govern the world next, . . . and shake it too before its empire is established."   The biographer of
Nelson devotes a whole conversation to the subject
of "steam and war."   But the theme of the book is
the question of moral and social progress, on which
the author inclines to the view that " the world will
continue to improve, even as it has hitherto been
continually improving ; and that the progress of
knowledge and the diffusion of Christianity will
bring about at last, when men become Christian in
reality as well as in name, something like that
Utopian state of which philosophers have loved
to dream."   This admission of Progress, cautious
though it was, circumscribed by reserves and compromised by hesitations, coming from such a
conservative pillar of Church and State as Southey,

is, a notable sign of the times, when we remember that the idea was still associated then with revolution and heresy.

It is significant too that at the same time an octogenarian mathematician of Aberdeen was composing a book on the same subject. Hamilton's *Progress of Society* is now utterly forgotten, but it must have contributed in its day to propagating the same moderate view of Progress, consistent with orthodoxy, which Southey held. " The belief of the perfectibility of human nature and the attainment of a golden age in which vice and misery have no place, will only be entertained by an enthusiast ; but an inquiry into the means of improving our nature and enlarging our happiness is consistent with sober reason, and is the most important subject, merely human, that can engage the mind of man." [1]

2

We have been told by Tennyson that when he went by the first train from Liverpool to Manchester (1830) he thought that the wheels ran in grooves. " Then I made this line :

Let the great world spin for ever down the ringing grooves of change." [2]

Locksley Hall, which was published in 1842, illustrates how the idea of Progress had begun to creep into the imagination of Englishmen. Though subsidiary to a love story, it is the true theme of the poem. The pulsation of eager interest in the terrestrial destinies of humanity, the large excitement

[1] P. 13. The book was published posthumously by Murray in 1830, a year after the author's death.

[2] See *Tennyson, Memoir by his Son*, vol. i. p. 195.

of living in a "wondrous Mother-age," dreams of
the future, quicken the passion of the hero's youth.
His disappointment in love disenchants him ; he
sees the reverse side of civilisation, but at last he
finds an anodyne for his palsied heart in a more
sober version of his earlier faith, a chastened belief
in his Mother-age. He can at least discern an
increasing purpose in history, and can be sure that
" the thoughts of men are widened with the process
of the suns." The novelty of the poem lay in finding
a cathartic cure for a private sorrow, not in religion
or in nature, but in the modern idea of Progress.
It may be said to mark a stage in the career of
the idea.

The view of civilisation which Tennyson took
as his *motif* had no revolutionary implications,
suggested no impatience or anger with the past.
The startling prospect unfolding itself before Europe
is " the long result of time," and history is justified
by the promise of to-day :

> The centuries behind me like a fruitful land reposed.

Very different was the spirit in which another
great poet composed, nearly twenty years later, a
wonderful hymn of Progress. Victor Hugo's *Plein
Ciel*, in his epic *La Légende des siècles*,[1] announces a
new era of the world in which man, the triumphant
rebel, delivered from his past, will move freely
forward on a glorious way. The poet is inspired
not by faith in a continuous development throughout
the ages, but by the old spirit of the Revolution,
and he sees in the past only a heavy chain which the
race at last flings off. The horrible past has gone,

[1] A.D. 1859.

not to return : " ce monde est mort " ; and the poem is at once a paean on man's victorious rebellion against it and a dithyramb on the prospect of his future.

Man is imagined as driving through the heavens an aerial car to which the four winds are harnessed, mounting above the clouds, and threatening to traverse the ether.

> Superbe, il plane, avec un hymne en ses agrès ;
> Et l'on voit voir passer la strophe du progrès.
>   Il est la nef, il est le phare !
> L'homme enfin prend son sceptre et jette son bâton.
> Et l'on voit s'envoler le calcul de Newton
>   Monté sur l'ode de Pindare.

But if this vision foreshadows the conquest of the air, its significance is symbolic rather than literal, and, like Pindar checking the steeds of his song, Hugo returns to earth :

> Pas si loin ! pas si haut ! redescendons.   Restons
> L'homme, restons Adam ; mais non l'homme à tâtons,
> Mais non l'Adam tombé !   Tout autre rêve altère
> L'espèce d'idéal qui convient à la terre.
> Contentons-nous du mot : meilleur ! écrit partout.

Dawn has appeared, after six thousand years in the fatal way, and man, freed by "the invisible hand" from the weight of his chains, has embarked for new shores :

> Où va-t-il ce navire ?   Il va, de jour vêtu,
> À l'avenir divin et pur, à la vertu,
>   À la science qu'on voit luire,
> À la mort des fléaux, à l'oubli généreux,
> À l'abondance, au calme, au rire, à l'homme heureux,
>   Il va, ce glorieux navire.

> Oh ! ce navire fait le voyage sacré !
> C'est l'ascension bleue à son premier degré ;
>   Hors de l'antique et vil décombre,

Hors de la pesanteur, c'est l'avenir fondé ;
C'est le destin de l'homme à la fin évadé,
          Qui lève l'ancre et sort de l'ombre !

The union of humanity in a universal commonwealth, which Tennyson had expressed as "the
Parliament of Man, the Federation of the World,"
the goal of many theorists of Progress, becomes
in Hugo's imagination something more sublime.
The magic ship of man's destiny is to compass
the cosmopolis of the Stoics, a terrestrial order in
harmony with the whole universe.

Nef magique et suprême ! elle a, rien qu'en marchant,
Changé le cri terrestre en pur et joyeux chant,
          Rajeuni les races flétries,
Établi l'ordre vrai, montré le chemin sûr,
Dieu juste ! et fait entrer dans l'homme tant d'azur
          Qu'elle a supprimé les patries !

Faisant à l'homme avec le ciel une cité,
Une pensée avec toute l'immensité,
          Elle abolit les vieilles règles ;
Elle abaisse les monts, elle annule les tours ;
Splendide, elle introduit les peuples, marcheurs lourds,
          Dans la communion des aigles.

3

Between 1830 and 1850 railway transport spread
throughout Great Britain and was introduced on the
Continent, and electricity was subdued to man's use
by the invention of telegraphy.   The great Exhibition of London in 1851 was, in one of its aspects, a
public recognition of the material progress of the
age and the growing power of man over the physical
world.   Its aim, said a contemporary, was "to seize
the living scroll of human progress, inscribed with
every successive conquest of man's intellect."[1]   The

---

[1] *Edinburgh Review* (October 1851), p. 562, in a review of the *Official
Catalogue* of the Exhibition.

Prince Consort, who originated the Exhibition, explained its significance in a public speech :

"Nobody who has paid any attention to the peculiar features of our present era will doubt for a moment that we are living at a period of most wonderful transition, which tends rapidly to accomplish that great end to which indeed all history points—*the realisation of the unity of mankind.* . . . The distances which separated the different nations and parts of the globe are rapidly vanishing before the achievements of modern invention, and we can traverse them with incredible ease ; the languages of all nations are known, and their acquirements placed within the reach of everybody ; thought is communicated with the rapidity, and even by the power, of lightning. On the other hand, the *great principle of division of labour*, which may be called the moving power of civilisation, is being extended to all branches of science, industry, and art. . . . Gentlemen, the Exhibition of 1851 is to give us a true test and a living picture of the point of development at which the whole of mankind has arrived in this great task, and a new starting-point from which all nations will be able to direct their further exertions." [1]

The point emphasised here is the "solidarity" of the world. The Exhibition is to bring home to men's consciousness the community of all the inhabitants of the earth. The assembled peoples, wrote Thackeray, in his " May-day Ode," [2]

---

[1] Martin, *Life of the Prince Consort* (ed. 3), iii. p. 247. The speech was delivered at a banquet at the Mansion House on March 21, 1850.

[2] Published in the *Times*, April 30, 1851. The Exhibition was opened on May 1.

> See the sumptuous banquet set,
> The brotherhood of nations met
> Around the feast.

And this was the note struck in the leading article of the *Times* on the opening day: "The first morning since the creation that all peoples have assembled from all parts of the world and done a common act." It was claimed that the Exhibition signified a new, intelligent, and moral movement which "marks a great crisis in the history of the world," and fore-shadows universal peace.

England, said another writer, produced Bacon and Newton, the two philosophers "who first lent direction and force to the stream of industrial science; we have been the first also to give the widest possible base to the watch-tower of international progress, which seeks the formation of the physical well-being of man and the extinction of the meaner jealousies of commerce." [1]

These quotations show that the great Exhibition was at the time optimistically regarded, not merely as a record of material achievements, but as a demonstration that humanity was at last well on its way to a better and happier state, through the falling of barriers and the resulting insight that the interests of all are closely interlocked. A vista was suggested, at the end of which far-sighted people might think they discerned Tennyson's "Federation of the World."

4

Since the Exhibition, western civilisation has advanced steadily, and in some respects more rapidly

---

[1] *Edinburgh Review, loc. cit.*

than any sober mind could have predicted—civilisation, at least, in the conventional sense, which has been not badly defined as "the development of material ease, of education, of equality, and of aspirations to rise and succeed in life."[1]   The most striking advance has been in the technical conveniences of life—that is, in the control over natural forces.   It would be superfluous to enumerate the discoveries and inventions since 1850 which have abridged space, economised time, eased bodily suffering, and reduced in some ways the friction of life, though they have increased it in others.   This uninterrupted series of technical inventions, proceeding concurrently with immense enlargements of all branches of knowledge, has gradually accustomed the least speculative mind to the conception that civilisation is naturally progressive, and that continuous improvement is part of the order of things.

So far the hopes of 1851 have been fulfilled. But against all this technical progress, with the enormous expansion of industry and commerce, dazzling to the man in the market-place when he pauses to reflect, have to be set the exploitation and sufferings of industrial workers, the distress of intense economic competition, the heavier burdens of preparation for modern war.   The very increase of "material ease" seemed unavoidably to involve conditions inconsistent with universal happiness; and the communications which linked the peoples of the world together modified the methods of warfare instead of bringing peace.   "Toutes nos merveilleuses inventions sont aussi puissantes pour le mal

[1] B. Kidd, *Social Evolution*, p. 368.

que pour le bien."[1]   One fact indeed might be taken as an index that humanity was morally advancing—the abolition of slavery in America at the price of a long and sanguinary war.   Yet some triumphs of philanthropy hardly seemed to endanger the conclusion that, while knowledge is indefinitely progressive, there is no good reason for sanguine hopes that man is "perfectible" or that universal happiness is attainable.   A thoughtful writer observed, discussing Progress in 1864, that the innumerable individual steps in the growth of knowledge and business organisation have not been combined, so far, to produce a general advance in the happiness of life; each step brings increase of pressure.[2]

Yet in spite of all adverse facts and many eminent dissenters the belief in social Progress has on the whole prevailed.   This triumph of optimism was promoted by the victory of a revolutionary hypothesis in another field of inquiry, which suddenly electrified the world.

---

[1] H. de Ferron, *Théorie du progrès* (1867), ii. 439.

[2] Lotze, *Microcosmus* (Eng. tr.), vol. ii. p. 396.

CHAPTER XIX

PROGRESS IN THE LIGHT OF EVOLUTION

I

In the sixties of the nineteenth century the idea of Progress entered upon the third period of its history. During the *first* period, up to the French Revolution, it had been treated rather casually; it was taken for granted and received no searching examination either from philosophers or from historians. In the *second* period its immense significance was apprehended, and a search began for a general law which would define and establish it. The study of sociology was founded, and at the same time the impressive results of science, applied to the conveniences of life, advertised the idea. It harmonised with the notion of "development" which had become current both in natural science and in metaphysics. Socialists and other political reformers appealed to it as a gospel.

By 1850 it was a familiar idea in Europe, but was not yet universally accepted as obviously true. The notion of social Progress had been growing in the atmosphere of the notion of biological development, but this development still seemed a highly precarious speculation. The fixity of species and the creation of man, defended by powerful interests and prejudices, were attacked but were not shaken. The hypothesis of organic evolution was much in the same position as the Copernican hypothesis in the sixteenth century. Then in 1859 Darwin intervened, like Galileo. The appearance of the *Origin of Species* changed the situation by disproving definitely the dogma of fixity of species and assigning real causes for "transformism." What might be set aside before as a brilliant guess was elevated to the rank of a scientific hypothesis, and the following twenty years were enlivened by the struggle around the evolution of life, against prejudices chiefly theological, resulting in the victory of the theory.

The *Origin of Species* led to the *third* stage of the fortunes of the idea of Progress. We saw how the heliocentric astronomy, by dethroning man from his privileged position in the universe of space and throwing him back on his own efforts, had helped that idea to compete with the idea of a busy Providence. He now suffers a new degradation within the compass of his own planet. Evolution, shearing him of his glory as a rational being specially created to be the lord of the earth, traces a humble pedigree for him. And this second degradation was the decisive fact which has established the reign of the idea of Progress.

2

Evolution itself, it must be remembered, does not necessarily mean, applied to society, the movement of man to a desirable goal. It is a neutral, scientific conception, compatible either with optimism or with pessimism. According to different estimates it may appear to be a cruel sentence or a guarantee of steady amelioration. And it has been actually interpreted in both ways.

In order to base Progress on Evolution two distinct arguments are required. If it could be shown that social life obeys the same general laws of evolution as nature, and also that the process involves an increase of happiness, then Progress would be as valid a hypothesis as the evolution of living forms. Darwin had concluded his treatise with these words :

As all the living forms of life are the lineal descendants of those which lived long before the Silurian epoch, we may feel certain that the ordinary succession by generation has never once been broken, and that no cataclysm has desolated the whole world. Hence we may look with some confidence to a secure future of equally inappreciable length. And as natural selection works solely by and for the good of each being, all corporeal and mental environments will tend to progress towards perfection.

Here the evolutionist struck the note of optimism. And he suggested that laws of Progress would be found in other quarters than those where they had hitherto been sought.

The ablest and most influential development of the argument from evolution to Progress was the work of Spencer. He extended the principle of evolution to sociology and ethics, and was the most conspicuous interpreter of it in an optimistic sense. He had been an evolutionist long before Darwin's decisive intervention, and in 1851 he had published his *Social Statics*, which, although he had not yet worked out the evolutionary laws which he began to formulate soon afterwards and was still a theist, exhibits the general trend of his optimistic philosophy. Progress here appears as the basis of a theory of ethics. The title indicates the influence of Comte, but the argument is sharply opposed to the spirit of Comte's teaching, and sociology is treated in a new way.[1]

Spencer begins by arguing that the constancy of human nature, so frequently alleged, is a fallacy. For change is the law of all things, of every single object as well as of the universe. "Nature in its infinite complexity is ever growing to a new development." It would be strange if, in this universal mutation, man alone were unchangeable, and it is not true. "He also obeys the law of indefinite variation." Contrast the houseless savages with Newtons and Shakespeares; between these extremes there are countless degrees of difference. If then humanity is indefinitely variable, perfectibility is possible.

In the second place, evil is not a permanent necessity. For all evil results from the non-adaptation of the organism to its conditions; this is true of everything that lives. And it is equally true that evil perpetually tends to disappear. In virtue of an essential principle of life, this non-adaptation of organisms to their conditions is ever being rectified, and one or both continue to be modified until the adaptation is perfect. And this applies to the mental as well as to the physical sphere.

In the present state of the world men suffer many evils, and this shows that their characters are

---

[1] *Social Statics, or the Conditions Essential to Human Happiness specified, and the first of them developed,* is the full title.

not yet adjusted to the social state. Now the qualification requisite for the social state is that each individual shall have such desires only as may fully be satisfied without trenching upon the ability of others to obtain similar satisfaction. This qualification is not yet fulfilled, because civilised man retains some of the characteristics which were suitable for the conditions of his earlier predatory life. He needed one moral constitution for his primitive state, he needs quite another for his present state. The resultant is a process of adaptation which has been going on for a long time, and will go on for a long time to come.

Civilisation represents the adaptations which have already been accomplished. Progress means the successive steps of the process. That by this process man will eventually become suited to his mode of life, Spencer has no doubts. All excess and deficiency of suitable faculties must disappear; in other words, all imperfection. "The ultimate development of the ideal man is logically certain— as certain as any conclusion in which we place the most implicit faith; for instance, that all men will die." Here is the theory of perfectibility asserted, on new grounds, with a confidence not less assured than that of Condorcet or Godwin.

Progress then is not an accident, but a necessity. Civilisation is a part of nature, being a development of man's latent capabilities under the action of favourable circumstances which were certain at some time or other to occur. Here Spencer's argument assumes a final cause. The ultimate purpose of creation, he asserts, is to produce the greatest amount of happiness, and to fulfil this aim it is necessary that each member of the race should possess faculties enabling him to experience the highest enjoyment of life, yet in such a way as not to diminish the power of others to receive like satisfaction.   Beings thus constituted cannot multiply in a world tenanted by inferior creatures; these, therefore, must be dispossessed to make room ; and to dispossess them aboriginal man must have an inferior constitution to begin with ; he must be predatory, he must have the desire to kill. In general, given an unsubdued earth, and the human being "appointed" to overspread and occupy it, then, the laws of life being what they are, no other series of changes than that which has actually occurred could have occurred.

The argument might be put in a form free from the assumption of a final cause, and without introducing the conception of a divine Providence which in this work Spencer adopted, though in his later philosophy it was superseded by the conception of the Unknowable existing behind all phenomena. But the *rôle* of the Divine ruler is simply to set in motion immutable forces to realise his design.   " In the moral as in the material world accumulated evidence is gradually generating the conviction that events are not at bottom fortuitous, but that they are wrought out in a certain inevitable way by unchanging forces."

The optimism of Spencer's view could not be surpassed.   " After patient study," he writes, " this chaos of phenomena into the midst of which he [man] was born has begun to generalise itself to him"; instead of confusion he begins to discern " the dim outlines of a gigantic plan.   No accidents, no chance, but everywhere order and completeness. One by one exceptions vanish, and all becomes systematic."

Always towards perfection is the mighty movement—towards a complete development and a more unmixed good ; subordinating in its universality all petty irregularities and fallings back, as the curvature of the earth subordinates mountains and valleys. Even in evils the student learns to recognise only a struggling beneficence. But above all he is struck with the inherent sufficingness of things.

But the movement towards harmony, the elimination of evil, will not be effected by idealists imposing their constructions upon the world or by authoritarian governments. It means gradual adaptation, gradual psychological change, and its life is individual liberty. It proceeds by the give and take of opposed opinions. Guizot had said, " Progress, and at the same time resistance." And Spencer conceives that resistance is beneficial, so long as it comes from those who honestly think that the institutions they defend are really the best and the proposed innovations absolutely wrong.

It will be observed that Spencer's doctrine of perfectibility rests on an entirely different basis from the doctrine of the eighteenth century. It is one thing to deduce it from an abstract psychology which holds that human nature is unresistingly plastic in the hands of the legislator and the instructor. It is another to argue that human nature is subject to the general law of change, and that the process by which it slowly but continuously tends to adapt itself more and more to the conditions of social life—children inheriting the acquired aptitudes of their parents—points to an ultimate harmony. Here profitable legislation and education are auxiliary to the process of unconscious adaptation, and respond to the psychological changes in the community, changes which reveal themselves in public opinion.

3

During the following ten years Spencer was investigating the general laws of evolution and planning his Synthetic Philosophy which was to explain the development of the universe. He aimed at showing that laws of change are discoverable which control all phenomena alike, inorganic biological, psychical, and social. In the light of this hypothesis the actual progression of humanity is established as a necessary fact, a sequel of the general cosmic movement and governed by the same principles; and, if that progression is shown to involve increasing happiness, the theory of Progress is established. The first section of the work, *First Principles*, appeared in 1862. The *Biology*, the *Psychology*, and finally the *Sociology*, followed during the next twenty years; and the synthesis of the world-process which these volumes lucidly and persuasively developed, probably did more than any other work, at least in England, both to drive home the significance of the doctrine of evolution and to raise the doctrine of Progress to the rank of a commonplace truth in popular estimation, an axiom to which political rhetoric might effectively appeal.

Many of those who were allured by Spencer's gigantic synthesis hardly realised that his theory of social evolution, of the gradual psychical improvement of the race, depends upon the validity of the assumption that parents transmit to their children faculties and aptitudes which they have themselves acquired.   On this question experts notoriously differ.   Some day it will probably be definitely decided, and perhaps in Spencer's favour.   But the theory of continuous psychical improvement by a process of nature encounters an obvious difficulty, which did not escape some critics of Spencer, in the prominent fact of history that every great civilisation of the past progressed to a point at which instead of advancing further it stood still and declined, to become the prey of younger societies, or, if it survived, to stagnate.   Arrest, decadence, stagnation has been the rule.   It is not easy to reconcile this phenomenon with the theory of mental improvement.

The receptive attitude of the public towards such a philosophy as Spencer's had been made possible by Darwin's discoveries, which were reinforced by the growing science of palaeontology and the accumulating material evidence of the great antiquity of man.   By the simultaneous advances of geology and biology man's perspective in time was revolutionised, just as the Copernican astronomy had revolutionised his perspective in space.   Many thoughtful and many thoughtless people were ready to discern—as Huxley suggested—in man's "long progress through the past, a reasonable ground of faith in his attainment of a nobler future."

The recorded portion of his long progress through the past was indeed not altogether pleasant to look back on for any one gifted with imagination, and Winwood Reade, a young African traveller, exhibited it in a vivid book as a long-drawn-out martyrdom.   But he was a disciple of Spencer, and his hopes for the future were as bright as his picture of the past was dark. *The Martyrdom of Man*, published in 1872, was so widely read that it reached an eighth edition twelve years later, and may be counted as one of the agencies which popularised Spencer's optimism.

That optimism was not endorsed by all the contemporary leaders of thought.   Lotze had asserted emphatically in 1864 that " human nature will not change," and afterwards he saw no reason to alter his conviction.

Never one fold and one shepherd, never one uniform culture for all mankind, never universal nobleness.   Our virtue and happiness can only flourish amid an active conflict with wrong.   If every stumbling-block were smoothed away, men would no longer be like men, but like a flock of innocent brutes, feeding on good things provided by nature as at the very beginning of their course.[1]

But even if we reject with Spencer the old dictum, endorsed by Lotze as by Fontenelle, that human nature is immutable, the dictum of ultimate harmony encounters the following objection.   " If the social environment were stable," it is easy to argue, " it could be admitted that man's nature, variable *ex hypothesi*, could gradually adapt itself

[1] *Microcosmus*, Bk. vii. 5 *ad fin.* (Eng. trans. p. 300).   The first German edition (three vols.) appeared in 1856–64, the third, from which the English translation was made, in 1876.   Lotze was optimistic as to the durability of modern civilisation : "No one will profess to foreknow the future, but as far as men may judge it seems that in our days there are greater safeguards than there were in antiquity against unjustifiable excesses and against the external forces which might endanger the continued existence of civilisation."

to it, and that finally a definite equilibrium would be established.   But the environment is continually changing as the consequence of man's very efforts to adapt himself; every step he takes to harmonise his needs and his conditions produces a new discord and confronts him with a new problem.   In other words, there is no reason to believe that the reciprocal process which goes on in the growth of society between men's natures and the environment they are continually modifying will ever reach an equilibrium, or even that, as the character of the discords changes, the suffering which they cause diminishes."

In fact, upon the neutral fact of evolution a theory of pessimism may be built up as speciously as a theory of optimism.   And such a theory was built up with great power and ability by the German philosopher E. von Hartmann, whose *Philosophy of the Unconscious* appeared in 1869.   Leaving aside his metaphysics and his grotesque theory of the destiny of the universe, we see here and in his subsequent works how plausibly a convinced evolutionist could revive the view of Rousseau that civilisation and happiness are mutually antagonistic, and that Progress means an increase of misery.

Huxley himself, one of the most eminent interpreters of the doctrine of evolution, did not, in his late years at least, entertain very sanguine views of mankind.   " I know of no study which is so saddening as that of the evolution of humanity as it is set forth in the annals of history. . . . Man is a brute, only more intelligent than other brutes " ; and " even the best of modern civilisations appears to me to exhibit a condition of mankind which neither embodies any worthy ideal nor even possesses the merit of stability." There may be some hope of a large improvement, but otherwise he would " welcome a kindly comet to sweep the whole affair away." And he came to the final conclusion that such an improvement could only set in by deliberately resisting, instead of co-operating with, the processes of nature. "Social progress means the checking of the cosmic process at every step and the substitution for it of another which may be called the ethical process." [1] How in a few centuries can man hope to gain the mastery over the cosmic process which has been at work for millions of years? "The theory of evolution encourages no millennial anticipations."

I have quoted these views to illustrate that evolution lends itself to a pessimistic as well as to an optimistic interpretation. The question whether it leads in a desirable direction or not is answered according to the temperament of the inquirer. In an age of prosperity and self-complacency the affirmative answer was readily received, and the term evolution attracted to itself in common speech the implications of value which belong to Progress.

It may be noticed that the self-complacency of the age was promoted by the popularisation of scientific knowledge. A rapidly growing demand (especially in England) for books and lectures, making the results of science accessible and interesting to the lay public, is a remarkable feature of the

[1] Huxley considers progress exclusively from an ethical, not from an eudaemonic point of view.

second half of the nineteenth century; and to supply this demand was a remunerative enterprise. This popular literature explaining the wonders of the physical world was at the same time subtly flushing the imaginations of men with the consciousness that they were living in an era which, in itself vastly superior to any age of the past, need be burdened by no fear of decline or catastrophe, but trusting in the boundless resources of science might securely defy fate.

4

Thus in the seventies and eighties of the last century the idea of Progress was becoming a general article of faith.   Some might hold it in the fatalistic form that humanity moves in a desirable direction, whatever men do or may leave undone; others might believe that the future will depend largely on our own conscious efforts, but that there is nothing in the nature of things to disappoint the prospect of steady and indefinite advance.   The majority did not inquire too curiously into such points of doctrine, but received it in a vague sense as a comfortable addition to their convictions.   But it became a part of the general mental outlook of educated people.

When Mr. Frederic Harrison delivered in 1889 at Manchester an eloquent discourse on the "New Era," in which the dominant note is "the faith in human progress in lieu of celestial rewards of the separate soul," his general argument could appeal to immensely wider circles than the Positivists whom he was specially addressing.

The dogma—for a dogma it remains, in spite of

the confidence of Comte or of Spencer that he had made it á scientific hypothesis—has produced an important ethical principle. Consideration for posterity has throughout history operated as a motive of conduct, but feebly, occasionally, and in a very limited sense. With the doctrine of Progress it assumes, logically, a preponderating importance ; for the centre of interest is transferred to the life of future generations who are to enjoy conditions of happiness denied to us, but which our labours and sufferings are to help to bring about. If the doctrine is held in an extreme fatalistic form, then our duty is to resign ourselves cheerfully to sacrifices for the sake of unknown descendants, just as ordinary altruism enjoins the cheerful acceptance of sacrifices for the sake of living fellow-creatures. Winwood Reade indicated this when he wrote, " Our own prosperity is founded on the agonies of the past. Is it therefore unjust that we also should suffer for the benefit of those who are to come ? " But if it is held that each generation can by its own deliberate acts determine for good or evil the destinies of the race, then our duties towards others reach out through time as well as through space, and our contemporaries are only a negligible fraction of the " neighbours " to whom we owe obligations. The ethical end may still be formulated, with the Utilitarians, as the greatest happiness of the greatest number ; only the greatest number includes, as Kidd observed, " the members of generations yet unborn or unthought of." This extension of the moral code, if it is not yet conspicuous in treatises on Ethics, has in late years been obtaining recognition in practice.

5

Within the last forty years nearly every civilised country has produced a large literature on social science, in which indefinite Progress is generally assumed as an axiom. But the "law" whose investigation Kant designated as the task for a Newton, which Saint-Simon and Comte did not find, and to which Spencer's evolutionary formula would stand in the same relation as it stands to the law of gravitation, remains still undiscovered. To examine or even glance at this literature, or to speculate how theories of Progress may be modified by recent philosophical speculation, lies beyond the scope of this volume, which is only concerned with tracing the origin of the idea and its growth up to the time when it became a current creed.

Looking back on the course of the inquiry, we note how the history of the idea has been connected with the growth of modern science, with the growth of rationalism, and with the struggle for political and religious liberty. The precursors (Bodin and Bacon) lived at a time when the world was consciously emancipating itself from the authority of tradition and it was being discovered that liberty is a difficult theoretical problem. The idea took definite shape in France when the old scheme of the universe had been shattered by the victory of the new astronomy and the prestige of Providence, *cuncta supercilio mouentis*, was paling before the majesty of the immutable laws of nature. There began a slow but steady reinstatement of the kingdom of this world. The otherworldly dreams of theologians,

ceux qui reniaient la terre pour patrie,

which had ruled so long lost their power, and men's earthly home again insinuated itself into their affections, but with the new hope of its becoming a place fit for reasonable beings to live in. We have seen how the belief that our race is travelling towards earthly happiness was propagated by some eminent thinkers, as well as by some "not very fortunate persons who had a good deal of time on their hands." And all these high-priests and incense-bearers to whom the creed owes its success were rationalists, from the author of the *Histoire des oracles* to the philosopher of the Unknowable.

EPILOGUE

In achieving its ascendency and unfolding its meaning, the Idea of Progress had to overcome a psychological obstacle which may be described as *the illusion of finality*.

It is quite easy to fancy a state of society, vastly different from ours, existing in some unknown place like heaven ; it is much more difficult to realise as a fact that the order of things with which we are familiar has so little stability that our actual descendants may be born into a world as different from ours as ours is from that of our ancestors of the pleistocene age.

The illusion of finality is strong. The men of the Middle Ages would have found it hard to imagine that a time was not far off in which the Last Judgement would have ceased to arouse any emotional interest. In the sphere of speculation Hegel, and even Comte, illustrate this psychological limitation : they did not recognise that their own systems could not be final any more than the system of Aristotle or of Descartes. It is science, perhaps, more than anything else—the wonderful history of science in the last hundred years—that has helped us to transcend this illusion.

But if we accept the reasonings on which the dogma of Progress is based, must we not carry them to their full conclusion? In escaping from the illusion of finality, is it legitimate to exempt that dogma itself? Must not it, too, submit to its own negation of finality? Will not that process of change, for which Progress is the optimistic name, compel " Progress" too to fall from the commanding position in which it is now, with apparent security, enthroned? Ἔσσεται ἦμαρ ὅταν . . . A day will come, in the revolution of centuries, when a new idea will usurp its place as the directing idea of humanity. Another star, unnoticed now or invisible, will climb up the intellectual heaven, and human emotions will react to its influence, human plans respond to its guidance. It will be the criterion by which Progress and all other ideas will be judged. And it too will have its successor.

In other words, does not Progress itself suggest that its value as a doctrine is only relative, corresponding to a certain not very advanced stage of civilisation; just as Providence, in its day, was an idea of relative value, corresponding to a stage somewhat less advanced? Or will it be said that this argument is merely a disconcerting trick of dialectic played under cover of the darkness in which the issue of the future is safely hidden by Horace's prudent god?

INDEX

1. PERSONAL NAMES

2. SUBJECTS

A CATALOG OF SELECTED DOVER BOOKS IN ALL FIELDS OF INTEREST

CONCERNING THE SPIRITUAL IN ART, Wassily Kandinsky. Pioneering work by father of abstract art. Thoughts on color theory, nature of art. Analysis of earlier masters. 12 illustrations. 80pp. of text. 5⅜ × 8½. 23411-8 Pa. $2.50

LEONARDO ON THE HUMAN BODY, Leonardo da Vinci. More than 1200 of Leonardo's anatomical drawings on 215 plates. Leonardo's text, which accompanies the drawings, has been translated into English. 506pp. 8⅜ × 11¾. 24483-0 Pa. $10.95

GOBLIN MARKET, Christina Rossetti. Best-known work by poet comparable to Emily Dickinson, Alfred Tennyson. With 46 delightfully grotesque illustrations by Laurence Housman. 64pp. 4 × 6¾. 24516-0 Pa. $2.50

THE HEART OF THOREAU'S JOURNALS, edited by Odell Shepard. Selections from *Journal*, ranging over full gamut of interests. 228pp. 5⅜ × 8½. 20741-2 Pa. $4.50

MR. LINCOLN'S CAMERA MAN: MATHEW B. BRADY, Roy Meredith. Over 300 Brady photos reproduced directly from original negatives, photos. Lively commentary. 368pp. 8⅜ × 11¼. 23021-X Pa. $14.95

PHOTOGRAPHIC VIEWS OF SHERMAN'S CAMPAIGN, George N. Barnard. Reprint of landmark 1866 volume with 61 plates: battlefield of New Hope Church, the Etawah Bridge, the capture of Atlanta, etc. 80pp. 9 × 12. 23445-2 Pa. $6.00

A SHORT HISTORY OF ANATOMY AND PHYSIOLOGY FROM THE GREEKS TO HARVEY, Dr. Charles Singer. Thoroughly engrossing non-technical survey. 270 illustrations. 211pp. 5⅜ × 8½. 20389-1 Pa. $4.95

REDOUTE ROSES IRON-ON TRANSFER PATTERNS, Barbara Christopher. Redouté was botanical painter to the Empress Josephine; transfer his famous roses onto fabric with these 24 transfer patterns. 80pp. 8¼ × 10⅞. 24292-7 Pa. $3.50

THE FIVE BOOKS OF ARCHITECTURE, Sebastiano Serlio. Architectural milestone, first (1611) English translation of Renaissance classic. Unabridged reproduction of original edition includes over 300 woodcut illustrations. 416pp. 9⅜ × 12¼. 24349-4 Pa. $14.95

CARLSON'S GUIDE TO LANDSCAPE PAINTING, John F. Carlson. Authoritative, comprehensive guide covers, every aspect of landscape painting. 34 reproductions of paintings by author; 58 explanatory diagrams. 144pp. 8⅜ × 11. 22927-0 Pa. $5.95

101 PUZZLES IN THOUGHT AND LOGIC, C.R. Wylie, Jr. Solve murders, robberies, see which fishermen are liars—purely by reasoning! 107pp. 5⅜ × 8½. 20367-0 Pa. $2.00

TEST YOUR LOGIC, George J. Summers. 50 more truly new puzzles with new turns of thought, new subtleties of inference. 100pp. 5⅜ × 8½. 22877-0 Pa. $2.25

SMOCKING: TECHNIQUE, PROJECTS, AND DESIGNS, Dianne Durand. Foremost smocking designer provides complete instructions on how to smock. Over 10 projects, over 100 illustrations. 56pp. 8¼ × 11. 23788-5 Pa. $2.00

AUDUBON'S BIRDS IN COLOR FOR DECOUPAGE, edited by Eleanor H. Rawlings. 24 sheets, 37 most decorative birds, full color, on one side of paper. Instructions, including work under glass. 56pp. 8¼ × 11. 23492-4 Pa. $3.95

THE COMPLETE BOOK OF SILK SCREEN PRINTING PRODUCTION, J.I. Biegeleisen. For commercial user, teacher in advanced classes, serious hobbyist. Most modern techniques, materials, equipment for optimal results. 124 illustrations. 253pp. 5⅝ × 8½. 21100-2 Pa. $4.50

A TREASURY OF ART NOUVEAU DESIGN AND ORNAMENT, edited by Carol Belanger Grafton. 577 designs for the practicing artist. Full-page, spots, borders, bookplates by Klimt, Bradley, others. 144pp. 8⅜ × 11¼. 24001-0 Pa. $5.95

ART NOUVEAU TYPOGRAPHIC ORNAMENTS, Dan X. Solo. Over 800 Art Nouveau florals, swirls, women, animals, borders, scrolls, wreaths, spots and dingbats, copyright-free. 100pp. 8⅛ × 11. 24366-4 Pa. $4.00

HAND SHADOWS TO BE THROWN UPON THE WALL, Henry Bursill. Wonderful Victorian novelty tells how to make flying birds, dog, goose, deer, and 14 others, each explained by a full-page illustration. 32pp. 6½ × 9¼. 21779-5 Pa. $1.50

AUDUBON'S BIRDS OF AMERICA COLORING BOOK, John James Audubon. Rendered for coloring by Paul Kennedy. 46 of Audubon's noted illustrations: red-winged black-bird, cardinal, etc. Original plates reproduced in full-color on the covers. Captions. 48pp. 8¼ × 11. 23049-X Pa. $2.25

SILK SCREEN TECHNIQUES, J.I. Biegeleisen, M.A. Cohn. Clear, practical, modern, economical. Minimal equipment (self-built), materials, easy methods. For amateur, hobbyist, 1st book. 141 illustrations. 185pp. 6⅛ × 9¼. 20433-2 Pa. $3.95

101 PATCHWORK PATTERNS, Ruby S. McKim. 101 beautiful, immediately useable patterns, full-size, modern and traditional. Also general information, estimating, quilt lore. 140 illustrations. 124pp. 7⅞ × 10¾. 20773-0 Pa. $3.50

READY-TO-USE FLORAL DESIGNS, Ed Sibbett, Jr. Over 100 floral designs (most in three sizes) of popular individual blossoms as well as bouquets, sprays, garlands. 64pp. 8¼ × 11. 23976-4 Pa. $2.95

AMERICAN WILD FLOWERS COLORING BOOK, Paul Kennedy. Planned coverage of 46 most important wildflowers, from Rickett's collection; instructive as well as entertaining. Color versions on covers. Captions. 48pp. 8¼ × 11. 20095-7 Pa. $2.50

CARVING DUCK DECOYS, Harry V. Shourds and Anthony Hillman. Detailed instructions and full-size templates for constructing 16 beautiful, marvelously practical decoys according to time-honored South Jersey method. 70pp. 9¼ × 12¼. 24083-5 Pa. $4.95

TRADITIONAL PATCHWORK PATTERNS, Carol Belanger Grafton. Cardboard cut-out pieces for use as templates to make 12 quilts: Buttercup, Ribbon Border, Tree of Paradise, nine more. Full instructions. 57pp. 8¼ × 11. 23015-5 Pa. $3.50

25 KITES THAT FLY, Leslie Hunt. Full, easy-to-follow instructions for kites made from inexpensive materials. Many novelties. 70 illustrations. 110pp. 5⅜ × 8½.
22550-X Pa. $2.25

PIANO TUNING, J. Cree Fischer. Clearest, best book for beginner, amateur. Simple repairs, raising dropped notes, tuning by easy method of flattened fifths. No previous skills needed. 4 illustrations. 201pp. 5⅜ × 8½. 23267-0 Pa. $3.50

EARLY AMERICAN IRON-ON TRANSFER PATTERNS, edited by Rita Weiss. 75 designs, borders, alphabets, from traditional American sources. 48pp. 8¼ × 11.
23162-3 Pa. $1.95

CROCHETING EDGINGS, edited by Rita Weiss. Over 100 of the best designs for these lovely trims for a host of household items. Complete instructions, illustrations. 48pp. 8¼ × 11. 24031-2 Pa. $2.25

FINGER PLAYS FOR NURSERY AND KINDERGARTEN, Emilie Poulsson. 18 finger plays with music (voice and piano); entertaining, instructive. Counting, nature lore, etc. Victorian classic. 53 illustrations. 80pp. 6½ × 9¼. 22588-7 Pa. $1.95

BOSTON THEN AND NOW, Peter Vanderwarker. Here in 59 side-by-side views are photographic documentations of the city's past and present. 119 photographs. Full captions. 122pp. 8¼ × 11. 24312-5 Pa. $6.95

CROCHETING BEDSPREADS, edited by Rita Weiss. 22 patterns, originally published in three instruction books 1939-41. 39 photos, 8 charts. Instructions. 48pp. 8¼ × 11. 23610-2 Pa. $2.00

HAWTHORNE ON PAINTING, Charles W. Hawthorne. Collected from notes taken by students at famous Cape Cod School; hundreds of direct, personal *apercus*, ideas, suggestions. 91pp. 5⅜ × 8½. 20653-X Pa. $2.50

THERMODYNAMICS, Enrico Fermi. A classic of modern science. Clear, organized treatment of systems, first and second laws, entropy, thermodynamic potentials, etc. Calculus required. 160pp. 5⅜ × 8½. 60361-X Pa. $4.00

TEN BOOKS ON ARCHITECTURE, Vitruvius. The most important book ever written on architecture. Early Roman aesthetics, technology, classical orders, site selection, all other aspects. Morgan translation. 331pp. 5⅜ × 8½. 20645-9 Pa. $5.50

THE CORNELL BREAD BOOK, Clive M. McCay and Jeanette B. McCay. Famed high-protein recipe incorporated into breads, rolls, buns, coffee cakes, pizza, pie crusts, more. Nearly 50 illustrations. 48pp. 8¼ × 11. 23995-0 Pa. $2.00

THE CRAFTSMAN'S HANDBOOK, Cennino Cennini. 15th-century handbook, school of Giotto, explains applying gold, silver leaf; gesso; fresco painting, grinding pigments, etc. 142pp. 6⅛ × 9¼. 20054-X Pa. $3.50

FRANK LLOYD WRIGHT'S FALLINGWATER, Donald Hoffmann. Full story of Wright's masterwork at Bear Run, Pa. 100 photographs of site, construction, and details of completed structure. 112pp. 9¼ × 10. 23671-4 Pa. $6.95

OVAL STAINED GLASS PATTERN BOOK, C. Eaton. 60 new designs framed in shape of an oval. Greater complexity, challenge with sinuous cats, birds, mandalas framed in antique shape. 64pp. 8¼ × 11. 24519-5 Pa. $3.50

CHILDREN'S BOOKPLATES AND LABELS, Ed Sibbett, Jr. 6 each of 12 types based on *Wizard of Oz, Alice,* nursery rhymes, fairy tales. Perforated; full color. 24pp. 8¼ × 11. 23538-6 Pa. $3.50

READY-TO-USE VICTORIAN COLOR STICKERS: 96 Pressure-Sensitive Seals, Carol Belanger Grafton. Drawn from authentic period sources. Motifs include heads of men, women, children, plus florals, animals, birds, more. Will adhere to any clean surface. 8pp. 8½ × 11. 24551-9 Pa. $2.95

CUT AND FOLD PAPER SPACESHIPS THAT FLY, Michael Grater. 16 colorful, easy-to-build spaceships that really fly. Star Shuttle, Lunar Freighter, Star Probe, 13 others. 32pp. 8¼ × 11. 23978-0 Pa. $2.50

CUT AND ASSEMBLE PAPER AIRPLANES THAT FLY, Arthur Baker. 8 aerodynamically sound, ready-to-build paper airplanes, designed with latest techniques. Fly *Pegasus, Daedalus, Songbird,* 5 other aircraft. Instructions. 32pp. 9¼ × 11¼. 24302-8 Pa. $3.95

SIDELIGHTS ON RELATIVITY, Albert Einstein. Two lectures delivered in 1920-21: *Ether and Relativity* and *Geometry and Experience.* Elegant ideas in non-mathematical form. 56pp. 5⅜ × 8½. 24511-X Pa. $2.25

FADS AND FALLACIES IN THE NAME OF SCIENCE, Martin Gardner. Fair, witty appraisal of cranks and quacks of science: Velikovsky, orgone energy, Bridey Murphy, medical fads, etc. 373pp. 5⅜ × 8½. 20394-8 Pa. $5.95

VACATION HOMES AND CABINS, U.S. Dept. of Agriculture. Complete plans for 16 cabins, vacation homes and other shelters. 105pp. 9 × 12. 23631-5 Pa. $4.95

HOW TO BUILD A WOOD-FRAME HOUSE, L.O. Anderson. Placement, foundations, framing, sheathing, roof, insulation, plaster, finishing—almost everything else. 179 illustrations. 223pp. 7⅞ × 10¾. 22954-8 Pa. $5.50

THE MYSTERY OF A HANSOM CAB, Fergus W. Hume. Bizarre murder in a hansom cab leads to engrossing investigation. Memorable characters, rich atmosphere. 19th-century bestseller, still enjoyable, exciting. 256pp. 5⅜ × 8. 21956-9 Pa. $4.00

MANUAL OF TRADITIONAL WOOD CARVING, edited by Paul N. Hasluck. Possibly the best book in English on the craft of wood carving. Practical instructions, along with 1,146 working drawings and photographic illustrations. 576pp. 6½ × 9¼. 23489-4 Pa. $8.95

WHITTLING AND WOODCARVING, E.J Tangerman. Best book on market; clear, full. If you can cut a potato, you can carve toys, puzzles, chains, etc. Over 464 illustrations. 293pp. 5⅜ × 8½. 20965-2 Pa. $4.95

AMERICAN TRADEMARK DESIGNS, Barbara Baer Capitman. 732 marks, logos and corporate-identity symbols. Categories include entertainment, heavy industry, food and beverage. All black-and-white in standard forms. 160pp. 8⅜ × 11. 23259-X Pa. $6.95

DECORATIVE FRAMES AND BORDERS, edited by Edmund V. Gillon, Jr. Largest collection of borders and frames ever compiled for use of artists and designers. Renaissance, neo-Greek, Art Nouveau, Art Deco, to mention only a few styles. 396 illustrations. 192pp. 8⅜ × 11¼. 22928-9 Pa. $6.00

THE MURDER BOOK OF J.G. REEDER, Edgar Wallace. Eight suspenseful stories by bestselling mystery writer of 20s and 30s. Features the donnish Mr. J.G. Reeder of Public Prosecutor's Office. 128pp. 5⅜ × 8½. (Available in U.S. only)
24374-5 Pa. $3.50

ANNE ORR'S CHARTED DESIGNS, Anne Orr. Best designs by premier needlework designer, all on charts: flowers, borders, birds, children, alphabets, etc. Over 100 charts, 10 in color. Total of 40pp. 8¼ × 11.
23704-4 Pa. $2.50

BASIC CONSTRUCTION TECHNIQUES FOR HOUSES AND SMALL BUILDINGS SIMPLY EXPLAINED, U.S. Bureau of Naval Personnel. Grading, masonry, woodworking, floor and wall framing, roof framing, plastering, tile setting, much more. Over 675 illustrations. 568pp. 6½ × 9¼.
20242-9 Pa. $8.95

MATISSE LINE DRAWINGS AND PRINTS, Henri Matisse. Representative collection of female nudes, faces, still lifes, experimental works, etc., from 1898 to 1948. 50 illustrations. 48pp. 8⅜ × 11¼.
23877-6 Pa. $2.50

HOW TO PLAY THE CHESS OPENINGS, Eugene Znosko-Borovsky. Clear, profound examinations of just what each opening is intended to do and how opponent can counter. Many sample games. 147pp. 5⅜ × 8½.
22795-2 Pa. $2.95

DUPLICATE BRIDGE, Alfred Sheinwold. Clear, thorough, easily followed account: rules, etiquette, scoring, strategy, bidding; Goren's point-count system, Blackwood and Gerber conventions, etc. 158pp. 5⅜ × 8½.
22741-3 Pa. $3.00

SARGENT PORTRAIT DRAWINGS, J.S. Sargent. Collection of 42 portraits reveals technical skill and intuitive eye of noted American portrait painter, John Singer Sargent. 48pp. 8¼ × 11⅛.
24524-1 Pa. $2.95

ENTERTAINING SCIENCE EXPERIMENTS WITH EVERYDAY OBJECTS, Martin Gardner. Over 100 experiments for youngsters. Will amuse, astonish, teach, and entertain. Over 100 illustrations. 127pp. 5⅜ × 8½.
24201-3 Pa. $2.50

TEDDY BEAR PAPER DOLLS IN FULL COLOR: A Family of Four Bears and Their Costumes, Crystal Collins. A family of four Teddy Bear paper dolls and nearly 60 cut-out costumes. Full color, printed one side only. 32pp. 9¼ × 12¼.
24550-0 Pa. $3.50

NEW CALLIGRAPHIC ORNAMENTS AND FLOURISHES, Arthur Baker. Unusual, multi-useable material: arrows, pointing hands, brackets and frames, ovals, swirls, birds, etc. Nearly 700 illustrations. 80pp. 8⅜ × 11¼.
24095-9 Pa. $3.75

DINOSAUR DIORAMAS TO CUT & ASSEMBLE, M. Kalmenoff. Two complete three-dimensional scenes in full color, with 31 cut-out animals and plants. Excellent educational toy for youngsters. Instructions; 2 assembly diagrams. 32pp. 9¼ × 12¼.
24541-1 Pa. $4.50

SILHOUETTES: A PICTORIAL ARCHIVE OF VARIED ILLUSTRATIONS, edited by Carol Belanger Grafton. Over 600 silhouettes from the 18th to 20th centuries. Profiles and full figures of men, women, children, birds, animals, groups and scenes, nature, ships, an alphabet. 144pp. 8⅜ × 11¼.
23781-8 Pa. $4.95

SURREAL STICKERS AND UNREAL STAMPS, William Rowe. 224 haunting, hilarious stamps on gummed, perforated stock, with images of elephants, geisha girls, George Washington, etc. 16pp. one side. 8¼ × 11.   24371-0 Pa. $3.50

GOURMET KITCHEN LABELS, Ed Sibbett, Jr. 112 full-color labels (4 copies each of 28 designs). Fruit, bread, other culinary motifs. Gummed and perforated. 16pp. 8¼ × 11.   24087-8 Pa. $2.95

PATTERNS AND INSTRUCTIONS FOR CARVING AUTHENTIC BIRDS, H.D. Green. Detailed instructions, 27 diagrams, 85 photographs for carving 15 species of birds so life-like, they'll seem ready to fly! 8¼ × 11.   24222-6 Pa. $2.75

FLATLAND, E.A. Abbott. Science-fiction classic explores life of 2-D being in 3-D world. 16 illustrations. 103pp. 5⅜ × 8.   20001-9 Pa. $2.00

DRIED FLOWERS, Sarah Whitlock and Martha Rankin. Concise, clear, practical guide to dehydration, glycerinizing, pressing plant material, and more. Covers use of silica gel. 12 drawings. 32pp. 5⅜ × 8½.   21802-3 Pa. $1.00

EASY-TO-MAKE CANDLES, Gary V. Guy. Learn how easy it is to make all kinds of decorative candles. Step-by-step instructions. 82 illustrations. 48pp. 8¼ × 11.
23881-4 Pa. $2.50

SUPER STICKERS FOR KIDS, Carolyn Bracken. 128 gummed and perforated full-color stickers: GIRL WANTED, KEEP OUT, BORED OF EDUCATION, X-RATED, COMBAT ZONE, many others. 16pp. 8¼ × 11.   24092-4 Pa. $2.50

CUT AND COLOR PAPER MASKS, Michael Grater. Clowns, animals, funny faces...simply color them in, cut them out, and put them together, and you have 9 paper masks to play with and enjoy. 32pp. 8¼ × 11.   23171-2 Pa. $2.25

A CHRISTMAS CAROL: THE ORIGINAL MANUSCRIPT, Charles Dickens. Clear facsimile of Dickens manuscript, on facing pages with final printed text. 8 illustrations by John Leech, 4 in color on covers. 144pp. 8⅜ × 11¼.
20980-6 Pa. $5.95

CARVING SHOREBIRDS, Harry V. Shourds & Anthony Hillman. 16 full-size patterns (all double-page spreads) for 19 North American shorebirds with step-by-step instructions. 72pp. 9¼ × 12¼.   24287-0 Pa. $4.95

THE GENTLE ART OF MATHEMATICS, Dan Pedoe. Mathematical games, probability, the question of infinity, topology, how the laws of algebra work, problems of irrational numbers, and more. 42 figures. 143pp. 5⅜ × 8½. (EBE)
22949-1 Pa. $3.50

READY-TO-USE DOLLHOUSE WALLPAPER, Katzenbach & Warren, Inc. Stripe, 2 floral stripes, 2 allover florals, polka dot; all in full color. 4 sheets (350 sq. in.) of each, enough for average room. 48pp. 8¼ × 11.   23495-9 Pa. $2.95

MINIATURE IRON-ON TRANSFER PATTERNS FOR DOLLHOUSES, DOLLS, AND SMALL PROJECTS, Rita Weiss and Frank Fontana. Over 100 miniature patterns: rugs, bedspreads, quilts, chair seats, etc. In standard dollhouse size. 48pp. 8¼ × 11.   23741-9 Pa. $1.95

THE DINOSAUR COLORING BOOK, Anthony Rao. 45 renderings of dinosaurs, fossil birds, turtles, other creatures of Mesozoic Era. Scientifically accurate. Captions. 48pp. 8¼ × 11.   24022-3 Pa. $2.50

THE BOOK OF WOOD CARVING, Charles Marshall Sayers. Still finest book for beginning student. Fundamentals, technique; gives 34 designs, over 34 projects for panels, bookends, mirrors, etc. 33 photos. 118pp. 7¾ × 10⅝.   23654-4 Pa. $3.95

CARVING COUNTRY CHARACTERS, Bill Higginbotham. Expert advice for beginning, advanced carvers on materials, techniques for creating 18 projects—mirthful panorama of American characters. 105 illustrations. 80pp. 8⅜ × 11.
24135-1 Pa. $2.50

300 ART NOUVEAU DESIGNS AND MOTIFS IN FULL COLOR, C.B. Grafton. 44 full-page plates display swirling lines and muted colors typical of Art Nouveau. Borders, frames, panels, cartouches, dingbats, etc. 48pp. 9⅜ × 12¼.
24354-0 Pa. $6.95

SELF-WORKING CARD TRICKS, Karl Fulves. Editor of *Pallbearer* offers 72 tricks that work automatically through nature of card deck. No sleight of hand needed. Often spectacular. 42 illustrations. 113pp. 5⅜ × 8½.   23334-0 Pa. $3.50

CUT AND ASSEMBLE A WESTERN FRONTIER TOWN, Edmund V. Gillon, Jr. Ten authentic full-color buildings on heavy cardboard stock in H-O scale. Sheriff's Office and Jail, Saloon, Wells Fargo, Opera House, others. 48pp. 9¼ × 12¼.
23736-2 Pa. $3.95

CUT AND ASSEMBLE AN EARLY NEW ENGLAND VILLAGE, Edmund V. Gillon, Jr. Printed in full color on heavy cardboard stock. 12 authentic buildings in H-O scale: Adams home in Quincy, Mass., Oliver Wight house in Sturbridge, smithy, store, church, others. 48pp. 9¼ × 12¼.   23536-X Pa. $4.95

THE TALE OF TWO BAD MICE, Beatrix Potter. Tom Thumb and Hunca Munca squeeze out of their hole and go exploring. 27 full-color Potter illustrations. 59pp. 4¼ × 5½. (Available in U.S. only)   23065-1 Pa. $1.75

CARVING FIGURE CARICATURES IN THE OZARK STYLE, Harold L. Enlow. Instructions and illustrations for ten delightful projects, plus general carving instructions. 22 drawings and 47 photographs altogether. 39pp. 8⅜ × 11.
23151-8 Pa. $2.50

A TREASURY OF FLOWER DESIGNS FOR ARTISTS, EMBROIDERERS AND CRAFTSMEN, Susan Gaber. 100 garden favorites lushly rendered by artist for artists, craftsmen, needleworkers. Many form frames, borders. 80pp. 8¼ × 11.
24096-7 Pa. $3.50

CUT & ASSEMBLE A TOY THEATER/THE NUTCRACKER BALLET, Tom Tierney. Model of a complete, full-color production of Tchaikovsky's classic. 6 backdrops, dozens of characters, familiar dance sequences. 32pp. 9⅜ × 12¼.
24194-7 Pa. $4.50

ANIMALS: 1,419 COPYRIGHT-FREE ILLUSTRATIONS OF MAMMALS, BIRDS, FISH, INSECTS, ETC., edited by Jim Harter. Clear wood engravings present, in extremely lifelike poses, over 1,000 species of animals. 284pp. 9 × 12.
23766-4 Pa. $9.95

MORE HAND SHADOWS, Henry Bursill. For those at their 'finger ends," 16 more effects—Shakespeare, a hare, a squirrel, Mr. Punch, and twelve more—each explained by a full-page illustration. Considerable period charm. 30pp. 6½ × 9¼.
21384-6 Pa. $1.95

JAPANESE DESIGN MOTIFS, Matsuya Co. Mon, or heraldic designs. Over 4000 typical, beautiful designs: birds, animals, flowers, swords, fans, geometrics; all beautifully stylized. 213pp. 11⅜ × 8¼. 22874-6 Pa. $7.95

THE TALE OF BENJAMIN BUNNY, Beatrix Potter. Peter Rabbit's cousin coaxes him back into Mr. McGregor's garden for a whole new set of adventures. All 27 full-color illustrations. 59pp. 4¼ × 5½. (Available in U.S. only) 21102-9 Pa. $1.75

THE TALE OF PETER RABBIT AND OTHER FAVORITE STORIES BOXED SET, Beatrix Potter. Seven of Beatrix Potter's best-loved tales including Peter Rabbit in a specially designed, durable boxed set. 4¼ × 5½. Total of 447pp. 158 color illustrations. (Available in U.S. only) 23903-9 Pa. $10.80

PRACTICAL MENTAL MAGIC, Theodore Annemann. Nearly 200 astonishing feats of mental magic revealed in step-by-step detail. Complete advice on staging, patter, etc. Illustrated. 320pp. 5⅜ × 8½. 24426-1 Pa. $5.95

CELEBRATED CASES OF JUDGE DEE (DEE GOONG AN), translated by Robert Van Gulik. Authentic 18th-century Chinese detective novel; Dee and associates solve three interlocked cases. Led to van Gulik's own stories with same characters. Extensive introduction. 9 illustrations. 237pp. 5⅜ × 8½.
23337-5 Pa. $4.50

CUT & FOLD EXTRATERRESTRIAL INVADERS THAT FLY, M. Grater. Stage your own lilliputian space battles.By following the step-by-step instructions and explanatory diagrams you can launch 22 full-color fliers into space. 36pp. 8¼ × 11. 24478-4 Pa. $2.95

CUT & ASSEMBLE VICTORIAN HOUSES, Edmund V. Gillon, Jr. Printed in full color on heavy cardboard stock, 4 authentic Victorian houses in H-O scale: Italian-style Villa, Octagon, Second Empire, Stick Style. 48pp. 9¼ × 12¼.
23849-0 Pa. $3.95

BEST SCIENCE FICTION STORIES OF H.G. WELLS, H.G. Wells. Full novel *The Invisible Man*, plus 17 short stories: "The Crystal Egg," "Aepyornis Island," "The Strange Orchid," etc. 303pp. 5⅜ × 8½. (Available in U.S. only)
21531-8 Pa. $4.95

TRADEMARK DESIGNS OF THE WORLD, Yusaku Kamekura. A lavish collection of nearly 700 trademarks, the work of Wright, Loewy, Klee, Binder, hundreds of others. 160pp. 8¾ × 8. (Available in U.S. only) 24191-2 Pa. $5.95

THE ARTIST'S AND CRAFTSMAN'S GUIDE TO REDUCING, ENLARGING AND TRANSFERRING DESIGNS, Rita Weiss. Discover, reduce, enlarge, transfer designs from any objects to any craft project. 12pp. plus 16 sheets special graph paper. 8¼ × 11. 24142-4 Pa. $3.50

TREASURY OF JAPANESE DESIGNS AND MOTIFS FOR ARTISTS AND CRAFTSMEN, edited by Carol Belanger Grafton. Indispensable collection of 360 traditional Japanese designs and motifs redrawn in clean, crisp black-and-white, copyright-free illustrations. 96pp. 8¼ × 11. 24435-0 Pa. $3.95

CHANCERY CURSIVE STROKE BY STROKE, Arthur Baker. Instructions and illustrations for each stroke of each letter (upper and lower case) and numerals. 54 full-page plates. 64pp. 8¼ × 11. 24278-1 Pa. $2.50

THE ENJOYMENT AND USE OF COLOR, Walter Sargent. Color relationships, values, intensities; complementary colors, illumination, similar topics. Color in nature and art. 7 color plates, 29 illustrations. 274pp. 5⅜ × 8½. 20944-X Pa. $4.95

SCULPTURE PRINCIPLES AND PRACTICE, Louis Slobodkin. Step-by-step approach to clay, plaster, metals, stone; classical and modern. 253 drawings, photos. 255pp. 8⅛ × 11. 22960-2 Pa. $7.50

VICTORIAN FASHION PAPER DOLLS FROM HARPER'S BAZAR, 1867-1898, Theodore Menten. Four female dolls with 28 elegant high fashion costumes, printed in full color. 32pp. 9¼ × 12¼. 23453-3 Pa. $3.50

FLOPSY, MOPSY AND COTTONTAIL: A Little Book of Paper Dolls in Full Color, Susan LaBelle. Three dolls and 21 costumes (7 for each doll) show Peter Rabbit's siblings dressed for holidays, gardening, hiking, etc. Charming borders, captions. 48pp. 4¼ × 5½. 24376-1 Pa. $2.25

NATIONAL LEAGUE BASEBALL CARD CLASSICS, Bert Randolph Sugar. 83 big-leaguers from 1909-69 on facsimile cards. Hubbell, Dean, Spahn, Brock plus advertising, info, no duplications. Perforated, detachable. 16pp. 8¼ × 11. 24308-7 Pa. $2.95

THE LOGICAL APPROACH TO CHESS, Dr. Max Euwe, et al. First-rate text of comprehensive strategy, tactics, theory for the amateur. No gambits to memorize, just a clear, logical approach. 224pp. 5⅜ × 8½. 24353-2 Pa. $4.50

MAGICK IN THEORY AND PRACTICE, Aleister Crowley. The summation of the thought and practice of the century's most famous necromancer, long hard to find. Crowley's best book. 436pp. 5⅜ × 8½. (Available in U.S. only) 23295-6 Pa. $6.50

THE HAUNTED HOTEL, Wilkie Collins. Collins' last great tale; doom and destiny in a Venetian palace. Praised by T.S. Eliot. 127pp. 5⅜ × 8½. 24333-8 Pa. $3.00

ART DECO DISPLAY ALPHABETS, Dan X. Solo. Wide variety of bold yet elegant lettering in handsome Art Deco styles. 100 complete fonts, with numerals, punctuation, more. 104pp. 8⅛ × 11. 24372-9 Pa. $4.50

CALLIGRAPHIC ALPHABETS, Arthur Baker. Nearly 150 complete alphabets by outstanding contemporary. Stimulating ideas; useful source for unique effects. 154 plates. 157pp. 8⅜ × 11¼. 21045-6 Pa. $5.95

ARTHUR BAKER'S HISTORIC CALLIGRAPHIC ALPHABETS, Arthur Baker. From monumental capitals of first-century Rome to humanistic cursive of 16th century, 33 alphabets in fresh interpretations. 88 plates. 96pp. 9 × 12. 24054-1 Pa. $4.50

LETTIE LANE PAPER DOLLS, Sheila Young. Genteel turn-of-the-century family very popular then and now. 24 paper dolls. 16 plates in full color. 32pp. 9¼ × 12¼. 24089-4 Pa. $3.50

TWENTY-FOUR ART NOUVEAU POSTCARDS IN FULL COLOR FROM CLASSIC POSTERS, Hayward and Blanche Cirker. Ready-to-mail postcards reproduced from rare set of poster art. Works by Toulouse-Lautrec, Parrish, Steinlen, Mucha, Cheret, others. 12pp. 8¼× 11. 24389-3 Pa. $2.95

READY-TO-USE ART NOUVEAU BOOKMARKS IN FULL COLOR, Carol Belanger Grafton. 30 elegant bookmarks featuring graceful, flowing lines, foliate motifs, sensuous women characteristic of Art Nouveau. Perforated for easy detaching. 16pp. 8¼ × 11. 24305-2 Pa. $2.95

FRUIT KEY AND TWIG KEY TO TREES AND SHRUBS, William M. Harlow. Fruit key covers 120 deciduous and evergreen species; twig key covers 160 deciduous species. Easily used. Over 300 photographs. 126pp. 5⅜ × 8½. 20511-8 Pa. $2.25

LEONARDO DRAWINGS, Leonardo da Vinci. Plants, landscapes, human face and figure, etc., plus studies for Sforza monument, *Last Supper*, more. 60 illustrations. 64pp. 8¼ × 11⅛. 23951-9 Pa. $2.75

CLASSIC BASEBALL CARDS, edited by Bert R. Sugar. 98 classic cards on heavy stock, full color, perforated for detaching. Ruth, Cobb, Durocher, DiMaggio, H. Wagner, 99 others. Rare originals cost hundreds. 16pp. 8¼ × 11. 23498-3 Pa. $3.25

TREES OF THE EASTERN AND CENTRAL UNITED STATES AND CANADA, William M. Harlow. Best one-volume guide to 140 trees. Full descriptions, woodlore, range, etc. Over 600 illustrations. Handy size. 288pp. 4½ × 6⅜. 20395-6 Pa. $3.95

JUDY GARLAND PAPER DOLLS IN FULL COLOR, Tom Tierney. 3 Judy Garland paper dolls (teenager, grown-up, and mature woman) and 30 gorgeous costumes highlighting memorable career. Captions. 32pp. 9¼ × 12¼. 24404-0 Pa. $3.50

GREAT FASHION DESIGNS OF THE BELLE EPOQUE PAPER DOLLS IN FULL COLOR, Tom Tierney. Two dolls and 30 costumes meticulously rendered. Haute couture by Worth, Lanvin, Paquin, other greats late Victorian to WWI. 32pp. 9¼ × 12¼. 24425-3 Pa. $3.50

FASHION PAPER DOLLS FROM GODEY'S LADY'S BOOK, 1840-1854, Susan Johnston. In full color: 7 female fashion dolls with 50 costumes. Little girl's, bridal, riding, bathing, wedding, evening, everyday, etc. 32pp. 9¼ × 12¼. 23511-4 Pa. $3.95

THE BOOK OF THE SACRED MAGIC OF ABRAMELIN THE MAGE, translated by S. MacGregor Mathers. Medieval manuscript of ceremonial magic. Basic document in Aleister Crowley, Golden Dawn groups. 268pp. 5⅜ × 8½. 23211-5 Pa. $5.00

PETER RABBIT POSTCARDS IN FULL COLOR: 24 Ready-to-Mail Cards, Susan Whited LaBelle. Bunnies ice-skating, coloring Easter eggs, making valentines, many other charming scenes. 24 perforated full-color postcards, each measuring 4¼ × 6, on coated stock. 12pp. 9 × 12. 24617-5 Pa. $2.95

CELTIC HAND STROKE BY STROKE, A. Baker. Complete guide creating each letter of the alphabet in distinctive Celtic manner. Covers hand position, strokes, pens, inks, paper, more. Illustrated. 48pp. 8¼ × 11. 24336-2 Pa. $2.50

KEYBOARD WORKS FOR SOLO INSTRUMENTS, G.F. Handel. 35 neglected works from Handel's vast oeuvre, originally jotted down as improvisations. Includes Eight Great Suites, others. New sequence. 174pp. 9⅜ × 12¼.
24338-9 Pa. $7.50

AMERICAN LEAGUE BASEBALL CARD CLASSICS, Bert Randolph Sugar. 82 stars from 1900s to 60s on facsimile cards. Ruth, Cobb, Mantle, Williams, plus advertising, info, no duplications. Perforated, detachable. 16pp. 8¼ × 11.
24286-2 Pa. $2.95

A TREASURY OF CHARTED DESIGNS FOR NEEDLEWORKERS, Georgia Gorham and Jeanne Warth. 141 charted designs: owl, cat with yarn, tulips, piano, spinning wheel, covered bridge, Victorian house and many others. 48pp. 8¼ × 11.
23558-0 Pa. $1.95

DANISH FLORAL CHARTED DESIGNS, Gerda Bengtsson. Exquisite collection of over 40 different florals: anemone, Iceland poppy, wild fruit, pansies, many others. 45 illustrations. 48pp. 8¼ × 11. 23957-8 Pa. $1.75

OLD PHILADELPHIA IN EARLY PHOTOGRAPHS 1839-1914, Robert F. Looney. 215 photographs: panoramas, street scenes, landmarks, President-elect Lincoln's visit, 1876 Centennial Exposition, much more. 230pp. 8⅜ × 11¾.
23345-6 Pa. $9.95

PRELUDE TO MATHEMATICS, W.W. Sawyer. Noted mathematician's lively, stimulating account of non-Euclidean geometry, matrices, determinants, group theory, other topics. Emphasis on novel, striking aspects. 224pp. 5⅜ × 8½.
24401-6 Pa. $4.50

ADVENTURES WITH A MICROSCOPE, Richard Headstrom. 59 adventures with clothing fibers, protozoa, ferns and lichens, roots and leaves, much more. 142 illustrations. 232pp. 5⅜ × 8½. 23471-1 Pa. $3.95

IDENTIFYING ANIMAL TRACKS: MAMMALS, BIRDS, AND OTHER ANIMALS OF THE EASTERN UNITED STATES, Richard Headstrom. For hunters, naturalists, scouts, nature-lovers. Diagrams of tracks, tips on identification. 128pp. 5⅜ × 8. 24442-3 Pa. $3.50

VICTORIAN FASHIONS AND COSTUMES FROM HARPER'S BAZAR, 1867-1898, edited by Stella Blum. Day costumes, evening wear, sports clothes, shoes, hats, other accessories in over 1,000 detailed engravings. 320pp. 9⅜ × 12¼.
22990-4 Pa. $10.95

EVERYDAY FASHIONS OF THE TWENTIES AS PICTURED IN SEARS AND OTHER CATALOGS, edited by Stella Blum. Actual dress of the Roaring Twenties, with text by Stella Blum. Over 750 illustrations, captions. 156pp. 9 × 12.
24134-3 Pa. $8.50

HALL OF FAME BASEBALL CARDS, edited by Bert Randolph Sugar. Cy Young, Ted Williams, Lou Gehrig, and many other Hall of Fame greats on 92 full-color, detachable reprints of early baseball cards. No duplication of cards with *Classic Baseball Cards*. 16pp. 8¼ × 11. 23624-2 Pa. $3.50

THE ART OF HAND LETTERING, Helm Wotzkow. Course in hand lettering, Roman, Gothic, Italic, Block, Script. Tools, proportions, optical aspects, individual variation. Very quality conscious. Hundreds of specimens. 320pp. 5⅜ × 8½.
21797-3 Pa. $4.95

THE RIME OF THE ANCIENT MARINER, Gustave Doré, S.T. Coleridge. Doré's finest work, 34 plates capture moods, subtleties of poem. Full text. 77pp. 9¼ × 12. 22305-1 Pa. $4.95

SONGS OF INNOCENCE, William Blake. The first and most popular of Blake's famous "Illuminated Books," in a facsimile edition reproducing all 31 brightly colored plates. Additional printed text of each poem. 64pp. 5¼ × 7. 22764-2 Pa. $3.50

AN INTRODUCTION TO INFORMATION THEORY, J.R. Pierce. Second (1980) edition of most impressive non-technical account available. Encoding, entropy, noisy channel, related areas, etc. 320pp. 5⅜ × 8½. 24061-4 Pa. $4.95

THE DIVINE PROPORTION: A STUDY IN MATHEMATICAL BEAUTY, H.E. Huntley. "Divine proportion" or "golden ratio" in poetry, Pascal's triangle, philosophy, psychology, music, mathematical figures, etc. Excellent bridge between science and art. 58 figures. 185pp. 5⅜ × 8½. 22254-3 Pa. $3.95

THE DOVER NEW YORK WALKING GUIDE: From the Battery to Wall Street, Mary J. Shapiro. Superb inexpensive guide to historic buildings and locales in lower Manhattan: Trinity Church, Bowling Green, more. Complete Text; maps. 36 illustrations. 48pp. 3⅞ × 9¼. 24225-0 Pa. $2.50

NEW YORK THEN AND NOW, Edward B. Watson, Edmund V. Gillon, Jr. 83 important Manhattan sites: on facing pages early photographs (1875-1925) and 1976 photos by Gillon. 172 illustrations. 171pp. 9¼ × 10. 23361-8 Pa. $7.95

HISTORIC COSTUME IN PICTURES, Braun & Schneider. Over 1450 costumed figures from dawn of civilization to end of 19th century. English captions. 125 plates. 256pp. 8⅜ × 11¼. 23150-X Pa. $7.50

VICTORIAN AND EDWARDIAN FASHION: A Photographic Survey, Alison Gernsheim. First fashion history completely illustrated by contemporary photographs. Full text plus 235 photos, 1840-1914, in which many celebrities appear. 240pp. 6½ × 9¼. 24205-6 Pa. $6.00

CHARTED CHRISTMAS DESIGNS FOR COUNTED CROSS-STITCH AND OTHER NEEDLECRAFTS, Lindberg Press. Charted designs for 45 beautiful needlecraft projects with many yuletide and wintertime motifs. 48pp. 8¼ × 11. 24356-7 Pa. $2.50

101 FOLK DESIGNS FOR COUNTED CROSS-STITCH AND OTHER NEEDLE-CRAFTS, Carter Houck. 101 authentic charted folk designs in a wide array of lovely representations with many suggestions for effective use. 48pp. 8¼ × 11. 24369-9 Pa. $2.25

FIVE ACRES AND INDEPENDENCE, Maurice G. Kains. Great back-to-the-land classic explains basics of self-sufficient farming. The one book to get. 95 illustrations. 397pp. 5⅜ × 8½. 20974-1 Pa. $4.95

A MODERN HERBAL, Margaret Grieve. Much the fullest, most exact, most useful compilation of herbal material. Gigantic alphabetical encyclopedia, from aconite to zedoary, gives botanical information, medical properties, folklore, economic uses, and much else. Indispensable to serious reader. 161 illustrations. 888pp. 6½ × 9¼. (Available in U.S. only) 22798-7, 22799-5 Pa., Two-vol. set $16.45

TOLL HOUSE TRIED AND TRUE RECIPES, Ruth Graves Wakefield. Popovers, veal and ham loaf, baked beans, much more from the famous Mass. restaurant. Nearly 700 recipes. 376pp. 5⅜ × 8½. 23560-2 Pa. $4.95

FAVORITE CHRISTMAS CAROLS, selected and arranged by Charles J.F. Cofone. Title, music, first verse and refrain of 34 traditional carols in handsome calligraphy; also subsequent verses and other information in type. 79pp. 8⅜ × 11. 20445-6 Pa. $3.50

CAMERA WORK: A PICTORIAL GUIDE, Alfred Stieglitz. All 559 illustrations from most important periodical in history of art photography. Reduced in size but still clear, in strict chronological order, with complete captions. 176pp. 8⅜ × 11¼. 23591-2 Pa. $6.95

FAVORITE SONGS OF THE NINETIES, edited by Robert Fremont. 88 favorites: "Ta-Ra-Ra-Boom-De-Aye," "The Band Played On," "Bird in a Gilded Cage," etc. 401pp. 9 × 12. 21536-9 Pa. $12.95

STRING FIGURES AND HOW TO MAKE THEM, Caroline F. Jayne. Fullest, clearest instructions on string figures from around world: Eskimo, Navajo, Lapp, Europe, more. Cat's cradle, moving spear, lightning, stars. 950 illustrations. 407pp. 5⅜ × 8½. 20152-X Pa. $5.95

LIFE IN ANCIENT EGYPT, Adolf Erman. Detailed older account, with much not in more recent books: domestic life, religion, magic, medicine, commerce, and whatever else needed for complete picture. Many illustrations. 597pp. 5⅜ × 8½. 22632-8 Pa. $7.95

ANCIENT EGYPT: ITS CULTURE AND HISTORY, J.E. Manchip White. From pre-dynastics through Ptolemies: scoiety, history, political structure, religion, daily life, literature, cultural heritage. 48 plates. 217pp. 5⅜ × 8½. (EBE) 22548-8 Pa. $4.95

KEPT IN THE DARK, Anthony Trollope. Unusual short novel about Victorian morality and abnormal psychology by the great English author. Probably the first American publication. Frontispiece by Sir John Millais. 92pp. 6½ × 9¼. 23609-9 Pa. $2.95

MAN AND WIFE, Wilkie Collins. Nineteenth-century master launches an attack on out-moded Scottish marital laws and Victorian cult of athleticism. Artfully plotted. 35 illustrations. 239pp. 6⅛ × 9¼. 24451-2 Pa. $5.95

RELATIVITY AND COMMON SENSE, Herman Bondi. Radically reoriented presentation of Einstein's Special Theory and one of most valuable popular accounts available. 60 illustrations. 177pp. 5⅜ × 8. (EUK) 24021-5 Pa. $3.95

THE EGYPTIAN BOOK OF THE DEAD, E.A. Wallis Budge. Complete reproduction of Ani's papyrus, finest ever found. Full hieroglyphic text, interlinear transliteration, word-for-word translation, smooth translation. 533pp. 6½ × 9¼. (USO) 21866-X Pa. $8.95

COUNTRY AND SUBURBAN HOMES OF THE PRAIRIE SCHOOL PERIOD, H.V. von Holst. Over 400 photographs floor plans, elevations, detailed drawings (exteriors and interiors) for over 100 structures. Text. Important primary source. 128pp. 8⅜ × 11¼. 24373-7 Pa. $5.95

READY-TO-USE BORDERS, Ted Menten. Both traditional and unusual interchangeable borders in a tremendous array of sizes, shapes, and styles. 32 plates. 64pp. 8¼ × 11. 23782-6 Pa. $3.50

THE WHOLE CRAFT OF SPINNING, Carol Kroll. Preparing fiber, drop spindle, treadle wheel, other fibers, more. Highly creative, yet simple. 43 illustrations. 48pp. 8¼ × 11. 23968-3 Pa. $2.50

HIDDEN PICTURE PUZZLE COLORING BOOK, Anna Pomaska. 31 delightful pictures to color with dozens of objects, people and animals hidden away to find. Captions. Solutions. 48pp. 8¼ × 11. 23909-8 Pa. $2.25

QUILTING WITH STRIPS AND STRINGS, H.W. Rose. Quickest, easiest way to turn left-over fabric into handsome quilt. 46 patchwork quilts; 31 full-size templates. 48pp. 8¼ × 11. 24357-5 Pa. $3.25

NATURAL DYES AND HOME DYEING, Rita J. Adrosko. Over 135 specific recipes from historical sources for cotton, wool, other fabrics. Genuine premodern handicrafts. 12 illustrations. 160pp. 5⅜ × 8½. 22688-3 Pa. $2.95

CARVING REALISTIC BIRDS, H.D. Green. Full-sized patterns, step-by-step instructions for robins, jays, cardinals, finches, etc. 97 illustrations. 80pp. 8¼ × 11. 23484-3 Pa. $3.00

GEOMETRY, RELATIVITY AND THE FOURTH DIMENSION, Rudolf Rucker. Exposition of fourth dimension, concepts of relativity as Flatland characters continue adventures. Popular, easily followed yet accurate, profound. 141 illustrations. 133pp. 5⅜ × 8½. 23400-2 Pa. $3.00

READY-TO-USE SMALL FRAMES AND BORDERS, Carol B. Grafton. Graphic message? Frame it graphically with 373 new frames and borders in many styles: Art Nouveau, Art Deco, Op Art. 64pp. 8¼ × 11. 24375-3 Pa. $3.50

CELTIC ART: THE METHODS OF CONSTRUCTION, George Bain. Simple geometric techniques for making Celtic interlacements, spirals, Kellstype initials, animals, humans, etc. Over 500 illustrations. 160pp. 9 × 12. (Available in U.S. only) 22923-8 Pa. $6.00

THE TALE OF TOM KITTEN, Beatrix Potter. Exciting text and all 27 vivid, full-color illustrations to charming tale of naughty little Tom getting into mischief again. 58pp. 4¼ × 5½. (USO) 24502-0 Pa. $1.75

WOODEN PUZZLE TOYS, Ed Sibbett, Jr. Transfer patterns and instructions for 24 easy-to-do projects: fish, butterflies, cats, acrobats, Humpty Dumpty, 19 others. 48pp. 8¼ × 11. 23713-3 Pa. $2.50

MY FAMILY TREE WORKBOOK, Rosemary A. Chorzempa. Enjoyable, easy-to-use introduction to genealogy designed specially for children. Data pages plus text. Instructive, educational, valuable. 64pp. 8¼ × 11. 24229-3 Pa. $2.50

Prices subject to change without notice.

Available at your book dealer or write for free catalog to Dept. GI, Dover Publications, Inc., 31 East 2nd St. Mineola, N.Y. 11501. Dover publishes more than 175 books each year on science, elementary and advanced mathematics, biology, music, art, literary history, social sciences and other areas.